Frommer's®

P9-BZM-063

French
PhraseFinder &
Dictionary

2nd Edition

WILEY
Wiley Publishing, Inc.

Published by:

Wiley Publishing, Inc.

111 River St.
Hoboken, NJ 07030-5774

ISBN-13: 978-0-470-93648-1

French Editor: Irene Shifman
Series Editor: Jessica Langan-Peck
Photo Editor: Richard H. Fox
Cover design by Paul Dinovo

With special thanks to Jennifer Reilly and Maureen Clarke.

Translation, Copyediting, Proofreading, Production, and Layout by:
Lingo Systems, 15115 SW Sequoia Pkwy, Ste. 200
Portland, OR 97224

For information on our other products and services or to obtain technical support, please contact our Customer Care Department within the U.S. at 800/762-2974, outside the U.S. at 317/572-3993 or fax 317/572-4002.

Wiley also publishes its books in a variety of electronic formats. Some content that appears in print may not be available in electronic formats.

Manufactured in the United States of America

5   4   3   2   1

Contents

An Invitation to the Reader

In researching this book, we discovered many wonderful sayings and terms useful to travelers in France. We're sure you'll find others. Please tell us about them, so we can share the information with your fellow travelers in upcoming editions. If you were disappointed with an aspect of this book, we'd like to know that, too. Please write to:

Frommer's French PhraseFinder & Dictionary, 2nd Edition
Wiley Publishing, Inc.
111 River St. • Hoboken, NJ 07030-5774

An Additional Note

The packager, editors, and publisher cannot be held responsible for the experiences of readers while traveling. Your safety is important to us, however, so we encourage you to stay alert and be aware of your surroundings. Keep a close eye on cameras, purses, and wallets, all favorite targets of thieves and pickpockets.

Frommers.com

Now that you have the language for a great trip, visit our website at **www.frommers.com** for travel information on more than 3,000 destinations. With features updated regularly, we give you instant access to the most current trip-planning information available. At Frommers. com, you'll also find the best prices on airfares, accommodations, and car rentals—and you can even book travel online through our travel booking partners. At Frommers.com, you'll also find:

- Online updates to our most popular guidebooks
- Vacation sweepstakes and contest giveaways
- Newsletter highlighting the hottest travel trends
- Online travel message boards with featured travel discussions

INTRODUCTION: HOW TO USE THIS BOOK

As a Romance language, French is closely related to Latin, Spanish, Italian, Portuguese, and Romanian. The most widely taught second language after English, French is spoken by more than 75 million people in countries throughout the world including France, Belgium, parts of Switzerland, Algeria, Tunisia, and Morocco, many nations of West Africa, Tahiti, several Caribbean islands, and Canada. French was also the official language of the English courts for centuries—from the Middle Ages until 1731—and its effect on English is extensive and indelible; roughly 45 percent of modern English vocabulary is of French origin.

Our intention is not to teach you French; we figure you'll find an audio program for that. Our aim is to provide a portable travel tool that's easy to use. The problem we noticed with most phrasebooks is that you practically have to memorize the contents before you know where to look for a term you might need on the spot. This phrasebook is designed for fingertip referencing, so you can whip it out and find the words you need fast.

Like most phrasebooks, part of this book organizes terms by chapters, like the chapters in a Frommer's guide—getting a room, getting a good meal, and so on. And within those sections, we tried to organize phrases intuitively, according to how frequently most readers are likely to use them. But let's say you're in a cab and you've received the wrong change, and you forget which chapter covers money. With Frommer's PhraseFinder, you can quickly look up "change" in the dictionary, and learn how to say "Sorry, but this isn't the right change." Then you can follow the cross reference for numbers, and quickly learn how to specify how much you're missing.

What will make this book most practical? What will make it easiest to use? These are the questions we asked ourselves constantly as we assembled these travel terms.

Our immediate goal was to create a phrasebook as indispensable as your passport. Our far-ranging goal, of course, is to enrich your experience of travel. And with that, we offer the following wish: *Bon voyage!*

CHAPTER ONE

SURVIVAL FRENCH

If you tire of toting around this phrasebook, tear out this section. With the right hand gestures, you'll get a lot of mileage from the terms in the next 43 pages.

BASIC GREETINGS

For a full list of greetings and introductions, see p119.

Hello.	**Bonjour !**
	boh~-zhoohr
How are you?	**Comment allez-vous ?**
	koh-maw~-tah-lay-voo
I'm fine, thanks.	**Bien, merci.**
	bee-yeh~ mayhr-see
And you?	**Et vous ?**
	ay voo
My name is ____.	**Je m'appelle ____.**
	zhuh mah-pehl
And yours?	**Et vous ?**
	ay voo
It's a pleasure to meet you.	**Ravi(e) de faire votre connaissance.**
	rah-vee duh fayhr voh-truh koh-nay-sans
Please.	**S'il vous plaît.**
	seel voo play
Thank you.	**Merci.**
	mayhr-see
Yes.	**Oui.**
	wee
No.	**Non.**
	noh~

OK.	**D'accord.** *dah-kohr*
No problem.	**Pas de problème.** *pah duh proh-blehm*
I'm sorry, I don't understand.	**Je suis désolé(e), je ne comprends pas.** *zhuh swee day-zoh-lay zhuh nuh koh~-praw~ pah*
Would you speak slower, please?	**Pouvez-vous parler plus lentement, s'il vous plaît ?** *poo-vay-voo pahr-lay plue law~-t-maw~ seel voo play*
Would you speak louder, please?	**Pouvez-vous parler plus fort, s'il vous plaît ?** *poo-vay-voo pahr-lay plue fohr seel voo play*
Do you speak English?	**Parlez-vous anglais ?** *parhr-lay-voo aw~-glay*
Do you speak any other languages?	**Parlez-vous d'autres langues ?** *pahr-lay-voo doh-truh law~g*
I speak ___ better than French.	**Je parle ___ mieux que le français.** *zhuh pahrl ___ mee-yeuh kuh luh fraw~-say*
Would you spell that, please?	**Pouvez-vous épeler cela ?** *poo-vay-voo ay-play suh-lah*
Would you please repeat that?	**Pouvez-vous répéter cela, s'il vous plaît ?** *poo-vay-voo ray-pay-tay suh-lah, seel voo play*
Would you point that out in this dictionary?	**Pouvez-vous me le montrer dans ce dictionnaire ?** *poo-vay-voo muh luh moh~-tray daw~ suh deek-see-oh~-ayhr*

THE KEY QUESTIONS

With the right hand gestures, you can get a lot of mileage from the following list of single-word questions and answers.

Who?	**Qui ?**
	kee
What?	**Quoi ?**
	kwah
When?	**Quand ?**
	kaw~
Where?	**Où ?**
	oo
Why?	**Pourquoi ?**
	poohr-kwah
How?	**Comment?**
	koh-maw~
Which?	**Quel / Quelle ?**
	kehl
How many / much?	**Combien ?**
	koh~-bee-yeh~

THE ANSWERS: WHO

For full coverage of pronouns, see p22.

him	**lui**
	lwee
her	**elle**
	ehl
them	**eux / elles**
	euh / ehl
I	**moi**
	mwah
you (singular)	**toi / vous**
	twah / voo
you (plural)	**vous**
	voo
us	**nous**
	noo

THE ANSWERS: WHEN

now	**maintenant**
	maw~t-naw~
later	**plus tard**
	plue tahr
afterwards	**ensuite**
	aw~sweet
earlier	**plus tôt**
	plue-toh
in a minute	**dans une minute**
	daw~-zoon mee-noot
today	**aujourd'hui**
	oh-zhoohr-dwee
tomorrow	**demain**
	duh-meh~
yesterday	**hier**
	yayhr
in a week	**dans une semaine**
	daw~-zoon smehn
next week	**la semaine prochaine**
	lah smehn proh-shen
last week	**la semaine dernière**
	lah smen dayhr-nyayhr
next month	**le mois prochain**
	luh mwah proh-sheh~
At _____	**À _____**
	ah
ten o'clock this morning.	**dix heures ce matin.**
	dee-zoehr suh mah-teh~
two o'clock this afternoon.	**deux heures cet après-midi.**
	doeh-zoehr seh-tah-pray-mee-dee
seven o'clock this evening.	**sept heures ce soir.**
	seh-toehr suh swahr

For a full list of numbers, see p7.

THE ANSWERS: WHERE

here	**ici**
	ee-see
there	**là**
	lah
near	**près**
	pray
closer	**plus près**
	plue pray
closest	**le plus près**
	luh plue pray
far	**loin**
	lweh~
farther	**plus loin**
	plue lweh~
farthest	**le plus loin**
	luh plue lweh~
across from	**de l'autre côté de**
	duh lo-truh koh-tay duh
next to	**à côté de**
	ah koh-tay duh
behind	**derrière**
	dayhr-yayhr
straight ahead	**tout droit**
	too dwah
left	**à gauche**
	ah gohsh
right	**à droite**
	ah dwaht
up	**en haut**
	aw~-oh
down	**en bas**
	aw~ bah
lower	**plus bas**
	plue bah
higher	**plus haut**
	plue-oh
forward	**en avant**
	aw~-nah-vaw~

SURVIVAL FRENCH

back	**en arrière**
	aw~-nah-ree-yayhr
around	**autour**
	oh-toohr
across the street	**de l'autre côté de la rue**
	loh-truh koh-tay duh lah rue
down the street	**bas de la rue**
	bah duh lah rue
on the corner	**au coin de la rue**
	oh kweh~ duh lah rue
kitty-corner	**à l'opposé**
	ah loh-poh-zay
____ blocks from here	**à ____ rues d'ici**
	ah ____ roo dee-see

For a full list of numbers, see the following page.

THE ANSWERS: WHICH

this one	**celui-ci / celle-ci**
	suh-lwee see / sehl see
that one	**celui-là / celle-là**
	suh-lwee lah / sehl lah
this (here)	**ceci**
	suh-see
that (there)	**cela**
	suh-lah
these ones (here)	**ceux-ci / celles-ci**
	soeh-see / sehl see
those ones (there)	**ceux-là / celles-là**
	soeh-lah / sehl lah

HELP/EMERGENCIES

Can you help me?	**Pouvez-vous m'aider ?**
	poo-vay voo may-day
I'm lost.	**Je suis perdu(e).**
	zhuh swee payr-due
Help!	**A l'aide !**
	ahl aid
Call the police!	**Appelez la police !**
	ah-pehl-ay la poh-lees
I need a doctor.	**J'ai besoin d'un médecin.**
	zhay buh~zweh~-deh~-med-seh~

Thief!	**Au voleur !**
	Oh vo-lehr
My child is missing.	**J'ai perdu mon enfant.**
	zhay payr-due moh~naw~faw~
Call an ambulance.	**Appelez une ambulance.**
	ah-pehl-ay oon awm~bue-lance

NUMBERS & COUNTING

one	**un**	sixteen	**seize**
	uh~		*sehz*
two	**deux**	seventeen	**dix-sept**
	deuh		*dee-seht*
three	**trois**	eighteen	**dix-huit**
	twah		*dee-zhweet*
four	**quatre**	nineteen	**dix-neuf**
	kah-truh		*deez-noehf*
five	**cinq**	twenty	**vingt**
	saw~k		*veh~t*
six	**six**	twenty-one	**vingt-et-un**
	sees		*veh~-tay-uh~*
seven	**sept**	twenty-two	**vingt-deux**
	seht		*veh~t-deuh*
eight	**huit**	thirty	**trente**
	hweet		*traw~t*
nine	**neuf**	forty	**quarante**
	noehf		*kah-raw~t*
ten	**dix**	fifty	**cinquante**
	dees		*seh~-kaw~t*
eleven	**onze**	sixty	**soixante**
	oh~z		*swah-saw~t*
twelve	**douze**	seventy	**soixante-dix**
	dooz		*swah-saw~t-dees*
thirteen	**treize**	seventy-one	**soixante-et-onze**
	trehz		*swah-saw~-tay-oh~z*
fourteen	**quatorze**	seventy-two	**soixante-douze**
	kah-tohrz		*swah-sa~t-dooz*
fifteen	**quinze**	eighty	**quatre-vingts**
	keh~z		*kah-truh-vaw~*

eighty-one	**quatre-vingt-un** *kah-truh-vaw~-uh~*	one hundred	**cent** *saw~*
ninety	**quatre-vingt-dix** *kah-truh-vaw~-dees*	two hundred	**deux cents** *doeh saw~*
		two hundred and one	**deux cent un** *doeh saw~-uh~*
		one thousand	**mille** *meel*
ninety-one	**quatre-vingt-onze** *kah-truh-vaw~-oh~z*	two thousand	**deux mille** *doeh meel*

FRACTIONS & DECIMALS

one-eighth	**un huitième** *uh~ hwee-tee-ehm*
one-quarter	**un quart** *uh~ kahr*
one-third	**un tiers** *uh~tyayhr*
one-half	**un demi / une demie** *uh~ duh-mee / oon duh-mee*
two-thirds	**deux tiers** *doeh tyayhr*
three-quarters	**trois quarts** *twah kahr*
double	**double** *doo-bluh*
triple	**triple** *tree-pluh*
one-tenth	**un dixième** *uh~ dee-zyehm*
one-hundredth	**un centième** *uh~ saw~-tyehm*
one-thousandth	**un millième** *uh~ meel-yehm*

MATH

addition	**l'addition** *lah-dee-syoh~*
2 + 1	**deux plus un** *doeh plue-zuh~*
subtraction	**la soustraction** *lah soo-strakh-syoh~*
2 − 1	**deux moins un** *doeh mweh~ uh~*
multiplication	**la multiplication** *lah muel-tee-plee-kah-syoh~*
2 x 3	**deux fois trois** *doeh fwah twah*
division	**la division** *lah dee-vee-zyoh~*
6 ÷ 3	**six divisé par trois** *sees dee-vee-say pahr twah*

ORDINAL NUMBERS

first	**premier / première** *preh-myay / preh-myayhr*
second	**deuxième** *doeh-zyehm*
third	**troisième** *twah-zyehm*
fourth	**quatrième** *kah-tree-yehm*
fifth	**cinquième** *saw~kyehm*
sixth	**sixième** *see-zyehm*
seventh	**septième** *seh-tyehm*
eighth	**huitème** *weet-yehm*
ninth	**neuvième** *noehv-yehm*

tenth	**dixième**
	deez-yehm
last	**dernier / dernière**
	dayhr-nyay / dayhr-nyayhr

MEASUREMENTS

Measurements will usually be metric, though you may need a few American measurement terms.

inch	**pouce**
	poos
foot	**pied**
	pyay
mile	**mile**
	meel
millimeter	**millimètre**
	mee-lee-meh-truh
centimeter	**centimètre**
	saw~-tee-meh-truh
meter	**mètre**
	meh-truh
kilometer	**kilomètre**
	kee-loh-meh-truh
hectare	**hectare**
	ehk-tahr
squared	**carrés**
	kah-ray
short	**court / courte**
	koohr / koohrt
long	**long / longue**
	loh~ / loh~g

VOLUME

milliliter	**millilitre**
	mee-lee-lee-truh
liter	**litre**
	lee-truh
kilo	**kilo**
	kee-loh

MEASUREMENTS 11

ounce	**once**
	oh~s
cup	**tasse**
	tahs
pint	**pinte**
	peh~t
quart	**quart**
	kahr
gallon	**gallon**
	gah-luhn

QUANTITY

some	**quelques**
	kehl-kuh
none	**aucun / aucune**
	oh-kuh~ / oh-kuen
all	**tous / toutes**
	toos / toot
many / much	**beaucoup**
	boh-koo
a little bit (can be used for quantity or for time)	**un peu**
	uh~ pueh
dozen	**une douzaine**
	oon doo-zeh~n

SIZE

small	**petit / petite**
	puh-tee / puh-teet
the smallest (literally "the most small")	**le plus petit / la plus petite**
	luh plue peh-tee / lah plue peh-teet
medium	**moyen / moyenne**
	mwah-yaw~ / mwah-yaw~n
a little medium	**un moyen de taille petit**
	uhn mwah-yaw~ duh tie ptee

big	**grand / grande**
	graw~ / graw~d
fat	**gros / grosse**
	groh / grohs
really fat	**très gros / très grosse**
	tray groh / tray grohs
the biggest	**le plus grand / la plus grande**
	luh plue graw~ / lah plue graw~d
wide	**large**
	lahrzh
narrow	**étroit / étroite**
	ay-twah / ay-twaht
too	**trop**
	troh
not enough	**pas assez**
	pah-zah-say

TIME

Remember that civilians in Europe and French-speaking Canada make use of the 24-hour clock. After 12 noon, hours continue upward, so that 1:00 PM is the 13th hour, 2:00 PM is the 14th hour, and so on. The French also write time differently: Instead of separating hours from minutes with a colon, they use a lowercase "h." For example: 11:30 AM is 11h30; 11:30 PM is 23h30.

For full coverage of numbers, see p7.

HOURS OF THE DAY

What time is it?	**Quelle heure est-il ?**
	keh-loehr ey-teel
At what time?	**À quelle heure ?**
	ah keh-loehr
For how long?	**Pendant combien de temps ?**
	paw~-daw~ koh~-bee-yeh~
	duh taw~

It's one o'clock.	**Il est une heure.**
	eel ay-oon oehr
It's two o'clock.	**Il est deux heures.**
	eel ay doeh-zoehr
It's two thirty.	**Il est deux heures trente.**
	eel ay doeh-zoehr traw~t
It's two fifteen.	**Il est deux heures et quart.**
	eel ay doeh-zoehr ay kahr
It's a quarter to three.	**Il est trois heures moins le quart.**
	eel ay twah-zoehr mwah luh kahr
It's noon.	**Il est midi.**
	eel ay mee-dee
It's midnight.	**Il est minuit.**
	eel ay mee-nwee
It's early.	**Il est tôt.**
	eel ay toh
It's late.	**Il est tard.**
	eel ay tahr
in the morning	**au matin**
	oh mah-taw~
in the afternoon	**dans l'après-midi**
	daw~ lah-pray mee-dee
at night	**dans la soirée**
	daw~ lah swahray
at dawn	**à l'aube**
	ah lohb

DAYS OF THE WEEK

Monday	**lundi**
	luh~-dee
Tuesday	**mardi**
	mahr-dee
Wednesday	**mercredi**
	mehr-kruh-dee

Thursday	**jeudi**
	zhoeh-dee
Friday	**vendredi**
	vaw~-druh-dee
Saturday	**samedi**
	sahm-dee
Sunday	**dimanche**
	dee-maw~-sh
today	**aujourd'hui**
	oh-zhohr-dwee
tomorrow	**demain**
	duh-maw~
yesterday	**hier**
	ee-yayhr
the day before yesterday	**avant-hier**
	ah-vaw~-tee-yayhr
one week	**une semaine**
	oon seh-meh~n
next week	**la semaine prochaine**
	lah smeh~n pro-sheh~n
last week	**la semaine dernière**
	lah smeh~n dayhr-nyayhr

MONTHS OF THE YEAR

January	**janvier**
	zhaw~-vyay
February	**février**
	fay-vree-yay
March	**mars**
	mahrs
April	**avril**
	ah-vreel
May	**mai**
	may

June	**juin**
	zhweh~
July	**juillet**
	zhoo-ee-ay
August	**août**
	oot
September	**septembre**
	seh-taw-bruh
October	**octobre**
	ohk-toh-bruh
November	**novembre**
	noh-vaw-bruh
December	**décembre**
	day-saw-bruh
next month	**le mois prochain**
	luh mwah proh-shaw~
last month	**le mois dernier**
	luh mwah dayhr~nyay

SEASONS OF THE YEAR

spring	**le printemps**
	luh preh~-taw~
summer	**l'été**
	lay-tay
autumn	**l'automne**
	loh-tuhn
winter	**l'hiver**
	lee-vayhr

WEATHER

What's the weather like?	**Quel est le temps ?**
	kel ay luh taw~
What's the temperature?	**Quelle est la température ?**
	kel ay lah temp-ay-rah-tuehr
What's the forecast?	**Quelles sont les prévisions météo ?**
	kel soh~ lay pray-vee-zyoh may-tay-oh

Faux Amis

If you try winging it with "Frenglish," beware of false cognates, known as faux amis, "false friends"—French words that sound like English ones, but with different meanings. Here are some of the most commonly confused terms.

gros(se)	fat
dégoutant(e)	gross
bras	arm
soutien-gorge	bra
main	hand
principal(e)	main
raisin	grape
raisin sec	raisin
pain	bread
douleur	pain
boulette	small ball (like a meatball)
balle	bullet
vacances	holiday
chambres libres	vacancies
injurier	to insult
blesser	to injure
résumé	synopsis
curriculum vitae	résumé
manger	to eat
mangeoire	manger
robe	dress
peignoir	robe
assister	to attend an event
aider	to help
attendre	to wait
librairie	bookstore
bibliothèque	library

FRENCH GRAMMAR BASICS

ALPHABET & PRONUNCIATION

French uses the same alphabet as English, with the addition of the ligature **œ**, used in words like **sœur** (sister) and **œil** (eye). French pronunciation can seem quite difficult. There are several **"nasal vowels"** that are sometimes used when **m** or **n** follows a vowel. Only the nasal is pronounced, not the **m** or n, unless another vowel comes along afterward.

The **nasal** will be represented with a ~ . Try this example by tightening your throat as if to whine, snort, or hum:

a good white wine   **un bon vin blanc**
                        uh~ boh~ veh~ blaw~

Another tricky bit is the guttural French **r**. It's sounded in the back of the throat, somewhere near a German "ach." Because the French **r** is all but impossible without practice or prior experience, we'll help you hint at it by adding *hr* to pronunciations.

Letter	Name	Pronunciation
a	*ah*	**ah** as in *father*
		au: oh as in *so*
		ai, aie: ay as in *paid*
		ail: ie as in *tie*
		an: aw~ as in *long*
b	*bay*	**b** as in *bay*
c	*say*	**ca, co, cu:** hard **k** sound as in *car*
		ce, ci: s sound before **i, e,** as in *cent*
d	*day*	**d** as in *day*
		d at end of word is usually silent
e	*uh*	**uh** as in *women*, unstressed, but with lips more pursed
		e at end of word is usually silent
		ein: eh~ as in *men*
		en, em: aw~ as in *long*
		ent: at end of word is usually silent
		er: at end of word, **ay** as in *face*

Letter	Name	Pronunciation
		es at end of word is usually silent
		et, ez: at end of word, **ay** as in *face*
		eu, eue: oeh like German oe, oeh
e stressed	*eh*	**eh** as in *vet*
e stressed (é)	*ay*	**ay** as in *say*
f	*ehf*	f as in *father*
g	*zhay*	**ga, go, gu:** hard **g** sound as in *gold*
		ge, gi: zh as **g** in *massage* or **s** in *vision*
h	*ahsh*	silent
i	*ee*	**ee** as in *machine*
		il: at end of word, **ee** as in *see*
		in, im: eh~ as in *men*
j	*zhee*	**zh** as **g** in *massage* or **s** in *vision*
k	*kah*	hard **k** sound as in *kitten*
l	*ehl*	l as in *million*
m	*ehm*	m as in *money*
n	*ehn*	n as in *nothing*
		n, nd, nt: at end of word, ~ nasalizes preceding vowel
		ne: at end of word, as in *phone*
o before	*oh*	**o:** inside word, at end of word, or silent final letter, **oh** as in *so*
in		**o:** before nonsilent final letter, **uh** as in *come*
		oe, œ: uh like German but lower
		oi: wah as in *bourgeois*
		on: oh~ as in *phone*
		ou: oo as in *routine*
p	*pay*	p as in *pay*
q	*koeh*	**qu:** hard **k** sound as in *liquor*
r	*ehr*	**r, hr:** r as in *argument*, usually far back in throat

Letter	Name	Pronunciation
s	*ehs*	s as in *sister*
		s: between vowels, including final silent e,
		z as in *misery*
		s at end of word is usually silent
t	*tay*	t as in *tea*
		t at end of word is usually silent
		tre, ttre: at end of word, as in *bet*
u	*ueh*	ue, ueh as in *due*, but shorter
		un, um: uh~ as in *under*
v	*vay*	v as in *volt*
w	*doo-bluh-vay*	v as in *volt*
x	*eeks*	x: before unstressed vowel, ks as in *fixed*
		x: before stressed vowel, gz as in *examine*
		x at end of word is usually silent
y	*ee-grehk*	ee as in *mighty*
		y: before vowel, y as in *yank*
z	*zehd*	z as in *zip*
		z at end of word is usually silent

GENDER & ADJECTIVE AGREEMENT

All nouns in French are assigned a masculine or feminine gender, most often accompanied by a masculine or feminine definite article (**le** or **la**). Definite articles (the), indefinite articles (a), and related adjectives must also be masculine or feminine and singular or plural, depending on the noun they're modifying (see the examples in the following boxes).

Unlike English adjectives, French adjectives generally follow the noun, and they must agree in number and gender with the nouns they modify. Some common adjectives do come before the noun, however. These generally have to do with beauty, age, number, goodness, and size.

Quirks of Gender

A group of people always takes the masculine form unless the group is completely composed of females.

John and his sisters are blonds.	**Jean et ses sœurs sont blonds.**
	zhah~-nay say soehr soh~ bloh~

The Definite Article ("The")

	Singular	Plural
Masculine	le petit magasin cher (the small, expensive store)	les petits magasins chers (the small, expensive stores)
Feminine	la petite chambre chère (the small, expensive room)	les petites chambres chères (the small, expensive rooms)

When a singular definite article appears directly in front of a noun that begins with a vowel, it is contracted with an apostrophe:

	Singular	Plural
Masculine	l'amour (love)	les amours (loves)
Feminine	l'église (the church)	les églises (the churches)

The Indefinite and Partitive Articles ("A", "An," and "Any" / "Some")

	Singular	Plural
Masculine	un grand magasin intéressant (a big, interesting store)	des grands magasins intéressants (some / any big, interesting stores)
Feminine	une grande chambre intéressante (a big, interesting room)	des grandes chambres intéressantes (some / any big, interesting rooms)

How Much Do You Really Want? (The "Partitive")

French often uses what's called "the partitive" to express some of a larger whole; the words "some" or "any" are never implied, as in English. In other words, if you went to the store for "milk" (rather than for "some" milk), it would suggest all the milk in the world to a French speaker. In French, the words "some" or "any" must always be explicit, as in the examples below.

de + la = de la glace   some ice
duh lah glas

de + le = du lait   some milk (or some
  doo lay   ice cream)

de + l' + vowel (f) = de l'essence   some gasoline
duh leh-saw~s

de + l' + vowel (m) = de l'apéritif   some drink
duh lah-pay-ree-teef

de + les (f) = des aubergines   some eggplant(s)
day-zoh-bayhr-zheen

de + les (m) = des haricots verts   some green beans
day-zay-ree-koh vayhr

THIS / THESE / THAT / THOSE

When modifying nouns, "this," "that," "these," and "those" must agree with the noun in gender and number.

	This / That	These / Those
Masculine	**ce château** (this / that castle) **cet immeuble** (this / that building)	**ces châteaux** (these / those castles) **ces immeubles** (these / those buildings)
Feminine	**cette maison** (this / that house) **cette usine** (this / that factory)	**ces maisons** (these / those houses) **ces usines** (these / those factories)

French does not usually make a distinction between "this and "that" or between "these" and "those." If necessary, the endings **-ci** (here, nearby) and **-là** (over there) can be added for emphasis:

I'd like this ring here, not that necklace there.	**Je voudrais cette bague-ci, pas ce collier-là.** *zhuh voo-dray seht bahg-see pah suh kohl-yay-lah*
You take these taxis right here, not those coaches over there.	**On prend ces taxis-ci, pas ces cars-là** *oh~ praw~ say tahk-see-see pah say kahr-lah*

When **ce** is used with **être** (to be) to mean "this is," it makes a contraction. The plural form of "these are" also uses **ce**, not **ces**:

That's his widow.	**C'est sa veuve.** *say sah voehv*
These are our husbands.	**Ce sont nos maris.** *say soh~ noh mah-ree*

PERSONAL PRONOUNS

English	French	Pronunciation
I	Je	zhuh
You (singular, familiar)	Tu	tueh
He / She / It	Il / Elle	eel / ehl
We	Nous	noo
You (plural / singular formal)	Vous	voo
They (*m* / *f*)	Ils / Elles	eel / ehl

Hey, You!

French has two words for "you": *tu*, spoken among friends and familiars when addressing only one person, and *vous*, used among strangers or as a sign of respect for elders and authority figures, and to address more than one person—even if you're speaking to a group of your family members or close friends. When speaking with a stranger, expect to use *vous* unless you are invited to use *tu*.

When a verb begins with a vowel, if the subject appears directly in front of it, **je** (I) forms a contraction. The plural subjects change in pronunciation, though:

English	French	Pronunciation
I like.	J'aime.	zhehm
You (singular, familiar) like.	Tu aimes.	tueh ehm
He / She / It likes.	Il / Elle aime.	ee-lehm / eh-lehm
We like.	Nous aimons.	noo-zeh-moh~
You (plural / singular, formal) like.	Vous aimez.	voo-zeh-may
They (*m* / *f*) like.	Ils / Elles aiment.	eel-zehm / ehl-zehm

REGULAR VERB CONJUGATIONS

French verb infinitives end in **ER** (**parler**, to speak), **IR** (**choisir**, to choose), and **RE** (**vendre**, to sell). Most verbs (known as "regular verbs") are conjugated according to the rules for those endings. These are the present-tense conjugations for regular verbs.

Present Tense

ER Verbs	PARLER "To Speak"	
I speak.	Je parle.	zhuh pahrl
You (singular, familiar) **speak.**	Tu parles.	tueh pahrl
He / She / It speaks.	Il / Elle parle.	eel / ehl pahrl
We speak.	Nous parlons.	noo pahr-loh~
You (plural / singular, formal) **speak.**	Vous parlez.	voo pahr-lay
They speak.	Ils / Elles parlent.	eel / ehl pahrl

IR Verbs	CHOISIR "To Choose"	
I choose.	Je choisis.	zhuh shwah-zee
You (singular, familiar) **choose.**	Tu choisis.	tueh shwah-zee
He / She / It chooses.	Il / Elle choisit.	eel / ehl shwah-zee
We choose.	Nous choisissons.	noo shwah-zee-soh~
You (plural / singular, formal) **choose.**	Vous choisissez.	voo shwah-zee-say
They choose.	Ils / Elles choisissent.	eel / ehl shwah-zees

RE Verbs	VENDRE "To Sell"	
I sell.	Je vends.	zhuh vaw~
You (singular, familiar) sell.	Tu vends.	tueh vaw~
He / She / It sells.	Il / Elle vend. (no ending)	eel / ehl vaw~
We sell.	Nous vendons.	noo vaw~-doh~
You (plural / singular, formal) sell.	Vous vendez.	voo vaw~-day
They sell.	Ils / Elles vendent.	eel / ehl vaw~d

Past Tense

One way of expressing past tense in French is the **passé composé**. The passé composé is formed like the construction "I have walked," in English—with a helping verb (the present tense of **avoir**, to have; or in rare cases, **être**, to be), plus the past participle of the action verb. For the verb "to walk," for example, it's equivalent to "I walked," "I did walk," or "I have walked" in English.

The past participle has a standard form for each type of regular verbs. The following boxes demonstrate how to conjugate **avoir** and then combine it with the past participle of regular **ER**, **IR**, and **RE** verbs to form the past tense.

Passé Composé / Past with Avoir

Present Tense	AVOIR "To Have"	
I have.	J'ai.	zhay
You (singular, familiar) have.	Tu as.	tueh ah
He / She / It has.	Il / Elle a.	eel / ehl ah
We have.	Nous avons.	noo-zah-voh~
You (plural / singular, formal) have.	Vous avez.	voo-zah-vay
They have.	Ils / Elles ont.	eel-zoh~ / ehl-zoh~

ER Verbs	AVOIR + PARLER "To Speak"	
I spoke.	J'ai parlé.	zhay pahr-lay
You (singular familiar) **spoke.**	Tu as parlé.	tueh ah pahr-lay
He / She / It spoke.	Il / Elle a parlé.	eel / ehl ah pahr-lay
We spoke.	Nous avons parlé.	noo-zah-voh~ pahr-lay
You (plural / singular, formal) **spoke.**	Vous avez parlé.	voo-zah-vay pahr-lay
They spoke.	Ils / Elles ont parlé.	eel-zoh~ / ehl-zoh~ pahr-lay
Past Participle:	parlé (with **être**; agrees with subject -- true for all past participles)	pahr-lay

IR Verbs	AVOIR + CHOISIR "To Choose"	
I chose.	J'ai choisi.	zhay shwah-zee
You (singular, familiar) **chose.**	Tu as choisi.	tueh ah shwah-zee
He / She / It chose.	Il / Elle a choisi.	eel / ehl ah shwah-zee
We chose.	Nous avons choisi.	noo-zah-voh~ shwah-zee
You (plural / singular, formal) **chose.**	Vous avez choisi.	voo-zah-vay shwah-zee
They chose.	Ils / Elles ont choisi.	eel-zoh~ / ehl-zoh~ shwah-zee
Past participle:	choisi	shwah-zee

RE Verbs	AVOIR + VENDRE "To Sell"	
I sold.	J'ai vendu.	zhay vaw~-doo
You (singular, familiar) **sold**.	Tu as vendu.	tueh ah vaw~-doo
He / She / It sold.	Il / Elle a vendu.	eel / ehl ah vaw~-doo
We sold.	Nous avons vendu.	noo-zah-voh~ vaw~-doo
You (plural / singular, formal) **sold**.	Vous avez vendu.	voo-zah-vay vaw~-doo
They sold.	Ils / Elles ont vendu.	eel-zoh~ / ehl-zoh~ vaw~-doo
Past participle:	vendu	vaw~-doo

Passé Composé / Past with Être

A few exceptional verbs—mostly involving verbs of motion—use **être** (to be) instead of **avoir** to form the **passé compose**. Like adjectives, past participles with **être** must agree with the subject in number and gender. Note that the pronunciation of the past participle never changes.

Present Tense	ÊTRE "To Be"	
I am.	Je suis.	zhuh swee
You (singular, familiar) **are**.	Tu es.	tueh ay
He / She / It is.	Il / Elle est.	eel / ehl ay
We are.	Nous sommes.	noo-suhm
You (plural / singular, formal) **are**.	Vous êtes.	voo-zeht
They are.	Ils / Elles sont.	eel soh~ / ehl soh~

IR Verbs	ÊTRE + PARTIR "To Leave"	
I left.	Je suis parti(e).	zhuh swee pahr-tee
You (singular, familiar) **left.**	Tu es parti(e).	tueh ay pahr-tee
He / She / It left.	Il est parti. / Elle est partie.	eel / ehl ay pahr-tee
We left.	Nous sommes parti(e)s.	noo-suhm pahr-tee
You (plural / singular, formal) **left.**	Vous êtes parti(e)s.	voo-zeht pahr-tee
They left.	Ils sont partis. / Elles sont parties.	eel soh~ / ehl soh~ pahr-tee

The following verbs use **être** as the helping verb for the **passé composé**:

aller (to go)	Je suis allé(e). (I went.)	zhuh swee-zah-lay
arriver (to arrive)	Je suis arrivé(e). (I arrived.)	zhuh swee-zah-ree-vay
descendre (to go down)	Je suis descendu(e). (I went down.)	zhuh swee day-saw~-doo
devenir (to become)	Je suis devenu(e). (I became.)	zhuh swee dehv-nueh
entrer (to come in)	Je suis entré(e). (I came in.)	zhuh swee-zaw~-tray
monter (to go up)	Je suis monté(e). (I went up.)	zhuh swee moh~-tay
mourir (to die)	Je suis mort(e). (I died.)	zhuh swee mohr / mohrt
naître (to be born)	Je suis né(e). (I was born.)	zhuh swee nay

partir (to leave)	**Je suis parti(e).** (I left.)	zhuh swee pahr-tee
rentrer (to come / go home)	**Je suis rentré(e).** (I went home.)	zhuh swee raw~-tray
rester (to stay)	**Je suis resté(e).** (I stayed.)	zhuh swee res-tay
retourner (to go back)	**Je suis retourné(e).** (I went back.)	zhuh swee ray-toohr-nay
revenir (to come back)	**Je suis revenu(e).** (I came back.)	zhuh swee reh-vnueh
sortir (to go out)	**Je suis sorti(e).** (I went out.)	zhuh swee sohr-tee
tomber (to fall)	**Je suis tombé(e).** (I fell.)	zhuh swee toh~-bay
venir (to come)	**Je suis venu(e).** (I came.)	zhuh swee vnueh

Having It All

Avoir means "to have," but it's also used to describe conditions, such as hunger or thirst, body pain, and age:

I'm hungry.	**J'ai faim.**	*zhay feh~*
I have a headache.	**J'ai mal à la tête.**	*zhay mah-lah lah teht*
I am ten years old.	**J'ai dix ans.**	*zhay dee-zah~*

Avoir is also used in the two common fixed expressions, *avoir besoin de*, "to need," and *il y a*, "there is," "there are":

I need a pillow.	**J'ai besoin d'un oreiller.** *zhay beh-zwah~ duh~-noh-ray-ay*
There are two seats available.	**Il y a deux places libres.** *eel-yah doeh plas lee-bruh*

The Future

For novice French speakers, the easiest way to express the future is to use the present tense of the irregular verb **aller** (to go) as a helping verb plus the infinitive. We use the same structure in English when we say things like "I'm going to eat."

Present Tense	ALLER "To Go"	
I go.	Je vais.	zhuh vay
You (singular, familiar) **go.**	Tu vas.	tueh vah
He / She / It goes.	Il / Elle va.	eel / ehl vah
We go.	Nous allons.	noo-zah-loh~
You (plural / singular, formal) **go.**	Vous allez.	voo-zah-lay
They go.	Ils / Elles vont.	eel / ehl voh~

ER Verbs	ALLER + PARLER "To Talk"	
I'm going to talk.	Je vais **parler.**	zhuh vay pahr-lay
You're (singular, familiar) **going to talk.**	Tu vas **parler.**	tueh vah pahr-lay
He / She / It is going to talk.	Il / Elle va **parler.**	eel / ehl vah pahr-lay
We're going to talk.	Nous allons **parler.**	noo-zah-loh~ pahr-lay
You're (plural / singular, formal) **going to talk.**	Vous allez **parler.**	voo-zah-lay pahr-lay
They're going to talk.	Ils / Elles vont **parler.**	eel / ehl voh~ pahr-lay

IRREGULAR VERBS

French has numerous irregular verbs that stray from the standard **ER**, **IR**, and **RE** conjugations. Rather than bog you down with too much grammar, we're providing the present tense conjugations for some of the most commonly used irregular verbs.

BOIRE "To Drink"

I drink.	Je bois.	zhuh bwah
You (singular, familiar) **drink.**	Tu bois.	tueh bwah
He / She / It drinks.	Il / Elle boit.	eel / ehl bwah
We drink.	Nous buvons.	noo bueh-voh~
You (plural / singular, formal) **drink.**	Vous buvez.	voo bueh-vay
They drink.	Ils / Elles boivent.	eel / ehl bwahv
Past participle:	bu	bueh

CONNAÎTRE "To Know" (a person / place)

I know Marc.	Je connais Marc.	zhuh koh-nay mahrk
You (singular, familiar) **know Nice.**	Tu connais Nice.	tueh koh-nay nees
He / She / It knows my parents.	Il / Elle connaît mes parents.	eel / ehl koh-nay mey par-aw~
We know your (girl)friends.	Nous connaissons vos amies.	noo koh-nay-soh~ voh-zah-mee
You (plural / singular, formal) **know this hostel.**	Vous connaissez cette auberge.	voo koh-nay-say seh-toh-bayrzh
They know our children.	Ils / Elles connaissent nos enfants.	eel / ehl koh-nehs noh-zaw~-faw~
Past participle:	connu	koh-nueh

DIRE "To Say", "To Tell"

I say.	Je dis.	zhuh dee
You (singular, familiar) say.	Tu dis.	tueh dee
He / She / It says.	Il / Elle dit.	eel / ehl dee
We say.	Nous disons.	noo dee-zoh~
You (plural / singular, formal) say.	Vous dites.	voo deet
They say.	Ils disent / Elles disent	eel deez / ehl deez
Past participle:	dit	dee

ÉCRIRE "To Write"

I write.	J'écris.	zheh-kree
You (singular, familiar) write.	Tu écris.	tueh eh-kree
He / She / It writes.	Il / Elle écrit.	eel / ehl eh-kree
We write.	Nous écrivons.	noo-zeh-kree-voh~
You (plural / singular, formal) write.	Vous écrivez.	voo-zeh-kree-vay
They write.	Ils écrivent / Elles écrivent.	eel-zeh-kreev / ehl-zeh-kreev
Past participle:	écrit	eh-kree

"Faire" Weather

The verb *faire* (to do, to make) is also used impersonally to describe the weather:

It's hot / cold out.	**Il fait chaud / froid.**
	eel fay shoh / fwah
The weather's nice / bad today.	**Il fait beau / mauvais aujourd'hui.**
	eel fay boh / moh-vay oh-zhoohr dwee

FAIRE "To Do," "To Make"

I do.	Je fais.	zhuh fay
You (singular, familiar) **do.**	Tu fais.	tueh fay
He / She / It does.	Il / Elle fait.	eel / ehl fay
We do.	Nous faisons.	noo feh-zoh~
You (plural / singular, formal) **do.**	Vous faites.	voo feht
They do.	Ils font / Elles font.	eel foh~ / ehl foh~
Past participle:	fait	fay

OUVRIR "To Open"

I open.	J'ouvre.	zhoovhr
You (singular, familiar) **open.**	Tu ouvres.	tueh oovhr
He / She / It opens.	Il / Elle ouvre.	eel / ehl oovhr
We open.	Nous ouvrons.	noo-zoo-vroh~
You (plural / singular, formal) **open.**	Vous ouvrez.	voo-zoo-vray
They open.	Ils ouvrent / Elles ouvrent	eel-zoovhr / ehl-zoovhr
Past participle:	ouvert	oo-vayhr

PARTIR "To Leave"

I leave.	Je pars.	zhuh pahr
You (singular, familiar) **leave.**	Tu pars.	tueh pahr
He / She / It leaves.	Il / Elle part.	eel / ehl pahr
We leave.	Nous partons.	noo pahr-toh~
You (plural / singular, formal) **leave.**	Vous partez.	voo pahr-tay
They leave.	Ils / Elles partent.	eel / ehl pahrt
Past participle:	parti	pahr-tee

POUVOIR "Can," "To Be Able"

I can.	Je peux.	zhuh poeh
You (singular, familiar) **can.**	Tu peux.	tueh poeh
He / She / It can.	Il / Elle peut.	eel / ehl poeh
We can.	Nous pouvons.	noo poo-voh~
You (plural / singular, formal) **can.**	Vous pouvez.	voo poo-vay
They can.	Ils / Elles peuvent.	eel / ehl poehv
Past participle:	pu	pue

PRENDRE "To Take"

I take.	Je prends.	zhuh praw~
You (singular, familiar) take.	Tu prends.	tueh praw~
He / She / It takes.	Il / Elle prend.	eel / ehl praw~
We take.	Nous prenons.	noo pruh-noh~
You (plural / singular, formal) take.	Vous prenez.	voo pruh-nay
They take.	Ils prennent / Elles prennent.	eel prehn / ehl prehn
Past participle:	pris	pree

SAVOIR "To Know" (a fact)

I know how to drive.	Je sais conduire.	zhuh say koh~-dweer
You (singular, familiar) know the route.	Tu connais la route.	tueh koh-nay lah root
He / She / It knows where.	Il / Elle sait où.	eel / ehl say oo
We know the answer.	Nous savons la réponse.	noo sah-voh~ lah ray-poh~s
You (plural / singular, formal) know his / her problem.	Vous savez son problème.	voo sah-vay soh~ praw-blehm
They know the truth.	Ils / Elles savent la vérité.	eel / ehl sahv lah vay-ree-tay
Past participle:	su	sue

SORTIR "To Go Out," "To Exit"

I go out.	Je sors.	zhuh sohr
You (singular, familiar) **go out.**	Tu sors.	tueh sohr
He / She / It goes out.	Il / Elle sort.	eel / ehl sohr
We go out.	Nous sortons.	noo sohr-toh~
You (plural / singular, formal) **go out.**	Vous sortez.	voo sohr-tay
They go out.	Ils / Elles sortent.	eel / ehl sohrt
Past participle:	sorti	sohr-tee

VENIR "To Come"

I come.	Je viens.	zhuh vee-yeh~
You (singular, familiar) **come.**	Tu viens.	tueh vyeh~
He / She / It comes.	Il / Elle vient.	eel / ehl vyeh~
We come.	Nous venons.	noo vnoh~
You (plural / singular, formal) **come.**	Vous venez.	voo vnay
They come.	Ils / Elles viennent.	eel / ehl vyehn
Past participle:	venu	vnueh

VOIR "To See"

I see.	Je vois.	zhuh vwah
You (singular, familiar) **see.**	Tu vois.	tueh vwah
He / She / It sees.	Il / Elle voit.	eel / ehl vwah
We see.	Nous voyons.	noo vwah-yoh~
You (plural / singular, formal) **see.**	Vous voyez.	voo vwah-yay
They see.	Ils / Elles voient.	eel / ehl vwah
Past participle:	vu	vue

You can say "I want" to make a request, but it's much more polite, just like in English, to say "I would like"—**je voudrais**. Therefore, we will provide this conditional tense rather than the present tense for this verb.

VOULOIR "To Want"

I would like to eat.	Je voudrais manger.	zhuh voo-dray mah~-zhay
You (singular, familiar) **would like a beer.**	Tu voudrais une bière.	tueh voo-dray oon bee-ayhr
He / She / It would like a knife.	Il / Elle voudrait un couteau.	eel / ehl voo-dray uh~ koo-toh
We would like some ketchup.	Nous voudrions du ketchup.	noo voo-dree-yon doo keht-shup
You (plural / singular, formal) **would like some books.**	Vous voudriez des livres.	voo voo-dree-yeh lee-vruh
They would like to stay.	Ils / Elles voudraient rester.	eel / ehl voo-dray ruh-stay

REFLEXIVE VERBS

French uses more reflexive verbs than English. A verb is reflexive when its subject and object both refer to the same person or thing:

Marie looks at herself in the mirror.	**Marie se regarde dans le miroir.** *mah-ree suh ruh-gahr-duh daw~ luh meer-wahr*

The following common verbs are often used reflexively: **s'habiller** (to get dressed, literally to dress oneself), **s'appeler** (to be named, literally to call oneself), **se baigner** (to bathe oneself), and **se lever** (to wake up, literally to raise oneself).

To indicate that a verb is reflexive, French attaches a reflexive pronoun to the verb according to the subject:

SE LEVER "To Get Up"

I get up.	Je me lève.	zhuh muh lehv
You (singular, familiar) **get up.**	Tu te lèves.	tueh tuh lehv
He / She / It gets up.	Il / Elle se lève.	eel / ehl suh lehv
We get up.	Nous nous levons.	noo noo leh-voh~
You (plural / singular, formal) **get up.**	Vous vous levez.	voo voo leh-vay
They get up.	Ils / Elles se lèvent.	eel / ehl suh lehv

When a reflexive pronoun ending with a vowel comes before a verb that starts with a vowel, all but the **nous** and **vous** forms make contractions. Note the contractions and pronunciation changes for the following verb.

Reflexive verbs use **être** in the **passé composé** (remember to make the verbs agree). The reflexive pronoun goes directly before the helping verb.

She woke up.	**Elle s'est levée.**	*ehl say luh-vay*
They (a group of females) woke up.	**Elles se sont levées.**	*ehl suh soh~ luh-vay*

An impersonal usage of a reflexive verb appears in two common, useful phrases:

What's happening?	**Qu'est-ce qui se passe ?**
	kehs kee suh pahs
What happened?	**Qu'est-ce qui s'est passé ?**
	kehs kee say pah-say

S'AMUSER "To Have a Good Time"

I am having a good time.	Je m'amuse.	zhuh mah-muehz
You (singular, familiar) **are having a good time.**	Tu t'amuses.	tueh tah-muehz
He / She / It is having a good time.	Il / Elle s'amuse.	eel / ehl sah-muehz
We are having a good time.	Nous nous amusons.	noo noo-zah-mueh-zoh~
You (plural / singular, formal) **are having a good time.**	Vous vous amusez.	voo voo-zah-meuh-zay
They are having a good time.	Ils / Elles s'amusent.	eel / ehl sah-muehz

Who's Calling, Please?

Many reflexive verbs can also be used in a nonreflexive sense. The reflexive pronoun makes all the difference between *j'appelle Jean* (I'm calling John) and *je m'appelle Jean* (my name is John, literally I call myself John).

NEGATIVES

To render a statement negative, bracket the verb with **ne . . . pas**, as in the examples below. **Ne** contracts to **n'** in front of a vowel. (In spoken French, the **ne** is often omitted, so you'll need to listen for the **pas**.)

ALLER "To Go"		
I am not going.	Je ne vais pas.	zhuh nuh vay pah
You (singular, familiar) are not going.	Tu ne vas pas.	tueh nuh vah pah
He / She / It is not going.	Il / Elle ne va pas.	eel / ehl nuh vah pah
We are not going.	Nous n'allons pas.	noo nah-loh~ pah
You (plural / singular, formal) are not going.	Vous n'allez pas.	voo nah-lay pah
They are not going.	Ils / Elles ne vont pas.	eel / ehl nuh voh~ pah

Other Negatives

Here are some other negative expressions that follow a similar pattern.

NEVER: ne . . . jamais

I never like dancing.	Je n'aime jamais danser.	zhuh neyhm zhah-mey dah~-say

NO LONGER: ne . . . plus

I no longer like this.	Je n'aime plus ça.	zhuh neyhm plue sah

NO ONE: ne . . . personne

I like no one.	Je n'aime personne.	zhuh neyhm payhr-suhn

NOTHING / ANYTHING: ne . . . rien

I don't like anything.	Je n'aime rien.	zhuh neyhm ree-yaw~

ONLY: ne . . . que

I only like you.	Je n'aime que toi.	zhuh neyhm kuh twah

QUESTIONS

There are several ways to ask a question in French: The very simplest is just to use the tone of your voice. Just like in English, a sentence that drops in pitch at the end is a statement, but a sentence that rises in pitch is instantly a question.

You have (some) soap.

Vous avez du savon.
voo-zah-vay due sah-voh~

Do you have (any) soap?

Vous avez du savon ?
voo-zah-vay due sah-voh~

Another easy and useful way to ask a question is to stick the fixed phrase **Est-ce que** onto the beginning of the sentence. There's no literal translation for **Est-ce que** that makes much sense; word-for-word it means "Is it that . . .?"

Do you have (any) soap?

Est-ce que vous avez du savon ?
ehs kuh voo-zah-vay doo sah-voh~

For other kinds of questions, see p3.

POSSESSIVES

French has no **'s** shorthand to show ownership. If you want to talk about "the girl's name," you have to say **le nom de la fille** (the name of the girl). The preposition de changes depending on which definite article follows it.

de + la = de la	le bouchon de la bouteille (the bottle's cork)	luh boo-shoh~ duh lah boo-tayh
de + le = du	les portes du restaurant (the restaurant's doors)	lay pohrt doo ruh-stoh-raw~
de + l' = de l'	la main de l'actrice (the actress's hand) le fil de l'ordinateur (the computer's cord)	lah meh~ duh lahk-trees luh feel duh lohr-dee-nah-toehr
de + les = des	la chanson des sœurs (the sisters' song) les valises des passagers (the passengers' suitcases)	lah shaw~-soh~ day soehr lay vah-lees day pah-sah-zhay

Possessive Adjectives

Masculine Noun

My dog is black.
Mon chien est noir.
moh~ shyeh~ ay nwahr

Your dog is pretty.
Ton chien est beau.
toh~ shyeh~ ay boh

His / Her / Its dog is small.
Son chien est petit.
soh~ shyeh~ ay ptee

Our dog is lost.
Notre chien est perdu.
nohtr shyeh~ ay pehr-due

Your dog is dirty.
Votre chien est sale.
vohtr shyeh~ ay sahl

Their book is dirty.
Leur livre est sale.
loehr lee-vuehr ay sahl

Feminine Noun

My car is black.
Ma voiture est noire.
mah vwah-tuehr ay nwahr

Your car is pretty.
Ta voiture est belle.
tah vwah-tuehr ay behl

His / Her / Its car is small.
Sa voiture est petite.
sah vwah-tuehr at puh-teet

Our car is lost.	**Notre voiture est perdue.**
	nohtr vwah-tuehr ay pehr-due
Your car is dirty.	**Votre voiture est sale.**
	vohtr vwah-tuehr ay sahl
Their table is dirty.	**Leur table est sale.**
	loehr tah-bluehr ay sahl

Plural Noun (Masculine or Feminine)

My luggage is black.	**Mes bagages sont noirs.**
	may bah-gahzh soh~ nwahr
Your luggage is pretty.	**Tes bagages sont beaux.**
	tay bah-gahzh soh~ boh
His / Her / Its luggage is small.	**Ses bagages sont petits.**
	say bah-gahzh soh~ ptee
Our luggage is lost.	**Nos bagages sont perdus.**
	noh bah-gahzh soh~ pehr-due
Your luggage is dirty.	**Vos bagages sont sales.**
	voh bah-gahzh soh~ sahl
Their luggage arrived.	**Leurs bagages sont arrivés.**
	loehr bah-gahzh soh~ tah-ree-vay

DIRECTIONS

Although they have many other uses, the prepositions **à** and **de** have a variety of translations—such as "to," "from," "at," "for," or "of"—when people talk about places. See the rules for using **de, du, de l'**, and **des** on p42. **À** changes very similarly to **de**.

à + la = à la	**Tu restes à la gare.** (You're staying at the train station.)	*tueh rehst ah lah gahr*
à + l' = à l'	**Elle est à l'hôtel.** (She's at the hotel.)	*ehl ay-tah loh-tehl*
à + le = au	**Nous partons au théâtre.** (We're leaving for the theatre.)	*noo pahr-toh~ oh tay-ahtr*
à + les = aux	**Ils vont aller aux musées.** (They're going to go to the museums.)	*eel voh~-ah-lay oh mueh-zay*

CHAPTER TWO
GETTING THERE & GETTING AROUND

This section deals with every form of automated transportation. Whether you've just reached your destination by plane or you're renting a car to tour the countryside, you'll find the phrase you need in the next 30 pages.

AT THE AIRPORT

I am looking for ____	**Je cherche ____**
	zhuh shayhrsh
a bus / train to city center.	**un bus / train pour le centre-ville.**
	uh~ buehs / truh~ poor leh centreh veel
a porter.	**un porteur.**
	uh~ pohr-toehr
the check-in counter.	**l'enregistrement.**
	law~-ruh-zhee-struh-maw~
the ticket counter.	**le guichet.**
	luh gee-shay
arrivals.	**les arrivées.**
	lay-zah-ree-vay
security.	**la sécurité.**
	lah say-cuh-ree-tay
immigration.	**le service immigration.**
	luh ser-vees ee-mee-grah-see-yoh~
customs.	**la douane.**
	lah dwan
departures.	**les départs.**
	lay day-pahrt
gate number ____.	**la porte numéro ____.**
	lah pohrt nue-may-roh

For a full list of numbers, see p7.

the waiting area.	**la salle d'attente.**
	lah sahl dah-taw~t
the men's restroom.	**les WC pour hommes.**
	lay vay-say poor uhm

the women's restroom.	**les WC pour femmes.**
	lay vay-say poor fahm
the police station.	**le poste de police.**
	luh post duh poh-lees
a security guard.	**un agent de sécurité.**
	uh~-nah-zhaw~ duh say-kue-ree-tay
the smoking area.	**la salle fumeur.**
	lah sahl fue-moehr
the information booth.	**le guichet d'information.**
	luh gee-shay daw~-fohr-mah-see-yoh~
a public telephone.	**un téléphone public.**
	uh~ tay-lay-fohn pue-bleek
an ATM.	**un distributeur automatique.**
	uh~ dees-tree-bue-toehr oh-toh-mah-teek
baggage claim.	**la zone de récupération des bagages.**
	lah zohn duh ray-kue-pay-rah-see-yoh~ day bah-gahzh
a luggage cart.	**un caddie.**
	uh~ kah-dee
a currency exchange.	**un bureau de change.**
	uh~ bue-roh duh shaw~zh
a mobile phone rental.	**un point de location de téléphone portable.**
	uh~ pwuh~ duh lo-kah-syoh~ duh tel-eh~phone pohr-ta-bleh
a café.	**un café.**
	uh~ kah-fay
a restaurant.	**un restaurant.**
	uh~ reh-stoh-raw~
a bar.	**un bar.**
	uh~ bahr
a bookstore or newsstand.	**une librairie ou un kiosque à journaux.**
	oon lee-brey-ree oo uh~ kee-yohsk ah zhoohr-noh

a duty-free shop.

une boutique hors taxe.
oon boo-teek ohr tahks

Is there Wi-Fi here?

Est-il possible d'accéder au wi-fi d'ici ?
ey-teel poh-see-bluh dahk-say-day oh wee-fee dee-see

May I have someone paged, please?

Pourriez-vous appeler quelqu'un par haut-parleur, s'il vous plaît ?
poo-ryay voo ah-play kehl-kuh~ pahr oh pahr-loehr seel voo play

Do you accept credit cards?

Acceptez-vous les cartes de crédit ?
ahk-sehp-tay-voo lay kahrt duh kray-dee

CHECKING IN

I would like a one-way ticket to _____.

Je voudrais un aller simple pour _____.
zhuh voo-dray uh~-nah-lay seh~-pluh poohr

I would like a round-trip ticket to _____.

Je voudrais un aller-retour pour _____.
zhuh voo-dray uh~-nah-lay ruh-toohr poohr

How much are the tickets?

Combien coûtent les billets ?
koh~-byeh~ koot lay bee-yay

Do you have anything less expensive?

Avez-vous quelque chose de moins cher ?
ah-vay-voo kehl-kuh shohz duh mwaw~ shayhr

What time does flight _____ leave?

À quelle heure le vol _____ part-il ?
ah keh-loehr luh vohl _____ pahr-teel

What time does flight _____ arrive?

À quelle heure le vol _____ arrive-t-il ?
ah keh-loehr luh vohl _____ ah-reev-teel

How long is the flight?

Combien de temps le vol dure-t-il ?
koh~-byeh~ duh taw~ luh vohl duehr-teel

Common Airport Signs

Arrivées	Arrivals
Départs	Departures
Terminal	Terminal
Porte	Gate
Guichets	Ticketing
Douane	Customs
Récupération des bagages	Baggage Claim
Pousser	Push
Tirer	Pull
Interdiction de fumer	No Smoking
Entrée	Entrance
Sortie	Exit
Hommes	Men's
Femmes	Women's
Navettes	Shuttle Buses
Taxis	Taxis

Do I have a connecting flight?	**Y a-t-il une correspondance ?** *yah-teel oon koh-ray-spoh~-daw~s*
Do I need to change planes?	**Dois-je changer d'avion ?** *dwah-zhuh shaw~-zhay dah-vee-yoh~*
My flight leaves at __:__ (time).	**Mon vol part à ____ heures ____.** *moh~ vohl pahr ah ____ oehr ____*
What time will the flight arrive?	**A quelle heure le vol va-t-il arriver ?** *ah keh-loehr luh vohl vah teel ah-ree-vay*
Is the flight on time?	**Le vol est-il à l'heure ?** *luh vohl ey-teel ah-loehr*
Is the flight delayed?	**Le vol est-il en retard ?** *luh vohl ey-teel aw~ ruh-tahr*

For full coverage of numbers, see p7.
For full coverage of time, see p12.

From which terminal is flight _____ leaving?

De quel terminal le vol _____ part-il ?
duh kehl tayhr-mee-nahl luh vohl _____ pahr-teel

From which gate is flight _____ leaving?

De quelle porte le vol _____ part-il ?
duh kehl pohrt luh vohl _____ pahr-teel

How much time do I need for check-in?

De combien de temps ai-je besoin pour l'enregistrement ?
duh koh~byeh~ duh taw~ ay-zhuh buh-zweh~ poohr law~-reh-zhee-struh-maw~

Is there an express check-in line?

Y a-t-il une file d'enregistrement express ?
yah-teel oon feel daw~-reh-zhee-struh-maw~ ehk-spress

Is online check-in available?

Y a-t-il un point d'enregistrement électronique ?
yah-teel uh~ pwah daw~-rehzh-ee-strumaw~ ay-lehk-troh~-ik

Questions you may be asked

Passeport s'il vous plaît ?
pahs-pohr seel voo play

Your passport, please.

Quel est le but de votre visite ?
keh-lay luh bue duh voh-tre vee-zeet

What is the purpose of your visit?

Quelle est la durée de votre séjour ?
keh-lay lah dueh-ray duh voh-tre seh-zhoohr

How long will you be staying?

Votre lieu de résidence ?
voh-tre lyoeh duh ray-zee-daw~s

Where are you staying?

**Avez-vous quelque chose
à déclarer ?**
ah-vay-voo kehl-kuh shohz ah day-klah-ray

Do you have anything to declare?

Ouvrez ce sac s'il vous plaît.
oov-ray suh sack seel voo play

Open this bag, please.

Seat Preferences

I would like _____
ticket(s) in _____

Je voudrais _____ billet(s) de _____
zhuh voo-dray _____ bee-yay duh _____

first class.

première classe.
preh-mee-yayhr klahs

business class.

classe affaires.
klahs ah-fayhr

economy class.

classe économique.
klahs ay-koh~-noh-meek

I would like _____

Je voudrais _____
zhuh voo-dray _____

Please don't give me _____

S'il vous plaît, ne me donnez pas_____
seel voo play nuh muh doh-nay pah

a window seat.

une place côté hublot.
oon plahs koh-tay oo-bloh

an aisle seat.

une place côté couloir.
oon plahs koh-tay kool-wahr

an emergency exit row
seat.

une place côté issue de secours.
*oon plahs koh-tay ee-sue duh
suh-koohr*

a bulkhead seat.

une place au premier rang.
oon plahs oh pruh-myay raw~

a seat by the restroom.	**une place près des toilettes.** *oon plahs pray day twah-leht*
a seat near the front.	**une place à l'avant de l'avion.** *oon plahs ah lah-vaw~ duh lah-vee-yoh~*
a seat near the middle.	**une place au milieu de l'avion.** *oon plahs oh meel-yoeh duh lah-vee-yoh~*
a seat near the back.	**une place à l'arrière de l'avion.** *oon plahs ah lah-ree-yayhr duh lah-vee-yoh~*
Is there a meal on the flight?	**Un repas sera-t-il servi durant le vol ?** *uh~ ruh-pah suh-rah-teel sayhr-vee due-raw~ luh vohl*
I'd like to order _____	**Je voudrais commander _____** *zhuh voo-dray koh-maw~-day*
a vegetarian meal.	**un repas végétarien.** *uh~ ruh-pah vay-zhay-tah-ree-yeh~*
a kosher meal.	**un repas kasher.** *uh~ ruh-pah kah-shayhr*
a gluten-free meal.	**un repas sans gluten.** *uh~ ruh-pah saw~ glue-ten*
a diabetic meal.	**un repas spécial diabétique.** *uh~ ruh-pah spay-see-yahl dee-ah-bay-teek*
I am traveling to _____.	**Je vais à _____.** *zhuh vay ah*
I am coming from _____.	**Je viens de _____.** *zhuh vee-yeh~ duh*
I arrived from _____.	**Je suis arrivé(e) de _____.** *zhuh sweez-ah-ree-vay duh*

For full coverage of countries, see English / French dictionary.

May I _____ my reservation?	**Puis-je _____ ma réservation ?** *Pwee-zhuh _____ mah ray-suhr-vah-see-yoh~*
change	**changer** *shaw~-zhay*

cancel	**annuler**
	aw~-nue-lay
confirm	**confirmer**
	koh~-feer-may
I have ____ bags / suitcases to check.	**J'ai ____ sacs / valises à enregistrer.**
	zhay ____ sahk / vah-leez ah aw~-reh-zhee-stray

For a full list of numbers, see p7.

Passengers with Special Needs

Is that handicapped accessible?	**Ce vol est-il accessible aux personnes à mobilité réduite ?**
	suh vohl ey-teel ahk-suhs-see-bluh oh payhr-suh-nah moh-bee-lee-tay ray-dweet
May I have a wheelchair / walker, please?	**Puis-je avoir un fauteuil roulant / un déambulateur, s'il vous plaît ?**
	Pwee-je ah-vwahr uh~ fo-teh~y roo-law~ / uh~ day-aw~-bue-lah-toehr seel voo play
I need some assistance boarding.	**J'ai besoin d'assistance à l'embarquement.**
	zhay buh-zweh~ dah-sees-taw~s ah law~-bahrk-maw~
I need to bring my service dog.	**J'ai besoin d'emmener mon chien car j'ai un handicap.**
	zhay buh-sweh~ daw~-m~nay moh-shyeh~ car zhay uh~ and-ee-cap
Do you have services for the deaf?	**Offrez-vous des services spéciaux aux malentendants ?**
	oh-fray-voo day sayhr-vees spay-see-yoh oh mah-law~-taw~-daw~
Do you have services for the blind?	**Offrez-vous des services spéciaux aux malvoyants ?**
	oh-fray-voo day sayhr-vees spay-see-yoh oh mahl-vwah-yaw~

Trouble at Check-In

| How long is the delay? | **Le retard est de combien de temps ?** |
| | *luh ruh-tahr ay duh koh~-bee-yeh~ duh taw~* |

My flight was late.	**Mon vol avait du retard.**
	moh~ voh-lah-vay due ruh-tahr
I missed my flight.	**J'ai manqué mon vol.**
	zhay maw~-kay moh~ vohl
When is the next flight?	**À quelle heure part le prochain vol ?**
	ah keh-loehr pahr luh pro-shaw~ vohl
May I have a meal voucher?	**Puis-je avoir un chèque-repas ?**
	pwee-zhuh ah-vwahr uh~ shek-ruh-pah
May I have a room voucher?	**Puis-je avoir un bon pour une chambre ?**
	pwee-zhuh ah-vwahr uh~ boh~-poor oon shaw~-bruh

AT CUSTOMS / SECURITY CHECKPOINTS

I'm traveling with a group.	**Je voyage avec un groupe.**
	zhuh vwah-yahzh ah-vek uh~ groop
I'm on my own.	**Je voyage seul(e).**
	zhuh vwah-yahzh soehl
I'm traveling on business.	**Je voyage pour affaires.**
	zhuh vwah-yahzh poohr-rah-fayhr
I'm on vacation.	**Je suis en vacances.**
	zhuh swee-zaw~ vah-kaw~s
I have nothing to declare.	**Je n'ai rien à déclarer.**
	zhuh nay ryeh~ nah day-klah-ray
I would like to declare ____.	**Je voudrais déclarer ____.**
	zhuh voo-dray day-klah-ray
I have some liquor.	**J'ai de l'alcool.**
	zhay duh lahl-kool
I have some cigars.	**J'ai des cigares.**
	zhay day see-gahr
They are gifts.	**Il s'agit de cadeaux.**
	eel sah-zee duh kah-doh
They are for personal use.	**Ils sont pour mon usage personnel.**
	eel soh~ poohr moh~-nue-sahzh payhr-suh-nehl

Listen Up: Security Lingo

Veuillez enlever vos chaussures / bijoux. *voeh-yay aw~-luh-vay voh shoh-shuehr / bee-zhooh*	Please remove your shoes / jewelry.
Veuillez enlever votre blouson / pull. *voeh-yay aw~-luh-vay voh-tre bloo-zoh~ / puell*	Please remove your jacket / sweater.
Veuillez placer vos bagages sur le tapis roulant. *voeh-yay plahsay voh bah-gazh shuehr luh ta-pee roo-law~*	Please place your bags on the conveyor belt.
Veuillez vous mettre sur le côté. *voeh-yay voo meht-treh shuehr luh koh-tay*	Please step to the side.
Nous désirons vous fouiller. *noo day-see-roh~ voo foo-wee-yay*	We have to do a hand search.

That is my medicine.	**Ce médicament est à moi.** *suh may-dee-ka-maw~ ey-tah mwah*
I have my prescription.	**J'ai l'ordonnance qui va avec.** *zhay lohr-doh~-naw~s kee vah ah-vek*
May I have a male / female officer conduct the search?	**Puis-je être fouillé(e) par un officier du sexe masculin / féminin ?** *pwee-zhuh eh-truh foo-wee-yay pahr uh~-noh-fee-see-yay due sehks mah-skue-law~ / fay-mee-naw~*

Trouble at Security

Help me. I've lost _____	**Veuillez m'aider. J'ai perdu _____**
	voeh-yay may-day; zhay payhr-due
my passport.	**mon passeport.**
	moh~ pahs-pohr
my boarding pass.	**ma carte d'embarquement.**
	mah~ kart daw~-bahrk-maw~
my identification.	**ma pièce d'identité.**
	mah pee-yehs dee-daw~-tee-tay
my wallet.	**mon portefeuille.**
	moh~ pohr-tuh-foeh-yuh
my purse.	**mon sac à main.**
	moh~ sah-kah meh~
Someone stole my purse / wallet!	**On a volé mon sac à main / mon portefeuille.**
	oh~-nah voh-lay moh~ sah-kah meh~ / moh~ pohr-tuh-foeh-yuh

IN-FLIGHT

It's unlikely you'll need much French on the plane, but these phrases will help if a bilingual flight attendant is unavailable or if you need to talk to a French-speaking neighbor.

I think that's my seat.	**Je pense que c'est ma place.**
	zhuh paw~s kuh say mah plahs
May I have _____	**Puis-je avoir _____**
	pwee-zhuh ah-vwahr
mineral water?	**de l'eau minérale ?**
	duh loh-mee-ney-rahl
water (plain)?	**de l'eau non-gazeuse ?**
	duh loh due noh~-gah-zoehz
sparkling water?	**de l'eau pétillante / de l'eau gazeuse ?**
	duh loh peh-tee-yaw~t / duh loh gaz-eh~s

orange juice?	**un jus d'orange ?** *uh~ zhue doh-raw~zh*
a soda?	**un soda ?** *uh~ saw-dah*
a diet soda?	**un soda allégé ?** *uh~ saw-dah ah-lay-zhay*
a beer?	**une bière ?** *oon bee-yahr*
some wine?	**du vin ?** *due veh~*

For a full list of drinks, see p96.

a pillow?	**un oreiller ?** *uh~-noh-ray-yay*
a blanket?	**une couverture ?** *oon koo-vayhr-tuehr*
headphones?	**un casque / des écouteurs ?** *uh~ kahsk / deh-z ay-koo-tehr*
a magazine or newspaper?	**un magazine ou un journal ?** *uh~ mah-gah-zeen oo uh~ zhoohr-nahl*
When will the meal be served?	**Quand le repas sera-t-il servi ?** *kaw~ luh ruh-pah suh-rah-teel sayhr-vee*
How long until we land?	**Dans combien de temps allons-nous atterrir ?** *daw~ koh~-bee-yeh~ duh taw~ ah-loh~-noo ah-teh-reehr*
May I move to another seat?	**Puis-je changer de place ?** *pwee-zhuh shaw~-zhay duh plahs*
How do I turn the light on / off?	**Comment allume-t-on / éteint-on la lumière ?** *koh-moh~ ah-luem-toh / ay-teh~-toh~ la lue-myayhr*

Trouble In-Flight

These headphones are broken.	**Mon casque ne marche pas.**
	moh~ kask nuh mahrsh pah
Excuse me, I spilled something.	**Pardon, je me suis renversé quelque chose dessus.**
	pahr-doh~ zhuh muh swee raw~- vayhr-say kehl-kuh shohz duh-sue
My child spilled something.	**Mon enfant s'est renversé quelque chose dessus.**
	moh~-naw~-faw~ say raw~-vayhr- say kehl-kuh shohz duh-sue
My child is sick.	**Mon enfant est malade.**
	moh~-naw~-faw~-tay mah-lahd
I need an airsickness bag.	**J'ai besoin d'un sac pour le mal de l'air.**
	zhay buh-zweh~ duh~ sahk poohr luh mahl duh layhr
I smell something strange.	**Je sens quelque chose de bizarre.**
	zhuh saw~ kehl-kuh shohz duh bee-zahr
That passenger is behaving suspiciously.	**Ce passager se comporte bizarrement.**
	suh pah-sah-zhay suh koh~-pohrt bee-zahr-maw~

BAGGAGE CLAIM

Where is baggage claim for flight ____?	**Où est la zone de récupération des bagages pour le vol ____ ?**
	oo ay lah zohn duh ray-kue-pay-rah- see-yoh~ day bah-gazh poohr luh vohl
Would you please help me with my bags?	**Pouvez-vous m'aider à trouver mes bagages, s'il vous plaît ?**
	poo-vay-voo may-day ah troo-vay may bah-gazh seel voo play
I am missing ____ bags / suitcases.	**Il me manque ____ sacs / valises.**
	eel muh maw~k ____ sahk / vah-leez
For a full list of numbers, see p7.	

My bag is / was _____	**Mon sac est / était** _____
	moh~ sah-kay / sah-kay-tay
lost.	**perdu.**
	payhr-due
damaged.	**abîmé.**
	ah-bee-may
stolen.	**volé.**
	voh-lay
a suitcase.	**une valise.**
	oon vah-leez
a briefcase.	**un porte-documents.**
	uh~ pohrt-doh-kue-maw~
a carry-on.	**un bagage à main.**
	uh~ bah-gah-zhah meh~
a suit bag.	**un porte-costume.**
	uh~ pohrt-koh-stuem
a trunk.	**une malle.**
	oon mahl
golf clubs.	**des clubs de golf.**
	day klueb duh gohlf
hard.	**à coques dures.**
	ah kohk duehr
made out of _____	**en** _____
	aw~
canvas.	**toile.**
	twahl
vinyl.	**vinyle.**
	vee-neel
leather.	**cuir.**
	kweer
hard plastic.	**plastique dur.**
	plah-steek duehr
aluminum.	**aluminium.**
	ah-lue-mee-nee-uhm

For a full list of colors, see the English / French dictionary.

RENTING A VEHICLE

Is there a car rental agency in the airport?

Y a-t-il une agence de location de voitures dans cet aéroport ?
yah-teel oo-nah-zhaw~s duh loh-kah-see-yoh~ duh vwah-tuehr daw~ seh-tay-roh-pohr

I have a reservation.

J'ai une réservation.
zhay oon ray-zayhr-vah-see-yoh~

VEHICLE PREFERENCES

I would like to rent ____

Je voudrais louer ____
zhuh voo-dray loo-ay

an economy car.

une voiture économique.
oon vwah-tuehr ay-koh-noh-meek

a midsize car.

une voiture intermédiaire.
oon vwah-tuehr aw~-tayhr-may-dee-yayhr

a convertible.

une décapotable.
oon day-kah-poh-tah-bluh

a van.

une camionnette.
oon ka-mioh-net

a sports car.

une voiture de sport.
oon vwah-tuehr duh spohr

a 4-wheel-drive vehicle.

un véhicule à quatre roues motrices.
uh~ vay-ee-kue-lah ka-truh roo moh-tree~s

a motorcycle.

une moto.
oon moh-toh

a scooter.

un scooter.
uh~ skoo-tayhr

Do you have one with ____	**En avez-vous une avec ____** *aw~-nah-vay-voo oon ah-vek*
air conditioning?	**la climatisation ?** *lah klee-mah-tee-zah-see-yoh~*
a sunroof?	**un toit ouvrant ?** *uh~ twah oov-raw~*
a CD player?	**un lecteur de CD ?** *uh~ lek-toehr duh say-day*
an iPod connection?	**une prise iPod ?** *oon preez iPod*
a GPS system?	**le GPS ?** *leh zhay pay S*
a DVD player?	**un lecteur de DVD ?** *uh~ lek-toehr duh day-vay-day*
child seats?	**des sièges pour enfant ?** *day see-yehz poohr aw~-faw~*
Do you have ____	**Avez-vous ____** *ah-vay-voo*
a smaller car?	**une voiture plus petite ?** *oon vwah-tuehr plue puh-teet*
a bigger car?	**une voiture plus grande ?** *oon vwah-tuehr plue graw~d*
a cheaper car?	**une voiture moins chère ?** *oon vwah-tuehr mweh~ shayhr*
Do you have a nonsmoking car?	**Avez-vous une voiture non-fumeur ?** *ah-vay-voo oon vwah-tuehr noh~-fue-moehr*
I need an automatic transmission.	**J'ai besoin d'une voiture à transmission automatique.** *zhay buh-zweh~ doon vwah-tuehr ah traw~-z-mee-shee-yoh~ ohtoh-mah-teek*

A standard transmission is okay.	**D'accord pour une boîte de vitesses** *dah-kohr poohr oon bwaht duh vee-tess*
May I have an upgrade?	**Puis-je bénéficier de la classe supérieure ?** *pwee-zhuh bay-nay-fee-see-yay duh lah klahs sue-pay-ree-yoehr*

MONEY MATTERS

What's the daily / weekly / monthly rate?	**Quel est le tarif journalier / hebdomadaire / mensuel ?** *keh-lay luh tah-reef zhoohr-nah-lee-yay / ehb-doh-mah-dayhr / maw~-swehl*
What is the mileage rate?	**Quel est le prix au kilomètre ?** *keh-lay luh pree oh kee-loh-meh-truh*
How much is insurance?	**Combien coûte l'assurance ?** *koh~-bee-yeh~ koot lah-sue-raw~s*
Are there other fees?	**Y a-t-il des frais supplémentaires ?** *yah-teel day fray suh-play-maw~-ter*
Is there a weekend rate?	**Y a-t-il un tarif spécial pour le week-end ?** *yah-teel uh~ tah-reef spay-see-yahl poohr luh wee-kend*

TECHNICAL QUESTIONS

What kind of gas does it take?	**Quel type d'essence consomme-t-elle ?** *kehl teep day-saw~s koh~-som-tehl*
Do you have the manual in English?	**Avez-vous un manuel en anglais ?** *ah-vay-voo uh~ maw~-nwehl aw~-naw~-glay*
Do you have an English booklet with the local traffic laws?	**Avez-vous une brochure en anglais sur le code de la route local ?** *ah-vay-voo oon broh-shuehr aw~-naw~-glay suehr luh kohd duh lah root loh-kahl*

Road Signs

Vitesse limitée	Speed Limit
Stop	Stop
Céder le passage	Yield
Danger	Danger
Voie sans issue	No Exit
Voie unique	One Way
Entrée interdite	Do Not Enter
Route fermée	Road Closed
Péage	Toll
Espèces uniquement	Cash Only
Parking interdit	No Parking
Parking payant	Parking Fee
Garage couvert	Parking Garage

CAR TROUBLES

The ____ doesn't work.

Le ____ ne marche pas.
luh ____ nuh mahrsh pah

See diagram on p62 for car parts.

It is already dented.

La carrosserie est déjà abîmée.
lah kah-roh-seh-ree ay day-zhah ah-bee-may

It is scratched.

La carrosserie est rayée.
lah kah-roh-seh-ree ay ray-ay

The windshield is cracked.

Il y a un impact sur le pare-brise.
eel ya uh~ uh~-pact sue~r luh pahr-breez.

The tires look low.

Les pneus ont l'air dégonflés.
lay puh-noeh oh~ layhr day-gon-flay

It has a flat tire.

L'un des pneus est à plat.
luh~ day puh-noeh ay-tah plah

Whom do I call for service?

Qui dois-je appeler pour me faire dépanner ?
kee dwah-zhuh ah-play poohr muh fayhr day-pah-nay

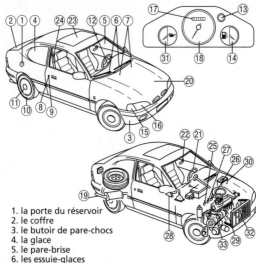

1. la porte du réservoir
2. le coffre
3. le butoir de pare-chocs
4. la glace
5. le pare-brise
6. les essuie-glaces
7. le lave-glace
8. la serrure
9. la serrure automatique
10. le pneu
11. la roue
12. l'allumage
13. les feux de détresse
14. la jauge d'essence
15. le clignotant
16. les feux avant
17. le compteur kilométrique
18. l'indicateur de vitesse
19. le silencieux
20. le capot
21. le volant
22. le rétroviseur

23. le toit ouvrant
24. la ceinture de sécurité
25. la pédale
26. l'embrayage
27. le frein
28. le frein à main
29. le moteur
30. la batterie
31. l'indicateur de niveau d'huile (à moteur)
32. le radiateur
33. la courroie du ventilateur

It won't start.	**Elle refuse de démarrer.**
	ehl ruh-fuez duh day-mah-ray
It's out of gas.	**Elle est en panne d'essence.**
	ehl ay-taw~ pahn day-saw~s
The check engine light is on.	**Le voyant de contrôle du moteur est allumé.**
	luh vwah-yaw~ duh koh~-trohl due moh-toehr ay-tah-lue-may
The oil light is on.	**Le voyant de niveau d'huile est allumé.**
	luh vwah-yaw~ duh nee-voh dweel ay-tah-lue-may
The brake light is on.	**Le voyant de contrôle des freins est allumé.**
	luh vwah-yaw~ duh koh~-trohl day frehn ay-tah-lue-may
It runs rough.	**La conduite est trop serrée.**
	lah koh~-dwee-tay troh suh-ray
The car is overheating.	**Le moteur chauffe.**
	luh moh-toehr shohf

Asking for Directions

Excuse me, please.	**Excusez-moi, s'il vous plaît.**
	ehks-kue-zay mwah seel voo play
How do I get to ____?	**Comment fais-je pour aller à ____ ?**
	koh-moh fay-zhuh pooh-rah-lay ah
Go straight.	**Allez tout droit.**
	ah-lay too dwah
Turn left / right.	**Tournez à gauche / à droite.**
	toohr-nay ah gohsh / ah dwaht
Continue right.	**Continuez à droite.**
	koh~-teen-yue-ay ah dwaht
It's on the right.	**C'est à droite.**
	say-tah dwaht
Can you show me on the map?	**Pouvez-vous me montrer sur la carte ?**
	poo-vay-voo muh moh~-tray suehr lah kahrt

What are the GPS coordinates?	**Quelles sont les coordonnées GPS ?** *kehl soh~ luh koh ohr-doh~-nay* *zhay pay ess*
Is it far from here?	**Est-ce loin d'ici ?** *ehs lweh dee-see*
Is this the right way for ____?	**Est-ce que c'est la bonne route pour ____ ?** *ehs kuh say lah buhn root pohr*
I've lost my way.	**Je me suis perdu(e).** *zhuh muh swee payhr-due*
Could you repeat that, please?	**Est-ce que vous pouvez répéter, s'il vous plaît ?** *ehs kuh voo poo-vay ruh-puh-tay seel voo play*
Thanks for your help.	**Merci pour votre aide.** *mayhr-see pohr voh-trehd*

For a full list of direction-related terms, see p5.

SORRY, OFFICER

What is the speed limit?	**Quelle est la limitation de vitesse ?** *keh-lay lah lee-mee-tay-see-yoh~ duh vee-tess*
I wasn't going that fast.	**Je n'allais pas si vite.** *zhuh nah-lay pah see veet*
Where do I pay the fine?	**Où dois-je payer l'amende ?** *oo dwah-zhuh pay-ay lah-maw~d*
How much is the fine?	**Combien coûte l'amende ?** *koh~-byeh~ koot lah-maw~d*
Do I have to go to court?	**Dois-je passer en justice ?** *dwah-zhuh pah-say aw~ zhues-tees*
I had an accident.	**J'ai eu un accident.** *zhay oo uh~-nahk-see-daw~*
The other driver hit me.	**C'est l'autre conducteur qui m'est rentré dedans.** *say loh-truh koh~-duek-toehr kee may raw~-tray duh-daw~*

I'm at fault.	**C'est moi qui suis responsable.**
	say mwah kee swee ruh-spoh~-sah-bluh

BY TAXI

Where is the taxi stand?	**Où est la station de taxi ?**
	oo ay lah stah-see-yon duh tahk-see
Is there a shuttle bus between the airport and my hotel?	**Y a-t-il une navette entre l'aéroport et mon hôtel ?**
	yah-teel oon nah-veht aw~-truh la-ay-roh-pohr ay moh~-noh-tel
I need to get to ____.	**Je désire aller à ____.**
	zhuh day-seer ah-lay ah ____
How much will that cost?	**Combien va coûter la course ?**
	koh~-bee-yeh~ vah koo-tay lah koohrs
Can you take me / us to the train / bus station?	**Pouvez-vous m'emmener / nous emmener à la gare / à la gare routière ?**
	poo-vay-voo maw~m-nay / nooz-ah~m-nay ah lah gahr / ah lah gahr roo-tee-yayhr
I am in a hurry.	**Je suis pressé(e).**
	zhuh swee pruh-say
Slow down.	**Veuillez ralentir.**
	voeh-yay rah-law~-teehr

GETTING THERE

Listen Up: Taxi Lingo

Montez ! *moh~-tay*	Get in!
Laissez vos bagages. Je m'en occupe. *leh-zay voh bah-gazh. zhuh maw~ ohk-kuep*	Leave your luggage. I got it.
C'est ____ euros par bagage. *say oeh-roh pahr bah-gazh*	It's ____ for each bag.
Combien de passagers ? *koh~-byeh~ duh pah-sah-zhay*	How many passengers?
Vous êtes pressés ? *vooz-eht pray-say*	Are you in a hurry?

Am I close enough to walk?	**Est-ce assez près pour y aller à pied ?** *eh-sah-say pray poohr yah-lay ah pee-ay*
Please let me out here.	**Laissez-moi descendre ici, s'il vous plaît.** *leh-zay mwah duh-saw~-druh ee-see seel voo play*
That's not the correct change.	**Vous ne m'avez pas rendu la bonne monnaie.** *voo nuh mah-vay pah raw~-due lah buhn moh-nay*

For a full list of numbers, see p7.

BY TRAIN

How do I get to the train station?	**Comment puis-je me rendre à la gare ?** *koh-maw~ pwee-zhuh muh raw~-drah lah gahr*
Would you take me to the train station?	**Pouvez-vous m'emmener à la gare ?** *poo-vay-voo maw~m-nay ah lah gahr*
How long is the trip to ____?	**Il y a combien de kilomètres jusqu'à ____ ?** *eel-yah koh~-bee-yeh~ duh kee-loh-meh-truh zhues-kah*
When is the next train?	**À quelle heure part le prochain train ?** *ah keh-loehr pahr luh pro-shaw~-treh~*
Do you have a schedule?	**Avez-vous un horaire des départs ?** *ah-vay-voo-zuh~-nohr-ayhr day day-pahr*

Do I have to change trains?	**Dois-je changer de train ?**
	dwah-zhuh shaw~-zhay duh treh~
a one-way ticket	**un aller simple**
	uh~-nah-lay seh~-pluh
a round-trip ticket	**un aller-retour**
	uh~-nah-lay ruh-toohr
Which platform does it leave from?	**De quel quai le train part-il?**
	duh kehl kay luh treh~ pahr-teel
Is there a bar car?	**Y a-t-il un service de boissons ?**
	yah-teel uh~ sayhr-vees duh bwah-soh~s
Is there a dining car?	**Y a-t-il un wagon-restaurant ?**
	yah-teel uh~ vah-goh~ reh-stoh-raw~
Which car is my seat in?	**Dans quel wagon se trouve ma place ?**
	daw~ kehl vah-goh~ suh troov mah plahs
Is this seat taken?	**Ce siège est-il pris ?**
	suh see-yehzh ey-teel pree
Where is the next stop?	**Quel est le prochain arrêt ?**
	keh-lay luh proh-sheh~-nah-rey
Would you please tell me how many stops to ____?	**Pouvez-vous me dire combien d'arrêts il y a avant ____ ?**
	poo-vay-voo muh deer koh~-bee-yeh~ dah-rey eel-yah ah-vaw~
What's the train number and destination?	**Quel est le numéro du train et sa destination ?**
	keh-lay luh nue-may-roh due treh~ ay sah deh-stee-nah-see-yoh~

BY BUS

How do I get to the bus station?

Comment puis-je me rendre à la gare routière ?
koh-maw~ pwee-zhuh muh raw~-druh ah lah gahr roo-tee-yayhr

Would you take me to the bus station?

Pouvez-vous m'emmener à la gare routière ?
poo-vay-voo maw~m-nay ah lah gahr roo-tee-yayhr

May I please have a bus schedule?

Puis-je avoir un horaire des cars ?
pwee-zhuh ah-vwahr uh~-noh-rayhr day kahr

Which bus goes to ____?

Quel car va à ____ ?
kehl kahr vah ah ____

Where does it leave from?

D'où part-il ?
due pahr-teel

How long does the bus take?

Combien de temps met le car ?
koh~-byeh~ duh taw~ may luh kahr

How much is it?

Combien ça coûte ?
koh~-bee-yeh~ sah koot

Is there an express bus?

Y a-t-il un service direct ?
yah-teel uh~ sayhr-vees dee-rekt

Does it make local stops?
Dessert-il toutes les villes ?
duh-zayhr-teel toot lay veel

Does it run at night?
Fonctionne-t-il pendant la nuit ?
*foh~k-see-yoh~-teel paw~-daw~
lah nwee*

When is the next bus?
À quelle heure part le prochain car ?
*ah keh-loehr pahr luh proh-sheh~
kahr*

a one-way ticket
un aller simple
uh~-nah-lay seh~-pluh

a round-trip ticket
un aller-retour
uh~-nah-lay ruh-toohr

How long will the bus be stopped?
Combien de temps dure l'arrêt ?
koh~-byeh~-duh taaw~ duhr lay-rey

Is there an air conditioned bus?
Y a-t-il un car climatisé ?
yah-teel uh~ kahr klee-mah-tee-zay

Is this seat taken?
Ce siège est-il pris ?
suh see-yehzh ey-teel pree

Where is the next stop?
Quel est le prochain arrêt ?
keh-lay luh proh-sheh~-nah-rey

Would you please tell me when we reach _____?
Pouvez-vous me dire quand nous atteindrons _____ ?
poo-vay voo muh deer kaw~ noo zah-teh~droh~

Would you please tell me how to get to _____?
Pouvez-vous me dire comment aller à _____, s'il vous plaît ?
*poo-vay-voo muh deer koh-maw~
ah-lay ah ___ seel voo play*

I'd like to get off here.
Je voudrais descendre ici.
zhuh voo-dray duh-saw~-druh ee-see

BY BOAT OR SHIP

Would you take me to the port?	**Pouvez-vous m'emmener au port?** *poo-vay-voo meh-men-ay oh pohr*
When does the boat sail?	**Quand le navire appareille-t-il ?** *kaw~ luh nah-veer ah-pah-ray teel*
How long is the voyage?	**Combien de temps la traversée dure-t-elle ?** *koh~-bee-yeh~-duh taw~ lah trah-vayhr-say duehr-tehl*
Where are the life preservers?	**Où sont les bouées de sauvetage ?** *oo soh~ lay boo-ay duh sohv-tazh*
I would like a private cabin.	**Je voudrais une cabine individuelle.** *zhuh voo-dray oon kah-been eh~-dee-vee-due-ehl*
Is the trip rough?	**Le voyage, est-il difficile ?** *luh vwah-yahzh ey-teel dee-fee-seel*
I feel seasick.	**J'ai le mal de mer.** *zhay luh mahl duh mayhr*
I need some Dramamine.	**Je voudrais de la Dramamine.** *zhuh voo-dray duh lah drah-mah-meen*
Where is the bathroom?	**Où puis-je trouver des WC ?** *oo pwee-zhuh troo-vay day vay-say*
Does the ship have a casino?	**Y a-t-il un casino à bord ?** *yah-teel uh~ kah-zee-noh ah bohr*
Will the ship stop at ports along the way?	**Le navire fera-t-il escale dans certains ports ?** *luh nah-veer fuh-rah teel ehs-kahl daw~ sayhr-teh~ pohr*

BY SUBWAY

A very convenient, fast, safe and inexpensive way to cruise through a French city is to take its **Métro**. Note that subways close at night (the Paris Métro closes from 12:50 AM to 5:30 AM), so do allocate enough time for your trip back to your hotel!

Where is the subway station?	**Où se trouve la station du métro ?** *oo suh troov lah stah-see-yoh~ due meh-troh*
Where can I buy a ticket?	**Où achète-t-on des billets ?** *oo ah-sheh-toh~ day bee-yay*
Could I have a map of the subway, please?	**Pouvez-vous me donner un plan de métro s'il vous plaît ?** *poo-vay voo mush duh-nay uh~ plaw~ duh meh-troh seel voo play*
Which line should I take for _____?	**Quelle ligne prend-on pour aller à _____ ?** *kehl lee-nyeh paw~ toh~ poor ah-lay ah*
Is this the right line for _____?	**Est-ce la bonne ligne pour aller à _____ ?** *ehs lah buhn lee-nyeh poor ah-lay ah*
Which stop is it for _____?	**Quel arrêt pour _____ ?** *keh-lah-rey poohr*
How many stops is it to _____?	**Combien d'arrêts jusqu'à _____ ?** *koh~-bee-yeh~ dah-rey zhues-kah*
Is the next stop _____?	**L' arrêt prochain, c'est _____ ?** *lah-rey proh-sheh~ say*
Where are we?	**Où sommes-nous ?** *oo suhm-noo*

Where do I change to _____?	**Où est-ce que je change pour aller à _____ ?** *oo ehs kuh zhuh shaw~ poor ah-lay ah _____*
What time is the last train to _____?	**À quelle heure part le dernier train pour _____ ?** *ah keh-loehr pahr luh dayhr-nyay treh~ poor _____*

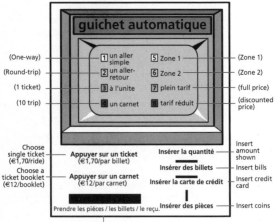

guichet automatique

(One-way)	**1** un aller simple	**5** Zone 1	(Zone 1)
(Round-trip)	**2** un aller-retour	**6** Zone 2	(Zone 2)
(1 ticket)	**3** à l'unite	**7** plein tarif	(full price)
(10 trip)	**4** un carnet	**8** tarif réduit	(discounted price)

Choose single ticket (€1,70) — **Appuyer sur un ticket** (€1,70/par billet)
Choose a ticket booklet (€12/booklet) — **Appuyer sur un carnet** (€12/par carnet)

Insérer la quantité — Insert amount shown
Insérer des billets — Insert bills
Insérer la carte de crédit — Insert credit card
Insérer des pièces — Insert coins

Prendre les piéces / les billets / le reçu. — Take change / tickets / receipt

TRAVELERS WITH SPECIAL NEEDS

Do you have wheelchair access?

Y a-t-il un accès pour fauteuils roulants ?
yah teel uh~ ak-say poor fo-teh~y roo-law~

Do you have elevators? Where?

Y a-t-il des ascenseurs ? Où ?
yah-teel day-zah-saw~-soehrs oo

Do you have ramps? Where?

Y a-t-il des rampes d'accès ?
yah teel day raw~-pah dak-say

Are the restrooms handicapped accessible?

Les toilettes sont-elles accessibles aux personnes à mobilité réduite ?
lay twah-leht soh~-tehl ahk-seh-see-bluh oh payhr-suhn ah moh-bee-lee-tay ray-dweet

Do you have audio assistance for deaf persons?

Offrez-vous des services audio aux malentendants ?
oh-fray-voo day sayhr-vees oh-dee-yoh oh mah-law~-taw~-daw~

I am deaf / hearing impaired.

Je suis sourd(e) / malentendant(e).
zhuh swee soohr(d) / mah-law~-taw~-daw~(t)

May I bring my service dog?

Puis-je emmener mon chien ? Je suis handicapé(e).
pwee-zhuh aw~-m-nay moh~-shyeh~ zhuh swee and-ee-ka-pay

I am blind / visually impaired.

Je suis aveugle / malvoyant(e).
zhuh swee ah-voeh-gluh / mahl-vwah-yaw~(t)

I need to charge my power chair.

J'ai besoin d'assistance pour recharger mon fauteuil électrique.
zhay buh-sweh~ dah-see-staw~s poor ruh-shar-jay moh~ fo-teh~y roo-law~

CHAPTER THREE

LODGING

This chapter will help you find the right accomodations, at the right price—and the amenities you might need during your stay.

ROOM PREFERENCES

Would you please recommend _____	**Pourriez-vous me recommander _____**
	pooh-ree-yay-voo muh ruh-koh-maw~-day
a clean hostel?	**une auberge propre ?**
	oo-noh-bayrzh proh-pruh
a moderately priced hotel?	**un hôtel à prix moyen ?**
	uh~ noh-tehl oh pree mwah-yaw~
a moderately priced B&B?	**une chambre d'hôtes / un bed and breakfast à prix moyen ?**
	oon shaw~-bruh doht / uh~ behd ahnd brehk-fahst oh pree mwah-yaw~
a good hotel / motel?	**un bon hôtel / motel ?**
	uh~ buh-noh-tehl / moh-tehl
Does the hotel have _____	**Cet hôtel a-t-il _____**
	seh-toh-tel ah-teel
an indoor/outdoor pool?	**une piscine intérieure / extérieure ?**
	oon pee-seen uh~-tay~r-year lex-tay~-r-year
a casino?	**un casino ?**
	uh~ kah-zee-noh
suites?	**des suites ?**
	day sweet
terraces?	**des chambres avec terrasse ?**
	day shaw~-bruh ah-vehk tay-rahs

a fitness center?	**une salle de musculation ?**
	oon sahl duh mues-kue-lah-see-yoh~
a spa?	**un spa ?**
	uh~ spah
a private beach?	**une plage privée ?**
	oon plazh pree-vay
a tennis court?	**un court de tennis ?**
	uh~ koohr duh tay-nees
air-conditioned rooms?	**chambres climatisées ?**
	shaw~-bruh klee-mah-tee-zay
free Wi-Fi?	**wi-fi gratuit ?**
	wee-fee grah-twee
I would like a room for ___ people.	**Je voudrais une chambre pour ___ personnes.**
	zhuh voo-dray oon shaw~-bruh poohr ___ payhr-suhn

For a full list of numbers, see p7.

I would like ___	**Je voudrais ___**
	zhuh voo-dray
a king-sized bed.	**une chambre à très grand lit.**
	oon shaw~-bruh ah tray graw~ lee
a double bed.	**une chambre à lit à une place.**
	oon shaw~-bruh ah lee ah oon plahs
twin beds.	**des lits jumeaux.**
	day lee zhue-moh

LODGING

Listen Up: Reservations Lingo

Nous sommes au complet. *noo sohm oh koh~-play*	We have no vacancies.
Combien de nuits désirez-vous rester ? *koh~-bee-yeh~ duh nwee day-zee-ray voo ruh-stay*	How long will you be staying?
Fumeur ou non-fumeur ? *fue-moehr oo noh~ fue-moehr*	Smoking or nonsmoking?

adjoining rooms.	**des chambres communicantes.**
	day shaw~-bruh koh-mue-neek-aw~t
a smoking room.	**une chambre fumeur**
	oon shaw~-bruh fue-moehr
nonsmoking room.	**une chambre non-fumeur.**
	oon shaw~-bruh noh~ fue-moehr
a private bathroom.	**une salle de bain privée.**
	oon sahl duh beh~ pree-vay
a room with a shower.	**une chambre avec douche.**
	oon shaw~-bruh ah-vehk doosh
a room with a bathtub.	**une chambre avec baignoire.**
	oon shaw~-bruh ah-vehk
	beh~-nwahr
air conditioning.	**la climatisation.**
	lah klee-mah-tee-zah-see-yoh
television.	**un poste de télévision.**
	pohst duh tay-lay-vee-zee-yoh~
cable.	**la télévision par câble.**
	lah tay-lay-vee-zee-yoh~ pahr
	kah-bluh
satellite TV.	**la télévision par satellite.**
	lah tay-lay-vee-zee-yoh~ pahr
	sah-teh-leet
a telephone.	**un téléphone.**
	un~ tay-lay-fohn
Internet access.	**accès à Internet.**
	ahk-say ah eh~-tayrh-neht
Wi-Fi.	**wi-fi**
	wee-fee
a refrigerator.	**un réfrigérateur.**
	uh~ ray-free-zheh-rah-toehr
a beach view.	**vue sur la mer.**
	vue suehr lah mayhr
a city view.	**vue sur la rue.**
	vue suehr lah rue

a kitchenette.	**une kitchenette.**
	oon kee-shee-neht
a balcony.	**un balcon.**
	uh~ bahl-koh~
a suite.	**une suite.**
	oon sweet
a penthouse.	**une chambre terrasse.**
	oon shaw~-bruh tay-rahs
I would like a room ____	**Je voudrais une chambre ____**
	zhuh voo-dray oon shaw~-bruh
on the ground floor.	**au rez-de-chaussée.**
	oh ray duh shoh-say
near the elevator.	**à proximité d'un ascenseur.**
	ah prok-see-mee-tay duh~ ah-saw~-soehr
near the stairs.	**à proximité d'un escalier.**
	ah prok-see-mee-tay duh~ ehs-kah-lee-yay
near the pool.	**à proximité de la piscine.**
	ah prok-see-mee-tay duh lah pee-zeen
away from the street.	**à l'écart de la rue.**
	ah lay-kahr duh lah rue
I would like a corner room.	**Je voudrais une chambre d'angle.**
	zhuh voo-dray oon shaw~-bruh daw~-gluh
Do you have ____	**Avez-vous ____**
	ah-vay-voo
a crib?	**un lit d'enfant ?**
	uh~ lee daw~-faw~
a foldout bed?	**un lit pliant ?**
	uh~ lee plee-yaw~

GUESTS WITH SPECIAL NEEDS

I need a room with _____	**J'ai besoin d'une chambre _____** *zhay buh-zweh~ doon shaw~-bruh*
wheelchair access.	**accessible en fauteil roulant.** *ahk-seh-see-bluh aw~ fo-teh~y roo-law~*
services for the visually impaired.	**équipée pour malvoyant.** *ay-kee-pay poohr mahl-vwahy-aw~*
services for the hearing impaired.	**équipée pour malentendant.** *ay-kee-pay poohr mah-law~-taw~-daw~*
I am traveling with a service dog.	**Je voyage avec un chien guide.** *zhuh vwah-yahzh ah-vek uh~ shyeh gee-d*

MONEY MATTERS

I would like to make a reservation.	**Je désire faire une réservation.** *zhuh day-zeer fayhr oon ray-zehr-vah-see-yoh~*
How much per night?	**Quel est le prix par nuit ?** *keh-lay luh pree pahr nwee*
Do you have a _____	**Avez-vous _____** *ah-vay-voo*
weekly rate?	**un tarif hebdomadaire ?** *uh~ tah-reef ehb-doh-mah-dayhr*
monthly rate?	**un tarif mensuel ?** *uh~ tah-reef maw~-swehl*
weekend rate?	**un tarif week-end ?** *uh~ tah-reef week-end*
a special rate?	**un tarif spécial ?** *uh~ tah-reef spay-cial*
a discount?	**une promotion ?** *oon pro-mo-tioh~*
We will be staying for _____ days / weeks / months.	**Nous désirons rester _____ nuits / semaines / mois.** *noo day-zeer-oh~ ruh-stay _____ nwee / smehn / mwah*

For full coverage of numbers, see p7.

When is checkout time?

À quelle heure la chambre doit-elle être libérée ?
ah keh-loehr lah shaw~-bruh dwah-tehl eh-truh lee-bay-ray

Do you accept credit cards?

Acceptez-vous les cartes de crédit ?
ahk-sehp-tay-voo lay kahrt duh kray-dee

May I see a room?

Puis-je visiter l'une de vos chambres ?
pwee-zhuh vee-zee-tay loon duh voh shaw~-bruh

How much extra are taxes?

A combien s'élève la taxe ?
Ah koh~-bee-yeh~ say-lay-vuh lah tahks

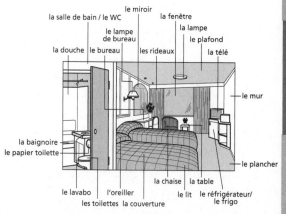

la salle de bain / le WC
le miroir
la fenêtre
le lampe de bureau
la lampe
le plafond
la douche
le bureau
les rideaux
la télé
le mur
la baignoire
le papier toilette
le plancher
la chaise
la table
le lavabo
l'oreiller
le lit
le réfrigérateur/ le frigo
les toilettes
la couverture

How much is the service charge, or is it included?

Combien coûte le service, ou est-il compris ?
koh~-bee-yeh~ koot luh suhr-vees oo ey-teel koh~-pree

I'd like to speak with the manager.

Je voudrais m'entretenir avec le directeur.
zhuh voo-dray maw~-truh-tuh-neer ah-vek luh dee-rehk-toehr

IN-ROOM AMENITIES

I'd like _____

Je voudrais _____
zhuh voo-dray

    to place an international call.

    passer un appel à l'étranger.
    pass-ay uh~-nah-pel ah lay-traw~-zhay

    to place a long-distance call.

    passer un appel longue distance.
    pass-ay uh~-nah-pel loh~g dee-staw~s

Instructions for Dialing the Hotel Phone

Pour appeler une autre chambre, composez le numéro de chambre. *poohr ah-play oon oh-truh shaw~-bruh koh~-poh-zay luh nue-may-roh duh shaw~-bruh*	To call another room, dial the room number.
Pour faire un appel local, composez d'abord le neuf. *poohr fayh-r un~ ah-pel loh-kahl koh~-poh-zay dah--bohr luh noehf*	To make a local call, first dial 9.
Pour appeler l'opératrice, composez le zéro. *poohr ah-play oh-pay-rah-tree~s koh~-poh-zay luh zay-roh*	To call the operator, dial 0.

directory assistance in English.	**les renseignements en anglais.** *lay raw~-seh~-nyuh-maw~- naw~-naw~-glay*
room service.	**le service en chambre.** *leh sayhr-vee-saw~ shaw~-bruh*
maid service.	**une femme de chambre.** *oon fahm duh shaw~-bruh*
the front desk.	**la réception.** *lah ray-sehp-see-yoh~*

Do you have room service?
Offrez-vous le service en chambre ?
oh-fray-voo leh sayhr-vee-saw~ shaw~-bruh

When is the kitchen open?
Quand peut-on dîner ?
kaw~ poeh-toh~ dee-nay

Do you serve breakfast?
Servez-vous le petit-déjeuner ?
sayhr-vay-voo luh ptee day-zhoeh-nay

When is breakfast served?
À quelle heure est le petit déjeuner ?
ah keh-loehr ey luh ptee day-zhuh-nay

For a full list of time-related terms, see p12.

Do you offer massages?
Offrez-vous un service de massage ?
oh-fray-voo uh~ sayhr-vees duh mah-sahzh

Do you have a lounge?
Y a-t-il un bar-salon dans l'hôtel ?
yah-teel uh~ bahr-sah-loh~ daw~ loh-tehl

Do you have a business center?
Avez-vous un centre d'affaires ?
ah-vay-voo uh~ saw~-truh dah-fayhr

Do you have Wi-Fi in rooms, or in the lobby only?
Y a-t-il le wi-fi dans les chambres ou seulement à la réception ?
yah-teel luh wee-fee daw~ lay shaw~-bruh~ oo suhl~-maw~ ah lah ray-sehp-see-yoh

May I have a newspaper in the morning?	**Puis-je avoir un journal le matin ?** *pwee-zhuh ah-vwahr uh~ zhoohr-ahl luh mah-teh~*
Do you offer a tailor service?	**Offrez-vous un service de raccommodage ?** *oh-fray-voo uh~ sayhr-vees duh rah-koh-moh-dazh*
Do you offer a laundry service?	**Offrez-vous un service de lessive ?** *oh-fray-voo uh~ sayhr-vees duh leh-seev*
Do you offer dry cleaning?	**Offrez-vous un service de nettoyage à sec ?** *oh-fray-voo uh~ sayhr-vees duh nuh-twah-yahzh ah sek*
May we have _____	**Pourrions-nous avoir _____** *pooh-ree-yoh~-noo-zah-vwahr*
clean sheets today?	**des draps propres aujourd'hui ?** *day drah proh-pruhz oh-zhoohr-dwee*
more towels?	**des serviettes supplémentaires ?** *day sayhr-vee-yeht sue-play-maw~-tayhr*
more toilet paper?	**du papier toilette ?** *due pah-pee-yay twah-leht*
extra pillows?	**des oreillers supplémentaires ?** *day-zoh-ray-ay sue-play-maw~-tayhr*
shampoo?	**du shampoing ?** *due shaw~-poeh~*
toothpaste?	**du dentifrice ?** *due daw~-tee-free~s*
a toothbrush?	**une brosse à dents ?** *oon bro~s ah daw~*
an adapter?	**un adaptateur ?** *uh~ ah-dap-tah-tur~*
a bottle opener?	**un décapsuleur / un tire-bouchon ?** *uh~ day-cap-sue-loer / uh~ teer-boo-cho~*

Do you have an ice machine?	**Y a-t-il une machine à glace dans l'hôtel ?**
	yah-teel oon mah-sheen ah glahs daw~ loh-tehl
Did I receive any ____	**Est-ce qu'il y a ____ pour moi ?**
	ehs keel-yah ____ poohr mwah
messages?	**des messages**
	day meh-sahzh
mail?	**du courriel**
	due kooh-ree-ehl
faxes?	**des télécopies**
	day tay-lay-koh-pee
May I have a spare key, please?	**Puis-je avoir une clé supplémentaire, s'il vous plaît ?**
	pwee-zhuh ah-vwahr oon klay sue-play-maw~-tayhr seel voo play
May I have more hangers, please?	**Puis-je avoir des cintres supplémentaires, s'il vous plaît ?**
	pwee-zhuh ah-vwahr day seh~-truh sue-play-maw~-tayhr seel voo play
I am allergic to down pillows.	**Je suis allergique aux oreillers à duvet d'oie.**
	zhuh swee-zah-layhr-zheek oh-zoh-ray-ay ah due-vay dwah
May I have a wake-up call?	**Puis-je demander un réveil téléphonique ?**
	pwee-zhuh duh-maw~-day uh~ ray-vay tay-lay-foh-neek

For a full list of time-related terms, see p12.

Do you have alarm clocks?	**Avez-vous des réveils ?**
	ah-vay-voo day ray-vay
Is there a safe in the room?	**Y a-t-il un coffre-fort dans la chambre ?**
	yah-teel uh~ koh-fruh fohr daw~ lah shaw~-bruh

LODGING

Does the room have a hair dryer?

Y a-t-il un sèche-cheveux dans la chambre ?
yah-teel uh~ sehsh-shuh-voeh daw~ lah shaw~-bruh

HOTEL ROOM TROUBLE

May I speak with the manager?

Puis-je parler au responsable de l'hôtel ?
pwee-zhuh pahr-lay oh ruh-spoh~sah-bluh duh loh-tehl

The _____ does not work.

_____ ne marche pas.
_____ nuh mahrsh pah

television

La télévision
lah tay-lay-vee-see-yoh~

telephone line

La ligne téléphonique
lah lee-nyuh tay-lay-foh-neek

air conditioning

La climatisation
lah klee-mah-tee-zah-see-yoh~

Internet access

L'accès à Internet
lahk-say ah eh~-tayrh-neht

cable TV

Les chaînes câblées
lay shehn kah-blay

There is no hot water.

Il n'y a pas d'eau chaude.
eel nyah pah doh shohd

The toilet is overflowing!

Les toilettes débordent !
lay twah-leht day-bohrd

This room is ____

  too loud.

  too cold.

  too warm.

  too smoky.

  dirty.

This room has ____

  bugs.

  mice.

May I have a different room, please?

Do you have a bigger room?

I locked myself out of my room.

I lost my keys.

Do you have a fan?

The sheets are not clean.

Cette chambre est ____
seht shaw~-bruh ay

  trop bruyante.
  troh bwee-yaw~t

  pas assez chauffée.
  pah-zah-say shoh-fay

  surchauffée.
  suehr-shoh-fay

  trop enfumée.
  troh aw~-fuh-may

  sale.
  sahl

Il y a ____ dans cette chambre.
eel-yah ____ daw~ seht shaw~-bruh

  des insectes
  day-zeh~-sehkt

  des souris
  day sooh-ree

Puis-je avoir une autre chambre, s'il vous plaît ?
pwee-zhuh ah-vwahr oon oh-truh shaw~-bruh seel voo play

Avez-vous une chambre plus spacieuse ?
ah-vay-voo-zoon shaw~-bruh plue spah-see-yoehz

J'ai oublié ma clé à l'intérieur de ma chambre.
zhay oo-blee-yay mah klay ah leh~-tay-ree-yoehr duh mah shaw~-bruh

J'ai perdu mes clés.
zhay pair-duh may clay

Avez-vous un ventilateur ?
ah-vay-voo uh~ vaw~-tee-lah-toehr

Les draps de mon lit sont sales.
lay drah duh moh~ lee soh~ sahl

The towels are not clean.	**Les serviettes de ma salle de bains sont sales.**
	lay sayhr-vee-yeht duh mah sahl duh beh~ soh~ sahl
The room is not clean.	**Ma chambre n'a pas été nettoyée.**
	mah shaw~bruh nah pah-zay-tay neh-twah-yay
This room smells like smoke. I am allergic to smoke.	**Cette chambre sent la fumée. Je suis allergique à la fumée.**
	seht shaw~-bruh saw~ lah fue-may; zhuh swee-zah-layhr-zhee-kah lah fue-may
The guests _____ are being very loud.	**Les occupants de la chambre _____ de la mienne sont très bruyants.**
	lay-zoh-kue-paw~ duh lah shaw~-bruh _____ duh lah mee-yehn soh~ trey bwee-yaw~
next door	**à côté**
	ah koh-tay
above	**au-dessus**
	oh duh-sue
below	**au-dessous**
	oh duh-soo

CHECKING OUT

May I leave these bags?	**Puis-je laisser ces sacs ?**
	pwee-zh~ lay-say say sack
I'm missing _____	**Il me manque ...**
	eel muh maw~k
I've lost _____	**J'ai perdu ...**
	zhay pair-duh~
I think this charge is a mistake.	**Je crois que ce montant-là est une erreur.**
	zhuh kwah kuh se moh~-taw~-lah ey-toon eh-roehr

Would you please explain this charge to me?

Pourriez-vous m'expliquer ce montant-là ?
poo-ree-yay-voo mehk-splee-kay suh moh~-taw~-lah

Thank you, we have enjoyed our stay.

Merci, nous avons passé un bon séjour.
mayhr-see noo-zah-voh~ pah-say uh~ boh~ say-zhoohr

The service was excellent.

Le service était excellent.
luh sayh-vee-zey-tay ehk-say-law~

Would you please call a cab for me?

Pouvez-vous m'appeler un taxi, s'il vous plaît ?
poo-vay-voo mah-play uh~ tahk-see seel voo play

Would someone please get my bags?

Pouvez-vous faire amener mes bagages ?
poo-vay-voo fayh-raw~-m-nay may bah-gazh

HAPPY CAMPING

I'd like a site for _____

Je voudrais un emplacement pour ___
zhuh voo-dray uh~-naw~-plah-smaw~ poohr

  a tent.

  une tente.
  oon taw~t

  a camper.

  un camping-car.
  uh~ kaw~-peeng kahr

Are there _____

Y a-t-il ___
yah-teel

  bathrooms?

  des toilettes dans ce camping ?
  day twah-leht daw~ suh kaw~-peeng

  showers?

  des douches?
  day doosh

Is there running water?

Y a-t-il l'eau courante ?
yah-teel loh kooh-raw~t

Is the water drinkable?

L'eau est-elle potable ?
loh ey-tehl poh-tah-bluh

Where is the electrical hookup?

Où est la borne de raccordement ?
oo ay lah bohrn duh rah-kohrd-maw~

CHAPTER FOUR

DINING

This chapter includes a menu reader and the language you need to communicate in a range of dining establishments and food markets.

FINDING A RESTAURANT

Would you please recommend a good _____ restaurant?

Pouvez-vous nous recommander un bon restaurant _____
poo-vay-voo noo ruh-koh-maw~-day uh~ boh-ruh-stoh-raw~

local	**à spécialités locales ?** *ah spay-see-yah-lee-tay loh-kahl*
Italian	**italien ?** *ee-tah-lee-yeh~*
French	**français ?** *fraw~-say*
German	**à spécialités allemandes ?** *ah spay-see-yah-lee-tay ahl-maw~d*
Spanish	**espagnol ?** *eh-spah~-nyohl*
Chinese	**chinois ?** *shee-nwah*
Japanese	**japonais ?** *zhah-poh~-neh*
Asian	**à spécialités asiatiques ?** *ah spay-see-yah-lee-tay ah-zee-yah-teek*
steakhouse	**spécialisé dans les steaks ?** *spay-see-yah-lee-zay daw~ lay stayk*

family	**familial ?**
	fah-mee-lee-yahl
seafood	**de fruits de mer ?**
	day fhwee duh mayhr
vegetarian	**végétarien ?**
	vay-zhay-tah-ree-yeh~
buffet-style	**de style buffet ?**
	duh steel bue-fay
Greek	**grec ?**
	grehk
budget	**pas cher ?**
	pah shayhr
Which is the best restaurant in town?	**Quel est le meilleur restaurant de la ville ?**
	keh-lay luh may-yoehr ruh-stoh-raw~ duh lah veel ?
Is there an all-night restaurant nearby?	**Y a-t-il un restaurant ouvert toute la nuit près d'ici ?**
	yah-teel uh~ ruh-stoh-raw~ oo-vayhr toot lah nwee pray dee-see
Is there a restaurant that serves breakfast nearby?	**Y a-t-il un restaurant qui sert des petits déjeuners près d'ici ?**
	yah-teel uh~ ruh-stoh-raw~ kee sayhr day ptee day-zhoeh-nay pray dee-see
Is it very expensive?	**Est-il très cher ?**
	ey-teel tray shayhr
Will I need a reservation?	**Aurai-je besoin d'une réservation ?**
	oh-ray-zhuh buh-zweh~ doon ray-suhr-vah-see-yoh~
Do they have a dress code?	**Y a-t-il une tenue de rigueur ?**
	yah-teel oon tuh-nue duh ree-goehr

Do they also serve lunch?	**Servent-ils aussi le déjeuner ?** *sayhrv-teel oh-see luh day- zheuh-nay*
What time do they serve dinner? Lunch?	**A quelle heure servent-ils le dîner ?** **Le déjeuner ?** *ah kehl-oehr sayhrv teel luh dee-nay luh day-zheuh-nay*
What time do they close?	**À quelle heure ferment-ils ?** *ah keh-loehr fayhrm-teel*
Do you have a take-out menu?	**Avez-vous des plats à emporter ?** *ah-vay-voo day plah ah aw~-pohr-tay*
Do you have a bar?	**Y a-t-il un bar ?** *yah teel uh~ bahr*
Is there a café nearby?	**Y a-t-il un café près d'ici** *yah-teel uh~ kah-fay pray dee-see*

GETTING SEATED

Are you still serving?	**Est-ce qu'il est encore possible de manger ?** *ehs keel ay-taw~-kohr poh-see- bluh duh maw~-zhay*
How long is the wait?	**De combien est l'attente ?** *duh koh~-bee-yeh~ ay lah-taw~t*
May I see a menu?	**Puis-je voir le menu ?** *pwee-zh-vwahr luh~muh-nue*
Do you have a non- smoking section?	**Y a-t-il une zone non-fumeur ?** *yah teel oon zone~ noh~ fue-moehr*
I'd like a table for ____, please.	**Je voudrais une table pour ____ personnes, s'il vous plaît.** *zhuh voo-dray oon tah-bluh poohr ____ payhr-suhn seel voo play*

For a full list of numbers, see p7.

Do you have a quiet table?	**Avez-vous une table calme ?** *ah-vay-voo-zoon tah-bluh kahlm*
Do you have highchairs?	**Avez-vous des chaises pour bébés ?** *ah-vay -voo day shay~z poor beh-beh*

Listen Up: Restaurant Lingo

Fumeur ou non-fumeur ?
fue-moehr oo noh~-fue-moehr
Smoking or
non-smoking?

**Vous devez porter une
cravate et une veste.**
*voo duh-vay pohr-tay
oon krah-vaht ay oon vehst*
You'll need a tie and
a jacket.

Les shorts sont interdits.
lay shohrt soh~-teh~-tayhr-dee
No shorts are allowed.

**Vous désirez quelque chose
à boire ?**
*voo day-zee-ray kehl-kuh
shohz ah bwahr*
May I bring you
something to drink?

**Vous désirez voir la carte
des vins ?**
*voo day-zee-ray vwahr
lah kahrt day veh~*
Would you like to see
a wine list?

**Vous désirez savoir quels
sont nos plats du jour ?**
*voo day-zee-ray sah-vwahr
kehl soh~ noh plah due zhoohr*
Would you like to hear
our specials?

**Vous êtes prêt à / prête(s)
à commander ?**
*voo-zeht preh ah /
preh-tah koh~-maw~-day*
Are you ready to order?

**Je suis désolé, votre carte
de crédit a été rejetée.**
*zhuh swee day-zoh-lay
voh-truh kahrt duh kray-
dee ah ay-tay ruh-zhuh-tay*
I'm sorry, your credit
card was declined.

May we sit outside /
inside, please?

**Pouvons-nous nous asseoir à
l'extérieur / à l'intérieur ?**
*poo-voh~-noo noo-zah-swahr ah lehk-
stay-ree-yoehr / ah leh~-tay-ree-yoehr*

May we sit at the counter?	**Pouvons-nous nous asseoir au comptoir ?** *poo-voh~-noo noo-zah-swahr oh koh-p-twahr*
I'd like to order.	**Je voudrais commander.** *zhuh voo-dray ko-maw~-day*

ORDERING

Do you have a special tonight?	**Avez-vous un plat du jour, ce soir ?** *ah-vay-voo uh~ plah due zhoor suh swahr*
What do you recommend?	**Qu'est-ce que vous recommandez ?** *keh-skuh voo ruh-koh-maw~-day*
May I see a wine list?	**Puis-je avoir la carte des vins ?** *pwee-zhuh ah-vwahr lah kahrt day veh~*
Do you serve wine by the glass?	**Servez-vous du vin au verre ?** *sayhr-vay-voo due veh~-noh vayhr*
May I see a drink list?	**Puis-je voir une liste des boissons ?** *pwee-zhuh vwahr oon leest day bwah-soh~*
I would like it cooked _____	**Je le voudrais _____** *zhuh luh voo-dray*

rare.	**bleu.** *bloeh*
medium rare.	**à point.** *ah pweh~*
medium.	**saignant.** *say-gnaw~*
medium well.	**cuit.** *kwee*

well.	**bien cuit.**
	bee-yeh~ kwee
charred.	**cuit à fond.**
	kwee-tah foh~
Do you have a ___ menu?	**Avez-vous un menu ___**
	ah-vay-voo-zuh~ muh-nue
diabetic	**pour diabétiques ?**
	poohr dee-yah-bay-teek
kosher	**kasher ?**
	kah-shayhr
gluten-free	**sans gluten ?**
	saw~ glue-ten
vegetarian	**végétarien ?**
	vay-zhay-tah-ree-yeh~
children's	**pour enfants ?**
	poohr aw~-faw~
Can you tell me what is in this dish?	**Pouvez-vous me dire ce qu'il y a dans ce plat ?**
	poo-vay-voo muh deer suh keel-yah ah daw~ suh plah
How is it prepared?	**Comment est-il cuit ?**
	koh-maw~ ey-teel kwee
What kind of oil is that cooked in?	**Avec quelle sorte d'huile est-il preparé ?**
	ah-vek kehl sohrt dweel ey-teel pruh-pah-ray
I'd like some oil, please.	**Je voudrais de l'huile, s'il vous plaît.**
	zhuh voo-dray de lweel seel voo play
Do you have any low-salt dishes?	**Avez-vous des plats à faible teneur en sel ?**
	ah-vay-voo day plah ah feh-bluh tuh-noehr aw~ sehl
No salt, please.	**Pas de sel, s'il vous plaît.**
	pah duh sehl seel voo play

May I have that on the side, please?	**Puis-je avoir cela dans une assiette séparée, s'il vous plaît ?** *pwee-zhuh ah-vwahr suh-lah daw~ oo-nah-see-yeht say-pah-ray seel voo play*
Dressing on the side, please.	**La sauce à part, s'il vous plaît.** *lah soh-sah pahr seel voo play*
May I make a substitution?	**Puis-je remplacer cela par autre chose ?** *Pwee-zhuh raw~-plah-say suh-lah pahr oh-truh shohz*
I'd like to try that.	**Je voudrais essayer cela.** *zhuh voo-dray eh-say-ay suh-lah*
Is that fresh?	**C'est frais ?** *say fray*
Waiter!	**Monsieur / Madame, s'il vous plaît !** *moh~-syoehr / mah-dahm seel voo play*
May I have extra butter, please?	**Puis-je avoir un peu plus de beurre, s'il vous plaît ?** *pwee-zhuh ah-vwahr uh~ poeh plue duh beur, seel voo play*
More bread, please.	**Plus de pain, s'il vous plaît.** *plues (+) duh peh~ seel voo play*
No butter, please.	**Pas de beurre, s'il vous plaît.** *pas duh boehr seel voo play*
I am lactose intolerant.	**Je suis allergique aux produits laitiers.** *zhuh swee-zah-layhr-zheek oh proh-dwee lay-tee-yay*
Would you recommend something without milk?	**Pouvez-vous me recommander quelque chose qui ne contienne pas de lait ?** *poo-vay-voo muh ruh-koh~-maw~day kehl-kuh shohz kee nuh koh~-tee-yeh~ pah duh lay*

I am allergic to ____	**Je suis allergique ____** *zhuh swee-zah-layhr-zheek*
seafood.	**aux poissons et aux fruits de mer.** *oh pwah-soh~-nay oh fhwee duh mayhr*
shellfish.	**aux fruits de mer.** *oh fhwee duh mayhr*
nuts.	**aux noix.** *oh nwah*
peanuts.	**aux cacahuètes.** *oh kah-kah-oo-eht*
Water ____, please.	**De l'eau ____, s'il vous plaît.** *duh loh ____ seel voo play*
with ice	**avec des glaçons** *ah-vehk day glah-soh~*
without ice	**sans glaçons** *saw~ glah-soh~*
sparkling water	**eau pétillante** *oh peh-tee-yaw~t*
still water	**eau plate** *oh plaht*
I'm sorry, I don't think this is what I ordered.	**Je suis désolé(e), mais je ne pense pas que c'est ce que j'ai commandé.** *zhuh swee day-zoh-lay may zhuh nuh paw~s pah kuh say skuh zhay koh~-maw~-day*
My meat is over / under cooked.	**Ma viande est trop cuite / pas assez cuite.** *mah vee-yahnd ay troh kweet / pahz ah-say kweet*
My vegetables are a little over / under cooked.	**Mes légumes sont un peu trop cuits / pas assez cuits.** *may lay-guem soh~-tuh~ poeh troh kwee / pah-zah-say kwee*
There's a bug in my food!	**Il y a un insecte dans ma nourriture !** *eel-yah uh~-neh~sekt daw~ mah nooh-ree-teuhr*

May I have a refill?	**Puis-je avoir la même boisson ?**
	pwee-zhuh ah-vwahr lah mehm
	bwah-soh~
A dessert menu, please?	**La carte des desserts, s'il vous plaît ?**
	lah kahrt day day-zayhr seel voo play

DRINKS

alcoholic	**de l'alcool / une boisson alcoolisée**
	duh lahl-kool / oon bwah-soh~-
	ahl-koo-lee-zay
cocktail	**cocktail**
	cock-tail
neat / straight	**sec**
	sehk
on the rocks	**avec des glaçons**
	ah-vehk day glah-soh~
with (seltzer or soda) water	**avec de l'eau seltzer**
	ah-vehk duh loh selt-zer
beer	**la bière**
	lah bee-yayhr
wine	**le vin**
	luh veh~
house wine	**le vin maison**
	luh veh~ may-zoh~
sweet wine	**le vin doux**
	luh veh~ doo
dry white wine	**le vin blanc**
	luh veh~ blaw~
rosé	**le vin rosé**
	luh~ veh~ roh-zay
a light-bodied wine	**le vin léger**
	luh veh~ lay-zhay
a full-bodied wine	**le vin corsé**
	luh veh~ kohr-say
red wine	**le vin rouge**
	luh veh~ roozh
sparkling sweet wine	**le vin mousseux et doux**
	luh beh~ moo-soeh ay doo

Champagne	**un champagne**
	uh~ champagne
liqueur	**une liqueur**
	oon lee-koehr
brandy	**le brandy**
	luh braw~-dee
cognac	**le cognac**
	luh koh~-nyak
gin	**le gin**
	luh zheen
vodka	**la vodka**
	lah vohd-kah
rum	**le rhum**
	luh ruhm
non-alcoholic	**non alcoolisée / une boisson non alcoolisée**
	noh~-nahl-koo-lee-zay / oon bwah-soh~ noh~-nahl-koo-lee-zay
hot chocolate	**un chocolat chaud**
	uh~ shoh-koh-lah shoh
lemonade	**une limonade**
	oon lee-moh-nah-duh
milk	**du lait**
	due lay
milkshake	**un milk-shake**
	uh~ meehlk-shayk
tea	**un thé**
	uh~ tay
coffee	**un café**
	uh~ kah-fay
latté	**un café au lait**
	uh~ kah-fay oh lay
iced coffee	**un café glacé**
	uh~ kah-fay glah-say
fruit juice	**du jus de fruit**
	due zhue duh fhwee

For a full list of fruit, see p113.

For a full list of fruit, see p113.

DINING

SETTLING UP

Check, please.	**L'addition, s'il vous plaît !** *lah-dee-see-yoh~ seel voo play*
I'm stuffed!	**Je n'en peux plus !** *zhuh naw~ poeh plue*
The meal was excellent.	**Ce repas était excellent.** *suh ruh-pah ay-tay ehk-suh-law~*
There's a problem with my bill.	**Il y a un problème avec l'addition.** *eel-yah uh~ proh-blehm ah-vek lah-dee-see-yoh~*
Is the tip included?	**Le service est-il compris ?** *luh sayhr-vees ey-teel koh~-pree*
My compliments to the chef!	**Tous mes compliments au chef !** *too may koh~-plee-maw~ oh shehf*

MENU READER

French cuisine varies broadly from region to region, but we've tried to make our list of classic dishes as encompassing as possible.

SOUPS (LES POTAGES)

crème d'asperges / de champignons / d'huîtres: cream of asparagus / mushroom / oyster soup

crème vichyssoise: cold potato-leek soup

gratinée à l'oignon: French onion soup

potage bilibi: cream of mussel soup

potage Crécy: carrot soup

potage cressonière: watercress soup

potage parmentier: potato soup

potage printanier: mixed vegetable soup

potage Saint-Germain: puréed split pea with ham soup

soupe au pistou: pesto soup with vegetables, white beans, and pasta

soupe aux moules: mussel soup

velouté de tomates / d'asperges / de volaille / d'huîtres: rich tomato / asparagus / chicken / oyster soup

TERRINES, PÂTÉS, CONFITS, & MEAT IN ASPIC

confit de canard / d'oie / de porc: preserved duck / goose / pork

foie gras: fattened goose / duck liver

galantine: boned meat or poultry, rolled or stuffed, served cold

gelée: aspic

pâté de campagne: country-style pâté, generally with a more rustic texture

pâté de canard: duck pâté

pâté en croûte: pâté baked in puff pastry

rillettes: pot of spreadable minced meat (pork, poultry) or fish

terrine / pâté de foie de volaille: poultry liver terrine / pâté

terrine de lapin: rabbit terrine

CLASSIC BISTRO / SIDE DISHES (LES ENTRÉES)

le croque-monsieur: grilled ham and cheese sandwich on sliced bread

l'omelette aux fines herbes: omelet with minced herbs

la pizza margarita: pizza topped with cheese and herbs, without vegetables or meat

les pommes frites: French fries

le sandwich mixte: gruyère and ham on French bread

la tarte à l'oignon: onion tart

FISH / SEAFOOD (LES POISSONS / LES FRUITS DE MER)

bouillabaisse: provençal fish stew

coquilles Saint-Jacques: lightly breaded scallops sautéed or baked with lemon juice, cayenne pepper, garlic, butter, and parsley

darne de saumon: salmon steak

homard cardinal: lobster cooked with mushrooms and truffles in béchamel sauce

homard Thermidor: Lobster baked in spicy mustard sauce and gratinéed

moules à la poulette: mussels in creamy white wine sauce

moules marinières: mussels in white wine with shallots, onions, and herbs

plateau de fruits de mer: assorted seafood platter

raie au beurre noir: skate in brown butter sauce

saumon à l'oseille: salmon with sorrel sauce

sole bonne femme: sole with potatoes, shallots, parsley, and mushrooms

truite au bleu: trout cooked in hot water and vinegar very soon after gutting, causing its skin to turn blue

truite aux amandes: sautéed trout in a crème fraîche and almond sauce

truite meunière: seasoned trout rolled in flour, fried in butter, and served with butter and lemon

For a full list of fish, see p111.

BEEF (LE BŒUF)

l'assiette anglaise: potted meat

bœuf bourguignon: beef stewed in red wine with onions, mushrooms, and bacon

carbonnade: beef stew

entrecôte maître d'hôtel: steak with butter and parsley

filet de bœuf Rossini: beef filet with foie gras

fondue bourguignonne: Burgundy-style fondue (small pieces of meat cooked in boiling oil and then dipped in various sauces)

la moelle: beef marrow

steak tartare: steak tartare

LAMB (L'AGNEAU)

carré d'agneau: rack of lamb

côtelettes d'agneau: lamb chops

épaule d'agneau farcie: stuffed lamb shoulder

navarin: lamb stew

navarin de mouton: mutton stew with spring vegetables

VEAL (LE VEAU)

l'agneau de lait: milk-fed lamb

l'agneau de pré-salé: salted lamb

blanquette de veau: veal stew

escalope de veau normande: thin slices of veal in cream sauce

escalope de veau milanaise: thin slices of veal in tomato sauce

PORK (LE PORC)

cassoulet: casserole with white beans and combinations of sausages, pork, lamb, goose, or duck

choucroute: sauerkraut with ham and sausages

le cochon de lait: suckling pig

côtelettes de porc: pork chops

croque-monsieur: toasted ham and cheese sandwich

RABBIT (LE LAPIN)

gibelotte de lapin: fricasseed rabbit in red or white wine

le lapereau: young rabbit

lapin à la Lorraine: rabbit in mushroom and cream sauce

lapin à la moutarde: rabbit in mustard sauce

le lapin de garenne: wild rabbit

râble de lièvre: saddle of hare

POULTRY (LA VOLAILLE)

aspic de volaille: poultry in aspic

le blanc de canard: duck breast

canard à l'orange: duck in orange sauce

canard aux cerises: duck in cherry sauce

le canard sauvage: wild duck

le caneton: duckling

filet de canard au poivre vert: duck filet in green peppercorn sauce

coq au vin: chicken in red wine sauce

poulet à l'estragon: chicken in tarragon-cream sauce

poulet chasseur: chicken with white wine and mushrooms

le poulet fermier: free-range chicken

suprême de volaille: boneless chicken breast

VEGETABLE DISHES (LES LEGUMES, LES CRUDITÉS, ET LES SALADES)

l'assiette de crudités: raw vegetables

chou-fleur au gratin: cauliflower baked in cream, topped with gruyere

épinards à la crème: creamed spinach

gratin dauphinois: thin-sliced potatoes baked with cheese

poivron farci: stuffed green pepper
salade composée: main-course salad (with meat, cheese, and raw
  vegetables)
salade mixte: mixed salad
salade verte: green salad
salade de tomates: tomato salad
salade russe: diced vegetables in mayonnaise
For a full list of vegetables, see p114.

DESSERTS / PASTRIES (LES DESSERTS / LES PÂTISSERIES)
baba au rhum: small rum-soaked cake
bavaroise: custard dessert with gelatin and cream
chausson aux pommes: apple turnover
chocolat amer: dark, bitter chocolate
clafoutis: custard and fruit tart
financier: small almond cake
fondant au chocolat: chocolate dessert akin to a brownie
gâteau au fromage: cheesecake
génoise: sponge cake
les flottantes / œufs à la neige: thin custard topped with
  soft meringue
madeleine: lemon tea cake
mille-feuille: napoleon
mont-blanc: pastry with whipped cream, chestnut purée, and baked
  meringue
pain au chocolat: croissant (chocolate-filled)
pâte feuilletée: puff pastry
pêche melba: vanilla ice cream with a poached peach and raspberry
  sauce
petits fours: bite-sized, beautifully-decorated pastries
poire belle-Hélène: pear with chocolate sauce
profiteroles: cream puffs
religieuse: cream puffs with chocolate icing
sabayon: thin custard made with Marsala

sablé: shortbread cookie

saint-Honoré: cake made with two types of pastry and cream filling

savarin: ring-shaped yeast cake in sweet syrup

soufflé au chocolat: chocolate soufflé

tarte au citron / aux fraises / aux pommes / aux abricots / aux framboises: lemon / strawberry / apple / apricot / raspberry tart

tarte tatin: upside-down apple tart

vacherin glacé: baked-Alaska-type dessert

SAUCES / METHODS OF PRESENTATION

basquaise: with ham, tomatoes, and peppers

béchamel: white sauce

bonne femme: with mushrooms and white wine

en brochette: on a skewer

aux câpres: in caper sauce

chasseur: with white wine and herbs

à la crème / à la normande: in cream sauce

au gratin: topped with cheese

jardinière: with mixed vegetables

maître d'hôtel: with butter and parsley

milanaise: in Italian-style tomato sauce

à la moutarde: in mustard sauce

à la nage: in wine and vegetable sauce

en papillote: baked in foil or parchment paper

piperade: with peppers and tomatoes

à la provençale: in olive oil (with herbs, garlic, and tomato)

sauce aurora: white sauce with tomato purée

sauce béarnaise: hollandaise sauce (with capers)

sauce au beurre noir: dark browned butter sauce

sauce cresson: watercress sauce

sauce Mornay: white sauce with cheese

sauce noisette: light browned butter sauce

sauce à l'oseille: sorrel sauce

au vin rouge: in red wine sauce

HERBS / SPICES / CONDIMENTS

l'ail / la gousse d'ail: garlic / garlic clove

l'aneth: dill

l'anis: anise

le basilic: basil

la feuille de laurier: bay leaf

le carvi: caraway

le chervil: chervil

les ciboulettes: chives

le clou de girofle: clove

la confiture: jam

la coriandre: cilantro / coriander

l'estragon: tarragon

l'huile: oil

le laurier: bay leaf

la marjolaine: marjoram

la marjolaine sauvage: oregano

la mayonnaise: mayonnaise

le mélange d'épices: allspice

le miel: honey

la moutarde: mustard

l'origan: oregano

le persil: parsley

le poivre rose / vert: pink / green peppercorns

le romarin: rosemary

le safran: saffron

la sauge: sage

le sel / le sel marin: salt / sea salt

le sucre en poudre: sugar (granular)

le sucre en morceaux: sugar cubes

le thym: thyme

la verveine: verbena

le vinaigre: vinegar

NUTS / LEGUMES / FANCY FUNGI

les amandes: almonds

l'arachide: peanut

les haricots blancs: white beans

les haricots d'Espagne: kidney beans

les lentilles: lentils

les marrons: chestnuts

les morilles: morels

la noisette: hazelnut

la noix: walnut

la pâte d'amandes: almond paste

les pignons: pine nuts

les pistaches: pistachio nuts

les truffes: truffles

BUYING GROCERIES

In France, like most other countries, locals shop for food either at outdoor markets, specialty stores or, less commonly than in the United States, large supermarkets.

GROCERY VENUES

bakery	**la boulangerie**
	lah boo-law~-zhree
butcher	**la boucherie**
	lah boo-shree
cheese shop	**la fromagerie**
	lah froh-mahzh-ree
delicatessen	**le traiteur**
	luh treh-toehr
open-air market	**le marché en plein air**
	luh mahr-shay ehn pleh~-nayhr
pastry shop	**la pâtisserie**
	lah pah-tee-sree
pork butcher	**la charcuterie**
	la shahr-kue-tree
supermarket	**le supermarché**
	luh sue-payhr-mahr-shay

AT THE SUPERMARKET

checkout counter	**le comptoir**
	luh koh~p-twahr
cash register	**la caisse**
	lah kehs
section / aisle	**le rayon**
	luh ray-oh~
produce	**les primeurs**
	lay pree-moehr
frozen food	**les plats congelés / surgelés**
	lay plah koh~zhlay / suehr-zhlay

Which aisle has _____	**Dans quel rayon se trouvent / trouve _____**
	daw~ kehl ray-oh~ suh troov
spices?	**les épices ?**
	lay-zay-pees
toiletries?	**les produits de toilette?**
	lay proh-dwee duh twah-leht
paper plates and napkins?	**les assiettes et les serviettes en papier ?**
	lay-zah-see-yeht ay lay sayhr-vee-yeh-taw~ pah-pee-yay
canned goods?	**les conserves ?**
	lay koh~-sayhrv
snack food?	**les amuse-gueules ?**
	lay-zah-muez goehl
baby food?	**la nourriture pour bébé ?**
	lah nooh-ree-teuhr poohr bay-bay
water?	**l'eau ?**
	loh
juice?	**le jus de fruits ?**
	luh zhues duh fhwee
bread?	**le pain ?**
	luh peh~
cheese?	**le fromage ?**
	luh froh-mahzh
fruit?	**les fruits ?**
	luh fhwee
cookies?	**les biscuits ?**
	lay bees-kwee

Bread and Rice

brown rice	**le riz brun**
	luh ree bruh~
white rice	**le riz blanc**
	luh ree blahn

wild rice	**le riz sauvage**
	luh ree sohvahzh
country-style loaf	**le pain de campagne**
	luh peh~ duh kaw~pah-nyuh
French bread: large / small	**la baguette / la flûte**
	lah bah-geht / lah fluet
rye bread	**le pain de seigle**
	luh peh~ duh seh-gluh
sourdough bread	**le pain au levain**
	luh peh~ oh luh-veh~
whole-grain bread	**le pain complet**
	luh peh~ koh~-play

Dairy

butter	**le beurre**
	luh boehr
cream	**la crème**
	lah krehm
milk, whole / skim	**le lait entier / écremé**
	luh lay aw~-tee-yay / ay-kray-may
yogurt	**le yaourt**
	luh yah-oohr

Cheese

bleu cheese	**le fromage bleu**
	luh froh-mahzh bloeh
cream cheese	**le fromage frais**
	luh froh-mahzh fray
goat cheese	**le (fromage de) chèvre**
	luh (froh-mahzh duh) sheh-vruh
firm	**un crottin**
	uh~ kroh-teh~
semisoft cheeses	**les fromages à croûte fleurie**
	lay fro-mahzh ah kroot fleuh-ree

Eggs

free-range	**les œufs de la ferme**
	lay-zoeh duh lah fayhrm
large / extra large	**les gros oeufs / très gros oeufs**
	grow zoeh / tray grow
small	**petits oeufs**
	puhtee zoeh

AT THE BUTCHER SHOP / AT THE FISH SHOP

Is the fish fresh?	**Le poisson est-il frais ?**
	luh pwah-soh~ ey-teel fray
Is the seafood fresh?	**Les fruits de mer sont-ils frais ?**
	lay fhwee duh mayhr soh~- teel fray
Do you sell _____ ?	**Vendez-vous de la viande de _____ ?**
	vaw~-day-voo duh lah vee- yand duh
I would like a cut of _____	**Je voudrais un morceau _____**
	zhuh voo-dray uh~ mohr-soh
tenderloin.	**de filet.**
	duh fee-lay
T-bone.	**d'aloyau.**
	dahl-wah-yoh
brisket.	**de poitrine.**
	duh pwah-treen
rump roast.	**de rôti de croupe.**
	duh roh-tee duh kroop
pork chops.	**de côtelette de porc.**
	duh koht-leht duh pohr
filet.	**tournedos.**
	toohr-nuh-doh

I would like ____	**Je voudrais____**
	zhuh voo-dray
the breast.	**le blanc.**
	luh blahn
chops.	**la côte.**
	lah koht
free-range.	**fermier.**
	fayhr-mee-yay
liver.	**le foie.**
	luh fwah
milk-fed.	**de lait.**
	duh lay
sweetbreads.	**le ris.**
	luh ree
Would you trim the fat?	**Pouvez-vous enlever le gras ?**
	poo-vay-voo aw~-luh-vay luh grah
May I smell it?	**Puis-je sentir ?**
	pwee-zhuh saw~-teer
Would you ____	**Pouvez-vous ____**
	poo-vay-voo
filet it?	**le couper en filets ?**
	luh koo-pay aw~ fee-lay
debone it?	**le désosser ?**
	luh day-zoh-say
remove the head and tail?	**enlever la tête et la queue ?**
	aw~-luh-vay lah teht ay lah koeh
Beef (Le Bœuf)	
ground beef	**le bœuf haché**
	luh boehf ah-shay
sirloin steak	**le faux-filet**
	luh foh-fee-lay
tripe	**les tripes**
	lay treep
veal	**le veau**
	luh voh

Other Meats

lamb	**l'agneau / le mouton** *lah-nyoh / luh moo-toh~*
leg of lamb	**le gigot** *luh zhee-goh*
rack of lamb	**le carré d'agneau** *luh kah-ray dah-nyoh*
horsemeat	**la viande de cheval** *lah vee-yand duh shuh-vahl*
pork	**le porc** *luh pohr*
rack of pork ribs	**le carré de porc** *luh kah-ray duh pohr*
ham	**le jambon** *luh zhahm-boh~*
bacon	**le lard** *luh lahr*
headcheese	**le fromage de tête** *luh froh-mazh duh teht*
sausage	**le saucisson** *luh soh-see-soh~*
dried sausage	**le saucisson sec** *luh soh-see-soh~ sehk*
fresh sausage	**la saucisse / le boudin** *lah soh-sees / luh boo-deh~*
rabbit	**le lapin** *luh lah-peh~*
hare	**le lièvre** *luh lee-yeh-vruh*
frog legs	**les cuisses de grenouille** *lay kwees duh gruh-nwee*
snails	**les escargots** *lay-zehs-kahr-goh*

Poultry

chicken	**le poulet**
	luh poo-lay
turkey	**la dinde**
	lah deh~d
duck	**le canard**
	luh kah-nahr
duck breast	**le blanc de canard**
	luh blaw~ duh kah-nahr
goose	**l'oie**
	lwah
pigeon / squab	**le pigeon**
	luh pee-zhyoh~
pheasant	**le faisan**
	luh fay-zaw~

Fish

catfish	**la barbotte**
	lah bahr-boht
flounder	**le flet**
	luh flay
halibut	**le flétan**
	luh flay-taw~
herring	**le hareng**
	luh ah-raw~g
mackerel	**le maquereau**
	luh mah-kroh
salmon	**le saumon**
	luh soh-moh~
sardine	**la sardine**
	lah sahr-deen
sea bass	**le bar**
	luh bahr
shark	**le requin**
	luh ruh-keh~

skate	**la raie**
	lah ray
sole	**la sole**
	lah sohl
swordfish	**l'espadon**
	leh-spah-doh~
trout	**la truite**
	lah tweet
turbot	**le turbot**
	luh tuehr-boh

Seafood

clams	**les palourdes**
	lay pah-loohrd
crab	**le crabe**
	luh krahb
crayfish	**l'écrevisse**
	lay-kray-vees
eel	**la lamproie**
	lah law~-pwah
lobster	**le homard**
	luh oh-mahr
mussels	**les moules**
	lay mool
octopus	**le poulpe**
	luh poolp
oyster	**l'huître**
	lwee-truh
scallop	**la coquille**
	lah koh-kee
shrimp	**la crevette**
	lah kruh-veht
squid	**le calmar**
	luh kahl-mahr

AT THE PRODUCE STAND / MARKET

Fruits

apple	**la pomme**
	lah puhm
apricot	**l'abricot**
	lah-bree-koh
banana	**la banane**
	lah bah-nahn
blackberries	**la mûre**
	lah muehr
blueberry	**la myrtille**
	lah meer-tee
cantaloupe	**le cantaloup**
	luh kaw~-tah-loo
cherry	**la cerise**
	lah suh-reez
coconut	**la noix de coco**
	lah nwah duh koh-koh
cranberry	**la canneberge**
	lah kah-nuh-bayhrzh
fig	**la figue**
	lah feeg
grapefruit	**le pamplemousse**
	luh paw~-pluh-moos
grapes (green, red)	**le raisin (vert, noir)**
	luh ray-zeh~ vayhr nwahr
gooseberry	**la groseille à maquereau**
	lah groh-zay ah mah-kroh
honeydew	**le melon miel**
	luh muh-loh~ mee-yehl
kiwi	**le kiwi**
	luh kee-wee
lemon	**le citron**
	luh see-troh~

lime	**le citron vert**
	luh see-troh~ vayhr
mango	**la mangue**
	lah maw~g
melon	**le melon**
	luh muh-loh~
orange	**l'orange**
	loh-raw~zh
blood orange	**la sanguine**
	lah saw~-gween
papaya	**la papaye**
	lah pah-pay
peach	**la pêche**
	lah pehsh
pear	**la poire**
	lah pwahr
pineapple	**l'ananas**
	law~-naw~-nahs
plum	**la prune**
	lah pruen
prune	**le pruneau**
	luh prue-noh
raspberry	**la framboise**
	lah fraw~-bwahz
strawberry	**la fraise**
	lah frehz
tangerine	**la mandarine**
	lah maw~-dah-reen
watermelon	**la pastèque**
	lah pah-stek

Vegetables

artichoke	**l'artichaut**
	lahr-tee-shoh
arugula	**la roquette**
	lah roh-keht

asparagus	**les asperges**
	lay-zah-spayrzh
avocado	**l'avocat**
	lah-voh-kah
beans	**les haricots**
	lay-zah-ree-koh
green beans	**les haricots verts**
	lay-zah-ree-koh vayhr
broccoli	**le brocoli**
	luh broh-koh-lee
cabbage	**le chou**
	luh shoo
carrot	**la carotte**
	lah kah-roht
cauliflower	**le chou-fleur**
	luh shoo-floehr
celery	**le céleri**
	luh say-lay-ree
corn	**le maïs**
	luh may-ees
cucumber	**le concombre**
	luh koh~-koh~-bruh
eggplant	**l'aubergine**
	loh-bayhr-zheen
endive	**la chicorée**
	lah shee-koh-ray
curly	**frisée**
	free-zay
Belgian	**l'endive**
	law~-deev
garlic	**l'ail**
	lie
leek	**le poireau**
	luh pwah-roh

lettuce	**la salade verte**
	lah sah-lahd vayhrt
romaine	**la laitue (romaine)**
	lah lay-tue
mushroom	**le champignon**
	luh shaw~-pee-nyoh~
black olives	**les olives noires**
	lay-zoh-leev nwahr
green olives	**les olives vertes**
	lay-zoh-leev vayhrt
onion	**l'oignon**
	loh-nyoh~
red pepper	**le poivron rouge**
	luh pwah-vroh roozh
green pepper	**le poivron vert**
	luh pwah-vroh vayhr
pepper (chili)	**le piment**
	luh pee-maw~
habañero pepper	**le piment habanero**
	luh pee-maw~ ah-bah-nyuh-roh
chipotle pepper	**le piment chipotle**
	luh pee-maw~ shee-poht-lay
jalapeno pepper	**le piment jalapeno**
	luh pee-maw~ yah-lah-peh-nyoh
cayenne (fresh) pepper	**le piment de cayenne**
	luh pee-maw~ duh kah-yehn
potato	**la pomme de terre**
	lah puhm duh tayhr
shallot	**l'échalote**
	lay-shah-loht
sorrel	**l'oseille**
	loh-zay
spinach	**les épinards**
	lay-zay-pee-nahr
squash	**la courge**
	lah koorzh

tomato	**la tomate**
	lah toh-maht
yam	**la patate douce**
	lah pah-taht doos
zucchini	**la courgette**
	lah koohr-zheht

AT THE DELI

What kind of salad is that?	**Quelle sorte de salade est-ce ?**
	kehl sohrt duh sah-lahd ehs
What kind of cheese is that?	**Quelle sorte de fromage est-ce ?**
	kehl sohrt duh froh-mahzh ehs
What kind of bread is that?	**Quelle sorte de pain est-ce ?**
	kehl sohrt duh peh~-nehs
I'd like some of this, please.	**J'en voudrais, s'il vous plaît.**
	zhaw~ voo-dray seel voo play
I'd like _____, please.	**Je voudrais _____, s'il vous plaît.**
	zheh voo-dray seel voo-play
a sandwich	**un sandwich**
	uh~ saw~d-weesh
a salad	**une salade**
	oon sah-lahd
tuna salad	**une salade au thon**
	oon sah-lahd oh toh~
chicken salad	**une salade au poulet**
	oon sah-lahd oh poo-lay
ham	**du jambon**
	due jaw~-boh~
roast beef	**du rosbif**
	due rohz-beef
some cole slaw	**du céleri rémoulade**
	due say-lay-ree ray-moo-lahd
mustard	**de la moutarde**
	duh lah moo-tahrd

mayonnaise	**de la mayonnaise** *duh lah may-oh-nehz*
a pickle	**un cornichon** *uh~ kohr-nee-shoh~*
about a pound	**cinq cent grammes** *seh~k saw~ grahm*
about a half-pound	**deux cent cinquante grammes** *doeh saw~ grahm*
about a quarter-pound	**cent vingt-cinq grammes** *saw~ veh~-seh~k grahm*
Is the salad fresh?	**La salade est-elle fraîche ?** *lah sah-lahd ey-tehl fresh*
Is that smoked?	**C'est fumé ?** *say fue-may*
May I have a package of tofu?	**Puis-je avoir du tofu ?** *pwee-zhuh ah-vwahr due toh-foo*

CHAPTER FIVE

SOCIALIZING

Whether you're meeting people in a bar or a park, you'll find the language you need, in this chapter, to make new friends.

GREETINGS

Hello!	**Bonjour !** *boh~-zhoohr*
How are you?	**Comment allez-vous ?** *formal /* **Ça va?** *informal* *koh-maw~-tah-lay-voo / sah vah*
Fine, thanks.	**Bien, merci.** *bee-yeh~ mayhr-see*
And you?	**Et vous ?** *formal /* **Et toi?** *informal* *ay voo / ay twah*
I'm exhausted.	**Je suis épuisé(e).** *zhuh swee-zay-pwee-zay*
I have a headache.	**J'ai mal à la tête.** *zhay mah-ah lah teht*
I'm terrible.	**Je vais très mal.** *zhuh vay treh mahl*
I have a cold.	**J'ai un rhume.** *zhay uh~ ruem*
Good morning.	**Bonjour !** *boh~-zhoohr*
Good evening.	**Bonsoir !** *boh~-swahr*
Good afternoon.	**Bon après-midi !** *boh~-nah-pray mee-dee*
Good night.	**Bonne nuit !** *buhn nwee*

Listen Up: Common Greetings

Bonjour !	Hello!
boh~-zhoohr	
Ravi(e) de faire votre connaissance.	It's a pleasure.
rah-vee duh fayhr voh-truh koh~-nay-saw~s	
Enchanté(e).	Charmed.
aw~-shaw~-tay	
Ravi(e).	Delighted.
rah-vee	
Ça va ?	How's it going?
sah vah	
Au revoir !	Goodbye!
oh r'vwahr	
À la prochaine !	See you around!
ah lah proh-shen	
À bientôt !	See you later!
ah bee-yeh~-toh	

THE LANGUAGE BARRIER

I'm sorry, I don't understand very well.	**Désolé(e), je ne comprends pas bien.**
	day-zoh-lay zhuh nuh koh~-praw~ pah byeh~
Would you speak slower, please?	**Pouvez-vous parler plus lentement, s'il vous plaît ?**
	poo-vay-voo pahr-lay plue law~t-maw~ seel voo play
Would you speak louder, please?	**Pouvez-vous parler plus fort, s'il vous plaît ?**
	poo-vay-voo pahr-lay plue fohr seel voo play
Do you speak English?	**Parlez-vous anglais ?**
	pahr-lay-voo aw~-glay

I speak _____ better than French.	**Je parle le _____ mieux que le français.**
	zhuh pahrl luh _____ mee-yoeh kuh luh fraw~-say
I'm sorry, would you spell that, please?	**Je suis désolé(e), pouvez-vous épeler, s'il vous plaît ?**
	zhuh swee day-zoh-lay poo-vay-voo-zeh-play seel voo play
Would you please repeat that?	**Pouvez-vous répéter, s'il vous plaît ?**
	poo-vay-voo ray-pay-tay seel voo play
How do you say _____?	**Comment dit-on _____ ?**
	koh-maw~ dee-toh~
Would you show me that in this dictionary?	**Pouvez-vous me montrer cela dans ce dictionnaire ?**
	poo-vay-voo muh moh~-tray suh-lah daw~ suh deek-syoh-nayhr

Common Curses

Merde alors !	Oh shit!
mayhr-dah-lohr	
Fils de pute !	Son of a bitch! (Son of a whore!)
fees duh puet	
Merde !	Damn!
mayhrd	
Trou du cul!	Asshole!
troo due kue	
Nous sommes foutus !	We're screwed! (We're fucked!)
noo suhm foo-tue	
Enfoiré! / Salaud !	Bastard!
aw~-fwah-ray / sah-loh	
Putain !	Fuck! / Fucker!
pue-teh~	
C'est foutu!	That's fucked up!
say foo-tue	

GETTING PERSONAL

Europeans are typically more formal than Americans. Remember to use the formal forms of speech until given permission to employ more familiar speech.

INTRODUCTIONS

What is your name?	**Comment vous appelez-vous ?**
	koh-maw~ voo-zah-play-voo
My name is ____.	**Je m'appelle ____.**
	zhuh mah-pehl
I'm very pleased to meet you.	**Ravi(e) de vous rencontrer.**
	rah-vee duh voo raw~-koh~-tray
May I introduce my ____.	**Laissez-moi vous présenter ____.**
	leh-zay-mwah voo pray-zaw~-tay
How is your ____	**Comment va votre ____**
	koh-maw~ vah voh-truh
wife?	**femme ?**
	fahm
husband?	**mari ?**
	mah-ree
son / daughter?	**fils / fille ?**
	fees / fee-yuh
friend?	**ami(e) ?**
	nah-mee
boyfriend / girlfriend?	**petit ami / petite amie ?**
	puh-tee-tah-mee / puh-tee-tah-mee
family?	**famille ?**
	fah-mee-yuh
mother?	**mère ?**
	mayhr
father?	**père ?**
	payhr
brother / sister?	**frère / sœur ?**
	frayhr / seuhr

neighbor?	**voisin / voisine ?**
	vwah-zeh~ / vwah-zeen
boss?	**patron / patronne ?**
	pah-troh~ / pah-truhn
cousin?	**cousine / cousine ?**
	koo-zeh~ / koo-zeen
aunt / uncle?	**oncle / tante ?**
	-noh~kluh / taw~t
fiancé / fiancée?	**fiancé / fiancée ?**
	fee-yaw~-say / fee-yaw~-say
partner?	**partenaire ?**
	pahrt-nayhr
nephew / niece?	**neveu / nièce ?**
	neh-voeh / nee-yehs
parents?	**parents ?**
	pah-raw~
grandparents?	**grand-parents ?**
	graw~-pah-raw~
grandchildren?	**vos petits-enfants ?**
	voh peh-teez aw~-faw~
Are you married / single?	**Vous êtes marié(e) / célibataire ?**
	voo-zeht mah-ree-yay / say-lee-bah-tayhr
I'm married.	**Je suis marié(e).**
	zhuh swee mah-ree-yay
I'm single.	**Je suis célibataire.**
	zhuh swee say-lee-bah-tayhr
I'm divorced.	**Je suis divorcé(e).**
	zhuh swee dee-vohr-say
I'm a widow / widower.	**Je suis veuf / veuve.**
	zhuh swee voehf / voehv
We're separated.	**Nous sommes séparés.**
	noo suhm say-pah-ray
I live with my boyfriend / girlfriend.	**Je vis avec mon petit ami / ma petite amie.**
	zhuh vee ah-vek moh~ puh-tee-tah-mee / mah puh-tee-tah-mee

I live with a roommate.	**Je vis en colocation.**
	zhuh vee aw~ ko-lo-kah-see-yoh~
How old are you / your children?	**Quel âge avez-vous / ont vos enfants ?**
	keh-lahzh ah-vay-voo / oh~ voh-zaw~faw~
Wow, that's very young.	**Oh là, c'est très jeune.**
	oh lah say tray zhoehn
What grade are they in?	**En quelle classe sont-ils ?**
	aw~ kehl klahs soh~-teel
Your wife / daughter is beautiful.	**Ta femme / fille est belle.**
	tah fahm / fee-yuh ay behl
Your husband / son is handsome.	**Ton mari / fils est beau.**
	toh~ mah-ree / fees ay boh
What a beautiful baby!	**Quel beau bébé !**
	kehl boh bay-bay
Are you here on business?	**Vous êtes ici en voyage d'affaires ?**
	voo-zeht ee-see aw~ vwah-yahz dah-fayhr
I am vacationing.	**Je suis en vacances.**
	zhuh swee-zaw~ vah-kaw~s
I'm attending a conference.	**Je participe à une conférence.**
	zhuh pahr-tee-see-pah oon koh~-fay-hraw~s
I'm traveling with my husband/wife.	**Je voyage avec mon mari/ma femme.**
	zhuh vwah-yahz ah-vek moh~ mah-ree/mah fahm
How long are you staying?	**Combien de temps restez-vous ici ?**
	koh~-byeh~ duh taw~ ruh-stay-voo-zee-see
What are you studying?	**Qu'étudiez-vous ?**
	kay-tue-dyay-voo
I'm a student.	**Je suis étudiant(e).**
	zhuh swee-zay-tue-dee-yaw~(t)
Where are you from?	**D'où êtes-vous ?**
	doo eht-voo

NATIONALITIES

I am _____	**Je suis _____**
	zhuh swee(z)
American.	**américain** *m* / **américaine** *f.*
	ah-may-ree-keh~ / ah-may-ree-kehn
Canadian.	**canadien** *m* /**canadienne** *f.*
	kah-nah-dee-yeh~ / kah-nah-dee-yehn
Chinese.	**chinois** *m* / **chinoise** *f.*
	shee-nwah / shee-nwahz
English.	**anglais** *m* / **anglaise** *f.*
	aw~-glay / aw~-glehz
French.	**français** *m* / **française** *f.*
	fraw~-say / fraw~-sehz
German.	**allemand** *m* /**allemande** *f.*
	ahl-maw~ / ahl-maw~d
Irish.	**irlandais** *m* / **irlandaise** *f.*
	eer-law~-day / eer-law~-dehz
Italian.	**italien** *m* / **italienne** *f.*
	ee-tahl-yeh~ / ee-tahl-yehn
Russian.	**russe** *m* / *f.*
	ruehs
Spanish.	**espagnol** *m* / **espagnole** *f.*
	ehs-pah-nyohl

See English / French dictionary for more nationalities.

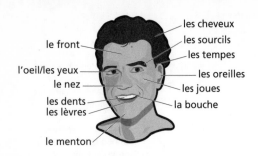

les cheveux
les sourcils
le front
les tempes
l'oeil/les yeux
les oreilles
le nez
les joues
les dents
la bouche
les lèvres
le menton

PERSONAL DESCRIPTIONS

blond(e)	**blond / blonde** *bloh~ / blohd*
brunette	**brun / brune** *bruh~ / bruen*
redhead	**roux / rousse** *roo / roos*
straight hair	**les cheveux raides** *lay shuh-voeh rayd*
curly hair	**les cheveux frisés** *lay shuh-voeh free-zay*
kinky hair	**les cheveux crépus** *lay shuh-voeh kray-pue*
long hair	**les cheveux longs** *lay shuh-voeh loh~*
short hair	**les cheveux courts** *lay shuh-voeh koohr*
tanned	**est bronzé(e)** *ay brow~-zay*
pale	**a le teint clair** *ah luh teh~ klayhr*

mocha-skinned	**a la peau sombre**
	ah lah po soh~-bruh
black	**est noir(e)**
	ay nwahr
white	**est blanc / blanche**
	ay blaw~ / blaw~sh
Asian	**est asiatique**
	ay ah-see-ah-teek
African-American	**est afro-américain(e)**
	ay ah-froh-ah-may-ree-keh~(n)
biracial	**est métis / métisse**
	ay may-tee / may-tee
tall	**est grand(e)**
	ay graw~(d)
short	**est petit(e)**
	ay puh-tee(t)
thin	**est mince**
	ay meh~s
fat	**est gros / grosse**
	ay groh(s)
blue eyes	**a les yeux bleus**
	ah lay-zyoeh bloeh
brown eyes	**a les yeux bruns**
	ah lay-zyoeh bruh~
green eyes	**a les yeux verts**
	ah lay-zyoeh veyhr
hazel eyes	**a les yeux noisette**
	ah lay-zyoeh nwah-zeht
eyebrows	**les sourcils**
	lay soohr-see
eyelashes	**les cils**
	lay see

freckles	**les taches de rousseur**
	lay tash duh roo-soehr
moles	**les grains de beauté**
	lay greh~ duh boh-tay
face	**le visage**
	luh vee-zahzh

See diagram, p126, for facial features.
See diagram, p196, for body parts.

DISPOSITIONS AND MOODS

sad	**triste**
	treest
happy	**heureux** *m* / **heureuse** *f*
	oeh-roeh / oeh-roehz
angry	**fâché(e)**
	fah-shay
tired	**fatigué(e)**
	fah-tee-gay
depressed	**déprimé(e)**
	day-pree-may
stressed	**stressé(e)**
	struh-say
anxious	**anxieux** *m* / **anxieuse** *f*
	aw~k-see-yoeh / aw~k-see-yoehz
confused	**confus(e)**
	koh~-fueh / koh~-fuehz
enthusiastic	**enthousiaste**
	aw~-too-zee-ahst

PROFESSIONS

What do you do for a living?	**Quelle est votre profession ?**
	keh-lay voh-truh proh-feh-syoh
Here is my business card.	**Voici ma carte de visite.**
	vwah-see mah kahrt duh vee-zeet
I am _____	**Je suis _____**
	zhuh swee
a doctor.	**médecin.**
	may-duh-seh~

an engineer.	**ingénieur.**
	eh~zhay-nyoehr
a lawyer.	**avocat(e).**
	ah-voh-kah(t)
a salesperson.	**représentant(e) commercial(e).**
	ruh-pray-saw~-taw~(t) koh-
	mayhr-see-yahl
a writer.	**écrivain.**
	ay-kree-veh~
an editor.	**rédacteur** *m* / **rédactrice** *f.*
	ruh-dahk-toehr / ruh-dahk-treese
a designer.	**styliste.**
	stee-leest
an educator.	**dans l'enseignement.**
	daw~ law~-seh~-nyuh-maw~
an artist.	**artiste.**
	ahr-teest
a craftsperson.	**artisan(e).**
	ahr-tee-saw~(n)
a homemaker.	**homme** *m* / **femme** *f.*
	au foyer.
	ohm / fahm oh fwah-yay
an accountant.	**comptable.**
	koh~-p-tah-bluh
a nurse.	**infirmier** *m* / **infirmière** *f.*
	eh~-feer-mee-yayh(r)
a musician.	**musicien** *m* / **musicienne** *f.*
	mue-zee-see-yeh~(n)
a military professional.	**dans l'armée.**
	daw~ lahr-may
a government employee.	**fonctionnaire.**
	foh~k-syoh~-nayhr
a web designer.	**concepteur web.**
	koh~-sayh-ptoehr web
a computer programmer.	**programmeur informatique.**
	pro-grah-moehr uh~-for-mah-teek

DOING BUSINESS

I'd like to make an appointment.

Je voudrais prendre rendez-vous.
zhuh voo-dray praw~-druh raw~-day-voo

I'm here to see _____.

J'ai rendez-vous avec _____.
zhay raw~-day-voo ah-vek

I need to photocopy this.

J'ai besoin de photocopier ceci.
zhay buh-zweh~ duh foh-toh-koh-pyay suh-see

May I use my laptop?

Puis-je utiliser mon ordinateur portable
pwee-zhuh oo-tee-lee-zay moh~nohr-dee-nah-toehr pohr-tah-bluh

What's the password?

Quel est le mot de passe ?
keh-lay luh moh duh pahs

May I access the Internet here?

Puis-je accéder à Internet d'ici ?
pwee-zhuh ahk-say-day ah eh~-tayhr-neht dee-see

May I send a fax?

Puis-je envoyer une télécopie?
pwee-zhuh aw~-vwah-yay oon tay-lay-koh-pee

May I use the phone?

Puis-je passer un appel ?
pwee-zhuh pah-say uh~-nah-pehl

Do you have a Wi-Fi network?

Avez-vous le wi-fi ?
ah-vay voo luh wee-fee

PARTING WAYS

Keep in touch.

Restons en contact.
ruh-stoh~-naw~ koh~-tahkt

Please write or e-mail.

Correspondons par courrier ou par mail.
koh-ruh-sph~-doh~ pahr kooh-ryeh oo pahr mail

Here's my phone number. Call me!

Voici mon numéro de téléphone. Appelez-moi !
vwah-see moh~-nue-may-roh duh tay-lay-fohn; ah-play mwah

May I have your phone number / e-mail, please?	**Puis-je avoir votre numéro de téléphone / adresse mail ?** *pwee-zhuh ah-vwahr voh-truh nue-may-roh duh tay-lay-fohn / ah-drehs mail*
May I have your card?	**Puis-je avoir votre carte de visite ?** *pwee-zhuh ah-vwahr voh-truh kahrt duh vee-zeet*
Are you on Facebook/Twitter?	**Êtes-vous sur Facebook/Twitter ?** *eht-voo suehr face-book/twee-tehr*

TOPICS OF CONVERSATION

As in the United States or anywhere in the world, the weather and current affairs are common conversation topics.

THE WEATHER

It's _____. / Is it always so _____?

sunny	**Il fait beau. / Fait-il toujours si beau ?** *eel fay boh / fay-teel too-zhoor see boh*
raining / rainy	**Il pleut. / Pleut-il toujours autant ?** *eel ploeh / ploeh-teel too-zhoor oh-taw~*
cloudy	**Le temps est nuageux. / Est-il toujours si nuageux ?** *luh taw~ ay nue-wah-zhoeh / ey-teel too-zhoor see nue-wah-zhoeh*
humid	**Le temps est humide. / Est-il toujours si humide ?** *luh taw~ ay-tue-meed / ey-teel too-zhoor see oo-meed*

warm	**Il fait chaud. / Fait-il toujours si chaud ?**
	eel fay shoh / fay-teel too-zhoor see shoh
cool	**Il fait frais. / Fait-il toujours si frais ?**
	eel fay fray / fay-teel too-zhoor see fray
windy	**Il y a du vent / Y a-t-il toujours autant de vent ?**
	eel yah due vaw~ / yah-teel too-zhoor oh-taw~ due vaw~
What's the forecast for tomorrow?	**Quel temps est prévu pour demain ?**
	kehl taw~ ay pray-vue poohr duh-meh~

THE ISSUES

What do you think about _____	**Quelle est votre position à propos _____**
	keh-lay voh-truh poh-zee-see-yoh~ ah proh-poh
the government?	**du gouvernement ?**
	due goo-vayhr-neh-maw~
democracy?	**de la démocracie en général ?**
	duh lah day-moh-krah-see aw~ zhay-nay-rahl
socialism?	**du socialisme ?**
	due soh-see-yah-lee-smuh
the environment?	**de l'environnement ?**
	duh leh~-vee-roh~-maw~
women's rights?	**des droits de la femme ?**
	day dhwah duh lah fahm
gay rights?	**des droits des homosexuels ?**
	day dhwah day-zoh-moh-sehk-sue-ehl

the French economy?	**de l'économie française ?** *duh lay-koh-noh-mee fraw~-sehz*
the French / American election?	**de l'élection française / américaine ?** *duh lehl-ehk-see-yoh~ fraw~-sehz / ah-may-ree-kehn*
the war in _____?	**de la guerre en _____?** *duh lah guehr aw~*
What party do you belong to?	**Vous êtes membre de quel parti politique ?** *voo-zeht maw~-bruh duh kehl pahr-tee poh-lee-teek*

RELIGION

Do you go to church / temple / mosque?	**Allez-vous à la messe / synagogue / mosquée ?** *ah-lay-voo-zah lah mehs / see-nah-guhg / muh-skay*
Are you religious?	**Êtes-vous pratiquant(e) ?** *eht-voo prah-tee-kaw~(t)*
I'm _____ / I was raised _____	**Je suis _____ / J'ai reçu une éducation _____** *zhuh swee / zhay ruh-sue oon ay-due-kah-see-yoh~*
Protestant.	**protestant(e).** *proh-teh-staw~(t)*
Catholic.	**catholique.** *kah-toh-leek*
Jewish.	**juif** *m* **/ juive** *f.* *zhweef / zhweev*
Muslim.	**musulman(e).** *mue-suel-maw~(n)*
Buddhist.	**bouddhiste.** *boo-deest*
Orthodox Christian.	**chrétien orthodoxe.** *khreh-tee-yeh~-nohr-toh-doks*

Hindu.	**hindouiste.**
	eh~-doo-eest
agnostic.	**agnostique.**
	ahg-noh-steek
atheist.	**athée.**
	ah-tay
I'm spiritual but I don't go to church.	**Je suis croyant *m* / croyante *f* mais je ne vais pas à la messe.**
	zhuh swee craw-yah~(t) may zhuh nuh vay pah-zah lah mehs
I don't believe in that.	**Je ne crois pas en cela.**
	zhuh nuh khwah pah-zaw~ suh-lah
That's against my beliefs.	**Cela va à l'encontre de mes croyances.**
	suh-lah vah ah law~-koh~truh duh may khwah-yaw~s
I'd rather not talk about it.	**Je préfère ne pas en parler.**
	zhuh pray-fayhr nuh pah-zaw~ pahr-lay

GETTING TO KNOW SOMEONE

Following are some fun topics for you to explore with friends you meet.

MUSICAL TASTES

What kind of music do you like?	**Quel type de musique aimez-vous ?**
	kehl teep duh mue-zeek ay-may-voo
I like _____	**J'aime _____**
	zhehm
rock'n'roll.	**le rock.**
	luh rohk
techno.	**la techno.**
	lah tehk-noh

disco.	**le disco.**
	luh dees-koh
classical.	**la musique classique.**
	lah mue-zeek klah-seek
jazz.	**le jazz.**
	luh zhahz
country and western.	**le country.**
	luh kuhn-tree
reggae.	**le reggae.**
	luh reh-gay
calypso.	**le calypso.**
	luh kah-leep-soh
opera.	**l'opéra.**
	loh-pay-rah
show-tunes / musicals.	**les comédies musicales.**
	lay koh-may-dee mue-zee-kahl
New Age.	**la musique New Age.**
	lah mue-zeek nyue ahzh
pop.	**la musique pop.**
	lah mue-zeek pohp

HOBBIES

What do you like to do in your spare time?	**Qu'est-ce que vous aimez faire pendant votre temps libre ?**
	kehs kuh voo-zay-may fayhr paw~-daw~ voh-truh taw~ lee-bruh
I like _____	**J'aime _____**
	zhehm _____
playing the guitar.	**jouer de la guitare.**
	zhoo-ay duh lah gee-tahr
playing the piano.	**jouer du piano.**
	zhoo-ay due pee-yah-noh

For other instruments, see English / French dictionary.

painting.	**peindre.**
	peh~-druh
drawing.	**dessiner.**
	deh-see-nay

dancing.	**danser.**
	daw~-say
reading.	**lire.**
	leer
watching TV.	**regarder la télé.**
	ruh-gahr-day lah tay-lay
blogging.	**tenir un/des blog(s).**
	teh-neer uh~/day blog
shopping.	**faire les magasins.**
	fayhr lay mah-gah-zeh~
going to the movies.	**aller au cinéma.**
	ah-lay oh see-nay-mah
hiking.	**faire de la marche.**
	fayhr duh lah mahrsh
camping.	**aller camper.**
	ah-lay kaw~-pay
hanging out.	**passer du temps avec mes amis.**
	pah-say due taw~ ah-vek may-
	zah-mee
traveling.	**voyager.**
	vwah-yah-zhay
eating out.	**manger au restaurant.**
	maw~-zhay oh ruh-stoh-raw~
cooking.	**cuisiner.**
	kwee-zee-nay
sewing.	**faire de la couture.**
	fayhr duh lah koo-tuehr
sports.	**faire du sport.**
	fayhr due spohr
Do you like to dance?	**Aimez-vous danser ?**
	ay-may-voo daw~-say
Would you like to go out?	**Voulez-vous sortir ?**
	voo-lay-voo sohr-teer
May I buy you dinner sometime?	**Puis-je vous inviter à dîner un de ces soirs ?**
	pwee-zhuh voo-zeh~-vee-tay ah dee-nay uh~ duh say swahr

What kind of food do you like?	**Quel type de nourriture aimez-vous ?** *kehl-teep duh nooh-ree-tuehr ay-may-voo*
For a full list of cuisines, see p88. Would you like to go _____	**Voulez-vous aller _____ avec moi ?** *voo-lay-voo-zah-lay _____ ah-vek mwah*
to a movie?	**au cinéma** *oh see-nay-mah*
to a concert?	**à un concert** *ah uh~ koh~-sayhr*
to the zoo?	**au zoo** *oh zoh*
to the beach?	**à la plage** *ah lah plah-zhuh*
to a museum?	**au musée** *oh mue-zay*
for a walk in the park?	**faire une promenade au parc** *fayhr oon proh-meh-nahd oh pahr*
dancing?	**danser** *daw~-say*
Would you like to get _____	**Voulez-vous _____ avec moi ?** *voo-lay-voo _____ ah-vek mwah*
lunch?	**déjeuner** *day-zhoeh-nay*
coffee?	**prendre un café** *preh~-druh uh~ kah-fay*
dinner?	**dîner** *dee-nay*

What kind of books do you like to read?	**Quel type de livres aimez-vous lire ?** *kehl teep duh lee-vruh ay-may-voo leer*
I like ____	**J'aime ____** *zhehm*
mysteries.	**les romans policiers.** *lay roh-maw~ poh-lee-see-yay*
Westerns.	**les romans-western.** *lay roh-maw~-vehs-tayhrn*
dramas.	**les romans dramatiques.** *lay roh-maw~ drah-mah-teek*
novels.	**les romans.** *lay roh-maw~*
biographies.	**les biographies.** *lay bee-yoh-grah-fee*
autobiographies.	**les autobiographies.** *lay-zoh-toh-bee-yoh-grah-fee*
romance.	**les romans d'amour.** *lay roh-maw~ dah-moohr*
history.	**les livres d'histoire.** *lay lee-vruh dees-twahr*

For dating terms, see Nightlife in Chapter 10.

CHAPTER SIX

MONEY & COMMUNICATIONS

This chapter covers money, the mail, phone and Internet service, and other tools you need to connect with the outside world.

MONEY

I need to exchange money.	**Je dois changer de l'argent.** *zhuh dwah shaw~-zhay duh lar-zhaw~*
Do you accept ____	**Acceptez-vous ____** *ahk-sehp-tay-voo*
Visa / MasterCard / Discover / American Express / Diners' Club?	**la carte Visa / MasterCard / Discover / American Express / Diners' Club ?** *lah kahrt vee-zah / mahs-tayhr-kahrd / dees-koh-vayhr / ah-may-ree-keh-nek-spres / day-nayhrz kloohb*
credit cards?	**les cartes de crédit ?** *lay kahrt duh kray-dee*
bills?	**les coupures / billets ?** *lay koo-puehr / bee-yay*
coins?	**les pièces ?** *lay pee-yes*
checks?	**les chèques ?** *lay shek*
money transfers?	**les virements ?** *lay veer-maw~*
May I wire transfer funds here?	**Puis-je virer des fonds d'ici ?** *pwee-zhuh vee-ray day foh~-dee-see*

Would you please tell me where to find ___	**Pouvez-vous m'indiquer ___** *poo-vay-voo meh~-dee-kay*
a bank?	**un bureau de banque?** *uh~ bue-roh duh baw~k*
a credit bureau?	**une institution de crédit ?** *oo-neh~-stee-tue-see-yoh~ duh kray-dee*
an ATM?	**une billeterie automatique ?** *uh~ bee-yeh-tree oh-toh-mah-teek*
a currency exchange?	**un bureau de change ?** *uh~ bueh-roh duh shaw~zh*
May I have a receipt, please?	**Puis-je avoir un reçu, s'il vous plaît ?** *pwee-zhuh ah-vwahr uh~ reh-sue seel voo play*
Would you please tell me the exchange rate for dollars to ___?	**Pouvez-vous me dire quel est le taux de change du dollar en ___ ?** *poo-vay-voo muh deer keh-lay luh toh duh shaw~zh due doh-lahr aw~*
Is there a service charge?	**Y a-t-il des frais bancaires ?** *yah-teel day frey baw~-kayhr*
May I have a cash advance on my credit card?	**Puis-je retirer de l'argent sur ma carte de crédit ?** *pwee-zhuh ruh-tee-ray duh lahr-zhaw~ suehr mah kahrt duh kray-dee*

En panne

Before you stick your coins or bills in a vending machine, watch out for the little sign that says *En panne* or *Hors service* (Out of Service).

Listen Up: Bank Lingo

Signez ici, s'il vous plaît.
seen-yay-zee-see
seel voo play

Please sign here.

Voici votre reçu.
vwah-see voh-truh ruh-sue

Here is your receipt.

**Puis-je voir une pièce
d'identité, s'il vous plaît ?**
*pwee-zhuh vwahr oon
pee-yes dee-deh~-tee-tay
seel voo play*

May I see your ID, please?

**Nous acceptons les
chèques de voyage.**
*noo-zahk-sehp-toh~ lay
shek duh vwah-yahzh*

We accept travelers' checks.

**Nous n'acceptons que
les espèces.**
*noo nahk-sehp-toh~ kuh
lay-zehs-pehs*

Cash only.

May I have smaller bills,
please?

**Puis-je avoir des billets plus petits,
s'il vous plaît ?**
*pwee-zhuh ah-vwahr day bee-yay
plue puh-tee seel voo play*

Can you make change?

Pouvez-vous faire de la monnaie ?
poo-vay-voo fayhr duh lah moh~-nay

I only have bills.

Je n'ai que des billets.
zhuh nay kuh day bee-yay

May I have some coins,
please?

**Puis-je avoir quelques pièces, s'il
vous plaît ?**
*pwee-zhuh ah-vwahr kehl-kuh
pee-yehs seel voo play*

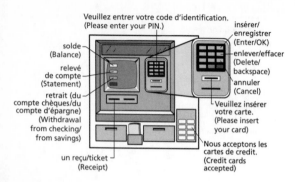

Veuillez entrer votre code d'identification.
(Please enter your PIN.)

solde
(Balance)

relevé
de compte
(Statement)

retrait (du
compte chèques/du
compte d'épargne)
(Withdrawal
from checking/
from savings)

un reçu/ticket
(Receipt)

insérer/
enregistrer
(Enter/OK)

enlever/effacer
(Delete/
backspace)

annuler
(Cancel)

Veuillez insérer
votre carte.
(Please insert
your card)

Nous acceptons les
cartes de credit.
(Credit cards
accepted)

PHONE SERVICE

Where can I buy or rent a cell phone?	**Où puis-je acheter ou louer un téléphone portable ?** *oo pwee-zhuh ahsh-tay oo loo-way uh~ tay-lay-fohn pohr-tah-bluh*
What rate plans do you have?	**Quels tarifs proposez-vous ?** *kehl tah-reef proh-poh-zay-voo*
Is this good in the whole country?	**Est-ce que c'est valable pour tout le pays ?** *ehs-kuh say vah-lah-bluh poohr too luh pay-ee*
Is data included in the rate?	**Le service données est-il compris dans le prix ?** *uh sayhr-vees do-nay ay-teel koh~-pree daw~ luh pree*
I'd like a pay-as-you-go SIM card.	**Je voudrais une carte SIM sans abonnement.** *zhuh voo-dray oon kart seem saw~-zah-bohn-maw~*

May I have a prepaid phone card?	**Puis-je avoir une carte téléphonique prépayée ?**
	pwee-zhuh ah-vwahr oon kahrt tay-lay-foh-neek pray-pay-ay
Where can I buy a phone card?	**Où puis-je acheter une carte téléphonique ?**
	oo pwee-zhuh ahsh-tay oon kahrt tay-lay-foh-neek
May I add more minutes to my phone card?	**Puis-je ajouter des minutes sur ma carte téléphonique ?**
	pwee-zhuh ah-zhoo-tay day mee-nuet suehr mah kahrt tay-lay-foh-neek

MAKING A CALL

May I dial direct?	**Puis-je composer le numéro directement ?**
	pwee-zhuh koh~-poh-zay luh nue-may-roh dee-rehkt-maw~
Operator, please.	**Je voudrais l'opératrice, s'il vous plaît.**
	zhuh voo-dray loh-pay-rah-trees seel voo play
I'd like to make an international call.	**Je voudrais passer un appel à l'étranger.**
	zhuh voo-dray pass-ay uh~-nah-peh-lah lay-traw~-zhay
I'd like to make a collect call.	**Je voudrais passer un appel en PCV.**
	zhuh voo-dray pass-ay uh~-nah-peh-law~ pay-say-vay
I'd like to use a calling card.	**Je voudrais passer un appel à l'aide d'une carte téléphonique.**
	zhuh voo-dray pass-ay uh~-nah-peh-lah lehd doon kahrt tay-lay-foh-neek

Listen Up: Phone Lingo

Bonjour.
boh~-zhoohr

Hello.

Quel numéro ?
kehl nue-may-roh

What number?

Désolé(e), la ligne est occupée.
day-zoh-lay lah lee-ney-toh-kue-pay

I'm sorry, the line is busy.

Veuillez raccrocher puis composer de nouveau le numéro.
voeh-yay rah-kroh-shay pwee koh~-poh-zay duh noo-voh luh nue-may-roh

Please hang up the phone and redial.

Désolé(e), ça ne répond pas.
day-zoh-lay sah nuh ray-poh~ pah

I'm sorry, nobody answers.

Il reste dix minutes sur votre carte.
eel rehst dee mee-nuet suehr voh-truh kahrt

Your card has ten minutes left.

I'd like to bill the call to my credit card.

Je voudrais facturer cet appel sur ma carte de crédit.
zhuh voo-dray fahk-tueh-ray seh-tah-pehl suehr mah kahrt duh kray-dee

May I bill the charges to my room?

Puis-je ajouter cet appel à ma note d'hôtel ?
pwee-zhuh ah-zhoo-tay seh-tah-pehl ah mah noht doh-tehl

Information, please.

Je voudrais les renseignements, s'il vous plaît.
zhuh voo-dray lay raw~-seh~-nyuh-maw~ seel voo play

Would you please give me the number for _____?

Je voudrais le numéro de _____, s'il vous plaît.
zhuh voo-dray luh nue-may-roh duh _____ seel voo play

I just got disconnected.

J'ai été coupé.
Zhay ay-tay koo-pay

The line is busy.

La ligne est occupée.
lah lee-ney-toh-kue-pay

INTERNET ACCESS

Would you tell me where to find an Internet café?

Pouvez-vous m'indiquer un cybercafé ?
poo-vay-voo meh~-dee-kay uh~-see-behr-kah-fay

Is there Wi-Fi?

Y a-t-il le wi-fi ?
yah-teel luh wee-fee

How much do you charge per minute / hour?

Combien prenez-vous par minute / heure ?
koh~-bee-yeh~ pruh-nay-voo pahr mee-nuet / oehr

Can I print here?	**Puis-je imprimer des documents ici ?** *pwee-zhuh eh~-pree-may day* *doh-kue-maw~-zee-see*
Can I burn a CD?	**Puis-je graver un CD ici ?** *pwee-zhuh grah-vay uh~ say-day* *ee-see*
Would you please help me change the preference to English?	**Pouvez-vous m'aider à configurer** **l'anglais comme langue préférée ?** *poo-vay-voo may-day ah koh~-fee-* *gueh-ray law~-glay kohm law~g* *pray-fay-ray*
May I scan something in here?	**Puis-je scanner quelque chose ici ?** *pwee-zhuh skah-nay kehl-kuh* *shoh-zee-see*
Can I upload photos from my digital camera?	**Puis-je télécharger des photos de** **mon appareil photo numérique ?** *pwee-zhuh tay-lay-shahr-zhay day* *foh-toh duh moh~-nah-pah-ray foh-* *toh nue-may-reek*
Do you have a Mac?	**Avez-vous un Mac ?** *ah-vay-voo-zuh~ mahk*
Do you have a PC?	**Avec-vous un PC ?** *ah-vay-voo-zuh~ pay-say*
Do you have a newer version of this software?	**Avez-vous une version plus** **récente de ce logiciel ?** *ah-vay-voo-zoon vayhr-see-yoh~* *plue ray-saw~t duh suh loh-zhee-* *see-yehl*

How fast is your connection speed?	**Quelle est la vitesse de connexion ?** *kehl ay lah vee-tess duh koh-nek-see-yoh~*
Do you have broadband?	**Avez-vous l'ADSL / le haut débit ?** *ah-vay-voo la-day-S-L / luh oh day-bee*

GETTING MAIL

Excuse me, can you tell me where to find the post office?	**Excusez-moi, pouvez-vous me dire où se trouve la poste ?** *ek-skue-zay mwah poo-vay-voo muh deer oo suh troov lah pohst*
May I send an international package?	**Puis-je envoyer un colis à l'étranger d'ici ?** *pwee-zhuh aw~-vwah-yay uh~-koh-lee ah lay-traw~-zhay dee-see*
Do I need a customs form?	**Ai-je besoin de remplir un formulaire de douane ?** *ay-zhuh buh-zweh~ duh raw~-pleer uh~ fohr-mue-layhr duh doo-wahn*
Do you sell insurance?	**Offrez-vous une formule assurance ?** *oh-fray-voo-zoon fohr-muel ah-sueh-raw~s*
Please, mark it fragile.	**Apposez un tampon « Fragile », s'il vous plaît.** *ah-poh-zay uh~ taw~-poh~ frah-zheel seel voo play*
Please, handle with care.	**Manipulez-le doucement, s'il vous plaît.** *mah-nee-pue-lay-luh doos-maw~ seel voo play*

Do you have more twine?

Avez-vous de la ficelle, s'il vous plaît ?
ah-vay-voo duh lah fee-sehl seel voo play

Would you please tell me where to find a DHL office?

Pouvez-vous me dire où se trouve l'agence DHL la plus proche ?
poo-vay-voo muh deer oo suh troov lah-zhaw~s day-ahsh-ehl lah plue prohsh

Do you sell stamps?

Est-ce que vous vendez des timbres ?
ehs kuh voo vaw~day day taw~-bruh

Do you sell postcards?

Est-ce que vous vendez des cartes postales ?
ehs kuh voo vaw~-day day kahrt poh-stahl

I'd like to send this first class / priority mail.

Je voudrais le service rapide / prioritaire.
zhuh voo-dray luh sayhr-vees rah-peed / pree-oh-ree-tayhr

Listen Up: Postal Lingo

Au suivant!	Next!
oh swee-vaw~	
Veuillez le poser ici.	Set it here.
voeh-yay luh poh-zay	
ee-see	
Quelle classe ?	Which class?
kehl klahs	
Vous désirez ?	What kind of service would you
voo day-zee-ray	like?
En quoi puis-je vous être	How can I help you?
utile ?	
aw~ kwah pwee-zhuh	
voo-zeh-truh oo-teel	
le guichet de dépôt	dropoff window
luh gee-shay duh day-poh	
le guichet de récupération	pickup window
luh gee-shay duh ray-kue-	
pay-rah-see-yoh~	

How much to send that express / air mail?	**Combien coûte l'envoi accéléré / par avion ?**
	koh~-bee-yeh~ koot law~-vwah ahk-say-lay-ray / pahr ah-vee-yoh~
Do you offer overnight delivery?	**Offrez-vous un service de livraison sous 24 heures ?**
	oh-fray-voo-zuh~ sayhr-vees duh lee-vray-zoh~ soo vaw~-kah-truh oehr
How long will that take?	**Combien de jours est-ce que l'envoi prendra ?**
	koh~-bee-yeh~ duh zhoohr ehs kuh law~-vwah praw~-drah

I'd like to buy an envelope, please.	**Je voudrais acheter une enveloppe, s'il vous plaît.** *zhuh voo-dray ahsh-tay oo-naw~-vuh-lohp seel voo play*
May I send it airmail?	**Puis-je l'envoyer par avion ?** *pwee-zhuh law~-vwah-yay pahr ah-vee-yoh~*
I'd like to send it certified / registered mail.	**Je voudrais l'envoyer en recommandé.** *zhuh voo-dray law~-vwah-yay aw~ ruh-koh-maw~-day*

CHAPTER SEVEN

CULTURE

CINEMA

Is there a movie theater nearby?

Y a-t-il un cinéma près d'ici ?
yah-teel uh~ see-nay-mah pray dee-see

Would you please tell me what's playing tonight?

Pouvez-vous me dire quels films passent ce soir ?
poo-vay-voo muh deer kehl feelm pahs suh swahr

Is that in English or French?

Est-ce un film en français ou en anglais ?
ehs uh~ feelm aw~ fraw~-say oo aw~-naw~-glay

Are there English subtitles?

Y a-t-il des sous-titres en anglais ?
yah-teel day soo-tee-truh aw~-naw~-glay

Is the theater air conditioned?

La salle est-elle climatisée ?
lah sahl ey-tehl klee-mah-tee-zay

How much is a ticket?

Combien coûte un billet ?
koh~-bee-yeh~ koo-tuh~ bee-yay

Do you have a discount for ____

Offrez-vous une réduction aux ____
oh-fray-voo oon ray-duek-syoh~

seniors?

personnes âgées ?
payhr-suh-nah-zhay

students?

étudiants ?
zay-tue-dee-yaw~

children?

enfants ?
zaw~-faw~

What time is the next showing?	**À quelle heure commence la prochaine séance ?** *ah keh-loehr koh~-maw~s lah proh-shen say-aw~s*
How long is the movie?	**Combien de temps dure ce film ?** *koh~-bee-yeh~ duh taw~ duehr suh feelm*
May I buy tickets in advance?	**Puis-je acheter des billets à l'avance ?** *pwee-zhuh ahsh-tay day bee-yay ah lah-vaw~s*
Is it sold out?	**C'est complet ?** *say koh~-play*
When does it begin?	**Quand commence-t-il ?** *kaw~ koh-maw~-steel*

PERFORMANCES

Are there any plays showing right now?	**Quelles pièces jouez-vous en ce moment ?** *kehl-pee-yehs zhoo-ay voo aw~ suh moh~-maw*
Is there a dinner theater?	**Y a-t-il une salle de dîner théâtre ?** *yah-teel oon sahl duh dee-nay tay-ah-truh*
Where can I buy tickets?	**Où achète-t-on des billets ?** *oo ah-sheh-toh~ day bee-yay*
Do you offer a student discount?	**Offrez-vous un tarif réduit aux étudiants ?** *oh-fray-voo-zuh~ tah-reef ray-dwee oh-zay-tue-dee-yaw~*

Listen Up: Box Office Lingo

Quel film désirez-vous voir ?
kehl feelm day-zee-ray-voo vwahr
What would you like to see?

Combien de personnes ?
koh~-bee-yeh~ duh payhr-suhn
How many?

Deux adultes ?
doeh-zah-duelt
For two adults?

Du popcorn ?
due pop-corn
Popcorn?

Avec du beurre ? Du sel ?
ah-vek due boehr; due sehl
With butter? Salt?

Désirez-vous autre chose ?
day-zee-ray-voo-zoh-truh shohz
Would you like anything else?

I need _____ seats.
J'ai besoin de places _____
zhay buh-zweh~ duh plahs

   aisle
   côté couloir.
   koh-tay kool-wahr

   orchestra
   parterre.
   pahr-tayhr

What time does the play start?
À quelle heure la pièce commence-t-elle ?
ah keh-loehr lah pee-yes koh~maw~s-tehl

Is there an intermission?
Y a-t-il un entracte ?
yah-teel uh~-naw~-trahkt

Is there an opera house?
Y a-t-il une salle d'opéra ?
yah-teel oon sahl doh-pay-rah

CULTURE

Is there a local symphony?

Y a-t-il un orchestre philharmonique local ?
yah-teel uh~-nohr-keh-struh fee-lahr-moh~-neek loh-kahl

May I purchase tickets over the phone /online?

Puis-je acheter des billets par tele phone / en ligne ?
pwee-zhuh ahsh-tay day bee-yay pahr tay-lay-fohn/aw~ lee-gneh

What time is the box office open?

À quelle heure le guichet ouvre-t-il ?
ah keh-loehr luh gee-shay~ oo-vruh-teel

I need space for a wheelchair.

J'ai besoin de suffisamment d'espace pour un fauteuil roulant.
zhay buh-zweh~ duh sue-fee-zah-maw~ day-spahs poohr uh~ fo-teh~y roo-law~

Do you have private boxes available?

Avez-vous des loges privées libres ?
ah-vay-voo day lohzh pree-vay lee-bruh

I'd like a program, please.

Je voudrais un programme, s'il vous plaît.
zhuh voo-dray uh~ proh-grahm seel voo play

Could you please show us our seats?

Pouvez-vous nous montrer où sont nos places ?
poo-vay-voo noo moh~-tray oo soh~ noh plahs

MUSEUMS, GALLERIES & SIGHTS

Do you have a museum guide?	**Avez-vous un guide des musées de la ville ?** *ah-vay-voo-zuh~ geed day mue-zay duh lah veel*
Do you have guided tours?	**Offrez-vous des visites guidées ?** *oh-fray-voo day-vee-zeet gee-day*
What are the museum hours?	**Quelles sont les heures d'ouverture de ce musée ?** *kehl soh~ lay-zoehr doo-vayhr-tuehr duh suh mue-zay*
Do I need to make an appointment?	**Ai-je besoin de m'inscrire à l'avance ?** *ay-zhuh buh-zweh~ duh meh~-skreer ah lah-vaw~s*
Is there an admission fee?	**L'entrée est-elle payante ?** *law~-tray ey-tehl pay-aw~t*
Do you offer _____	**Offrez-vous _____** *oh-fray-voo*
student discounts?	**des tarifs réduits aux étudiants ?** *day tah-reef ray-dwee oh-zay-tue-dee-yaw~*
senior discounts?	**des tarifs réduits aux personnes âgées ?** *day tah-reef ray-dwee oh payhr-suh-nah-zhay*
services for the hearing impaired?	**des services pour malentendants ?** *day sayhr-vees poohr mah-law~-taw~-daw~*
audio tours in English?	**une visite avec un audioguide en anglais ?** *oon vee-zeet ah-vehk oh-toh-gee-day aw~-naw~-glay*

CHAPTER EIGHT

SHOPPING

This chapter covers the phrases you'll need for shopping in a variety of settings: from the mall to the town square artisan market. We also throw in the terminology you'll need to visit the barber or hairdresser.

For coverage of food and grocery shopping, see Chapter 4, Dining.

GENERAL SHOPPING TERMS

Would you please tell me _____	**S'il vous plaît, pouvez-vous m'indiquer _____** *seel voo play poo-vay-voo meh~-dee-kay*
how to get to a mall?	**comment aller au centre commercial le plus proche ?** *koh~-maw~-tah-lay oh saw~-truh koh~-mayhr-see-yahl luh plue pro-sh*
the best place for shopping?	**le meilleur endroit pour faire des courses ?** *luh may-yoehr aw~-dhwah poohr fayhr day koohrs*
how to get downtown?	**comment aller au centre-ville ?** *koh~-maw~-tah-lay oh saw~-truh veel*
Where can I find a _____	**Où puis-je trouver _____** *oo pwee-zhuh troo-vay*
shoe store?	**un magasin de chaussures ?** *uh~ mah-gah-zeh~ duh shoh-suehr*
clothing store?	**un magasin de vêtements ?** *uh~ mah-gah-zeh~ duh veht-maw~*

designer fashion boutique?	**une boutique haute couture ?** *oon boo-teek oht koo-tuehr*
vintage clothing store?	**une friperie ?** *oon fhree-pay-ree*
jewelry store?	**une bijouterie ?** *oon bee-zhoo-tree*
bookstore?	**une librairie ?** *oon lee-bray-ree*
toy store?	**un magasin de jouets ?** *uh~ mah-gah-zeh~ duh zhoo-ay*
stationery store?	**une papeterie ?** *oon pah-pay-tree*
cigar store / tobacco shop?	**un bureau de tabac ?** *uh~ bueh-roh duh tah-bah*
antique shop?	**un antiquaire ?** *uh~-naw~-tee-kwayhr*
souvenir shop?	**un magasin de souvenirs ?** *uh~ mah-gah-zeh~ duh soov-neer*
flea market?	**un marché aux puces ?** *uh~ mahr-shay oh pues*

CLOTHES SHOPPING

I'd like to buy _____	**Je voudrais acheter _____** *zhuh voo-dray ahsh-tay*
some men's shirts.	**des chemises pour homme.** *day shmeez pooh-ruhm*
some women's shoes.	**des chaussures pour femme.** *day shoh-suehr poohr fahm*
some children's clothes.	**des vêtements pour enfant.** *day veht-maw~ pooh-raw~-faw~*

les boucles d'oreille
le collier
la robe
la montre

la chemise
la cravate
le veston
la ceinture
le pantalon
les chaussures

I'm looking for a size _____	**Je cherche une taille _____** *zhuh shayhrsh oon tie*

For a full list of numbers, see p7.

small.	**petite.** *puh-teet*
medium.	**moyenne.** *mwah-yehn*
large.	**grande.** *graw~-deh*
extra-large.	**extra-large.** *ehk-strah-lahrzh*
I'm looking for _____	**Je suis à la recherche _____** *zhuh sweez ah lah ruh-shayhrsh*
a silk blouse.	**d'un chemisier en soie.** *duh~ shmee-zee-yay aw~ swah*
cotton pants.	**d'un pantalon en coton.** *duh~ paw~-tah-loh~-naw~ koh-toh~*

- les lunettes
- le tee-shirt
- le jean
- les chaussures de tennis

a hat.	**d'un chapeau.** *duh~ shah-poh*
sunglasses.	**de lunettes de soleil.** *duh lue-neht duh soh-lay*
some underwear.	**de sous-vêtements.** *duh soo veht-maw~*
socks.	**de chaussettes.** *duh shoh-seht*
a sweater.	**d'un pull.** *duh~ puehl*
a swimsuit.	**d'un maillot de bain.** *duh~ mie-yoh duh beh~*
a coat.	**d'un manteau.** *duh~ maw~-toh*
May I try it on?	**Puis-je l'essayer ?** *pwee-zhuh leh-say-yay*
Do you have fitting rooms?	**Avez-vous des cabines d'essayage ?** *ah-vay-voo day kah-been deh-say-yazh*

SHOPPING

This is ____	**C'est ____**
	say
too tight.	**trop serré.**
	troh say-ray
too loose.	**trop large.**
	troh lahr-ge
too long.	**trop long.**
	troh loh~g
too short.	**trop court.**
	troh koohr
This fits great!	**C'est parfait comme taille!**
	say pahr-fay kohm tie
Thanks, I'll take it.	**Merci, je le _m_ / la _f_ / les _pl_.**
	mayhrsee zhuh luh / lah / lay praw~
Do you have that ____	**Est-ce que vous avez cet article**
	____
	ehs kuh voo-zah-vay seh-tahr-tee-kluh
in a smaller / larger size?	**dans une taille plus petite / grande ?**
	daw~-zoon tie plue puh-teet / graw~d
in a different color?	**dans une autre couleur ?**
	daw~-zoo-noh-truh koo-loehr
How much is it?	**Combien ça coûte ?**
	koh-byeh~ sah koot

ARTISAN MARKET SHOPPING

Is there a craft / artisans market?	**Y a-t-il un marché d'artisans ?**
	yah-teel uh~ mahr-shay dahr-tee-zaw~
That's beautiful. May I take a look at it?	**C'est très beau. Puis-je regarder de plus près ?**
	say tray boh; pwee-zhuh ruh-gahr-day duh plue pray

When is the farmers' market open?	**Quelles sont les heures d'ouverture du marché de producteurs ?** *kehl soh~ lay-zoehr doo-vayhr-tuehr due mahr-shay duh proh-duek-toehr*
Is that open every day of the week?	**Est-il ouvert tous les jours de la semaine ?** *ey-teel oo-vayhr too lay zhoohr duh lah smehn*
How much does that cost?	**Combien est-ce que cela coûte ?** *koh~-bee-yeh~ ehs kuh suh-lah koot*
Oh, that's too expensive!	**Oh la, c'est trop cher !** *oh lah say troh shayhr*
How much for both?	**Combien pour les deux ?** *koh~-byeh~ poor lay doeh*
Is there a cash discount?	**Y a-t-il une réduction en caisse ?** *yah-teel uhn ray-duc-syoh~ aw~ kehs*
No thanks. Maybe I'll come back.	**Non, merci. Je reviendrai peut-être.** *noh~ mayhr-see; zhuh ruh-vyeh~-dray poeh-teh-truh*
Would you take €____?	**Accepteriez-vous ____ euros ?** *ahk-sehp-tay-ree-yay-voo ____ oeh-roh*
For a full list of numbers, see p7. Okay, it's a deal. I'll take it / them!	**D'accord. Je le *m* / la *f* / les *pl* prends !** *dah-kohr; zhuh luh / lah / lay praw~*
Do you have a less expensive one?	**Est-ce que vous en avez un / une moins cher ?** *ehs kuh voo-zaw~-nah-vay uh~ / oon mweh~-shayhr*
Is tax included?	**La taxe est-elle comprise ?** *lah tahks ey-tehl koh~-preez*
May I have a VAT form?	**Puis-je avoir un formulaire TVA ?** *pwee-zhuh ah-vwahr uh~ fohr-mue-layhr tay-vay-ah*

For a full list of numbers, see p7.

SHOPPING

BOOKSTORE / NEWSSTAND SHOPPING

Is there a bookstore / newsstand nearby?	**Y a-t-il un libraire / kiosque à journaux près d'ici?** *yah-teel uh~ lee-brayhr / kee-ohsk ah zhoohr-noh pray dee-see*
Do you have ____	**Avez-vous ____** *ah-vay-voo*
books in English?	**des livres en anglais?** *day lee-vruh-zaw~-naw~-glay*
current newspapers?	**des journaux récents?** *day zhoohr-noh ray-saw~*
international newspapers?	**des journaux internationaux?** *day zhoohr-noh eh~-tayhr-nah-see-yoh~-noh*
magazines?	**des magazines?** *day mah-gah-zeen*
books about local history?	**des livres sur l'histoire de cette région?** *day lee-vruh suehr lees-twahr duh seht ray-zhee-yoh~*
picture books?	**des livres d'images?** *day lee-vruh dee-mahzhs*

SHOPPING FOR ELECTRONICS

With some exceptions, shopping for electronic goods in France is generally not recommended for North Americans. Many DVDs, CDs, and other products contain different signal coding than what is used in the United States and Canada to help deter piracy. Radios are probably the biggest exception, though, and lots of U.S. market goods are available.

Can I play this in the United States?	**Est-ce que cela va marcher aux États-Unis?** *ehs kuh suh-lah vah mahr-shay oh-zay-tah-zue-nee*

Will this game work on my game console in the United States?

Est-ce que ce jeu va marcher sur ma console aux États-Unis ?

ehs kuh suh zhoeh vah mahr-shay suehr mah koh~-sohl oh-zay-tah-zue-nee

Is this DVD region encoded?

Ce DVD est-il muni d'un code régional?

suh day-vay-day ay-teel mue-nee duh~ cohd ray-zhee-yoh-nal

Will this work with a 110 VAC adapter?

Est-ce que cela va marcher avec un adaptateur 110 VCA ?

ehs kuh suh-lah vah mahr-shay ah-vek uh~-nah-dahp-toehr saw~-dees vay-say-ah

Do you have an adapter plug for 110 to 220?

Est-ce que vous avez un adaptateur 110 à 220 ?

ehs kuh voo-zah-vay-zuh~-nah-dahp-toehr saw~-dee-zah saw~-veh~

Do you sell electronics adapters here?

Est-ce que vous vendez des adaptateurs pour appareils électroniques ?

ehs kuh voo vaw~-day day-zah-dahp-toehr poohr ah-pah-ray ay-lehk-troh-neek

Is it safe to use my laptop with this adapter?

Est-ce sans risque d'utiliser mon ordinateur portable avec cet adaptateur ?

ehs saw~ reesk due-tee-lee-zay moh~-nohr-dee-nah-toehr pohr-tah-bluh ah-vek seh-tah-dahp-toehr

If it doesn't work, may I return it?

Si cela ne marche pas, puis-je le ramener ?

see suh-lah nuh mahrsh pah pwee-zhuh luh rah-mnay

May I try it here in the store?	**Puis-je l'essayer ici, dans le magasin ?**
	pwee-zhuh leh-say-ay ee-see daw~luh mah-gah-zeh~

AT THE BARBER / HAIRDRESSER

Do you have a style guide?	**Avez-vous un magazine avec des modèles ?**
	ah-ay-voo uh~ mah-gah-zeen ah-vek day moh-day-l~
I'd like a trim.	**Je voudrais une coupe.**
	zhuh voo-dray-zoon koop
I'd like it bleached.	**Je voudrais une couleur.**
	zhuh voo-dray-zoon koo-loehr
Would you change the color?	**Pouvez-vous changer ma couleur ?**
	poo-vay-voo shaw~-zhay mah koo-loehr
I'd like it darker.	**Je la voudrais plus foncée.**
	zhuh lah voo-dray plue foh~-say
I'd like it lighter.	**Je la voudrais plus claire.**
	zhuh lah voo-dray plue klayhr
Would you just touch it up a little?	**Pouvez-vous faire une simple retouche ?**
	poo-vay-voo fayhr oon seh~-pluh ruh-toosh
I'd like it curled.	**Je voudrais une mise en plis.**
	zhuh voo-dray-zoon mee-zaw~ plee
Do I need an appointment?	**Ai-je besoin d'un rendez-vous ?**
	ay-zhuh buh-zweh~ duh~ raw~-day-voo
Do you do perms?	**Faites-vous des permanentes ?**
	feht-voo day payhr-maw~-naw~t

Please use low heat.	**Vérifiez que le sèche-cheveux ne soit pas trop chaud, s'il vous plaît.** *vay-ree-fee-yay kuh luh say-shuh-shuh-vuh~ nuh swah pah troh shoh seel voo play*
Please don't blow dry it.	**Pas de brushing, s'il vous plaît.** *pah duh bruh-sheen seel voo play*
Please dry it curly.	**Faites-les boucler, s'il vous plaît.** *feht-lay boo-klay seel voo play*
Please dry it straight.	**Lissez-les, s'il vous plaît.** *lee-say lay seel voo play*
Would you fix my highlights?	**Pouvez-vous me refaire mes mèches ?** *poo-vay-voo muh ruh-fayhr may mehsh*
Do you wax?	**Est-ce que vous faites des épilations à la cire ?** *ehs kuh voo feht day-zay-pee-lah-see-yoh~ ah lah seer*
I'd like a Brazilian wax.	**Je voudrais un maillot brésilien.** *zhuh voo-dray uh~ mah-yo bray-zeel-yu~*
Please wax my ____	**Épilez-moi ____ à la cire, s'il vous plaît.** *ay-pee-lay mwah ____ ah lah seer seel voo play*
legs.	**les jambes** *lay zhahmb*
bikini line.	**le maillot** *luh mah-yoh*
eyebrows.	**les sourcils** *lay soohr-seel*
under my nose.	**la moustache** *lah moos-tah-shuh*

Please trim my beard.	**Raccourcissez-moi un peu la barbe, s'il vous plaît.** *rah-koohr-see-say mwah uh~ poeh lah bahrb seel voo play*
May I have a shave, please?	**Puis-je me faire raser, s'il vous plaît ?** *pwee-zhuh muh fayhr rah-zay seel voo play*
Use a fresh blade, please.	**Utilisez une lame neuve, s'il vous plaît.** *oo-tee-lee-zay oon lahm noehv seel voo play*
Sure, cut it all off.	**D'accord, coupez-la f / coupez-les pl complètement.** *dah-kohr koo-pay lah / les koh~-pleht-maw~*

CHAPTER NINE
SPORTS & FITNESS

GETTING FIT

Is there a gymnasium
nearby?

Y a-t-il un gymnase près d'ici ?
*yah-teel uh~ zheem-nahz prey
dee-see*

Does the hotel have a gym?

**L'hôtel dispose-t-il d'une salle de
sport ?**
*loh-tell dees-poz-teel doon sahl
duh spor*

Do you have free weights?

Avez-vous des haltères ?
ah-vay-voo day-zahl-tayhr

Is there a pool?

Y a-t-il une piscine ?
yah-teel oon pee-seen

Do I have to be a member?

**L'entrée est-elle réservée aux
membres ?**
*law~-tray ey-tehl ray-zehr-vay oh
maw~-bruh*

May I come here for one
day?

**Puis-je entrer pour une séance à
l'unité ?**
*pwee-zhuh aw~-tray poohr oon
say-aw~s ah lue-nee-tay*

How much does a membership cost?	**Combien coûte l'abonnement ?** *koh~-bee-yeh~ koot lah-buhn-maw~*
I need to get a locker, please.	**Je voudrais un casier, s'il vous plaît.** *zhuh voo-dray uh~ kahz-yay seel voo play*
Do you have locks for those?	**Avez-vous des cadenas pour les casiers ?** *ah-vay-voo day kahd-nah poohr lay kahz-yay*
Do you have a treadmill?	**Y a-t-il un tapis de course ici ?** *yah-teel uh~ tah-pee duh koor-sue ee-see*
Do you have a stationary bike?	**Y a-t-il un vélo d'exercice ?** *yah-teel uh~ vaylo dehk-sayhr-sees*
Do you have a handball / squash court?	**Avez-vous un terrain de handball / squash ?** *ah-vay-voo-zuh~ tuh-reh~ duh ahnd bahl / skwahsh*
Are they indoors?	**Sont-ils couverts ?** *soh~-teel koo-vayhr*
I'd like to play tennis.	**J'aime jouer au tennis.** *zhehm zhoo-ay oh teh-nees*
Would you like to play?	**Voulez-vous jouer avec moi ?** *voo-lay-voo zhoo-ay ah-vek mwah*
I'd like to rent a racquet.	**Je voudrais louer une raquette.** *zhuh voo-dray loo-ay oon rah-keht*
I need to buy some new balls.	**Je voudrais acheter des balles neuves.** *zhuh voo-dray ahsh-tay day bahl noehv*
I lost my safety glasses.	**J'ai perdu mes lunettes de protection.** *zhay payhr-due may lue-neht duh pro-tek-syoh~*

May I rent a court for tomorrow?	**Puis-je louer un court pour demain ?**
	pwee-zhuh loo-ay uh~ koohr poohr duh-meh~
Do you have clean towels?	**Avez-vous des serviettes propres ?**
	ah-vay-voo day sayhr-vee-yeht proh-pruh
Where are the showers / locker rooms?	**Où sont les douches / vestiaires, s'il vous plaît ?**
	oo soh~ lay doosh / vehs-tee-yayhr seel voo play
Do you have a workout room for women only?	**Avez-vous une salle d'entraîne-ment réservée aux femmes ?**
	ah-vay-voo-zoon sahl daw~-treh~-maw~ ray-zehr-vay oh fahm
Do you have aerobics classes?	**Avez-vous des cours d'aérobic ?**
	ah-vay-voo day koohr dah-eyh-roh-beek
Are there Yoga/Pilates classes?	**Y a-t-il des cours de yoga / pilates ?**
	yah-teel day koor duh yo-gah/ peel-aht
Do you have a women's pool?	**Avez-vous une piscine réservée aux femmes ?**
	ah-vay-voo-zoon pee-seen ray-sehr-vay oh fahm
Let's go for a jog.	**Allons faire un jogging.**
	ah-loh~ fayhr uh~ zhoh-gheeng
That was a great workout.	**Je me suis bien entraîné(e).**
	zhuh muh swee bee-yeh~ aw~-treh~-nay

CATCHING A GAME

Where is the stadium?	**Où se trouve le stade ?**
	oo suh troov luh stahd
Who's playing?	**Qui joue ?**
	kee-zhoo

Who is the best goalie?	**Qui est le meilleur gardien de but ?** *kee ay luh may-yoehr gahr-dee-yeh~ duh bue*
Do you have any amateur / professional teams?	**Avez-vous des équipes amateurs / professionnelles ?** *ah-vay-voo day-zay-keep ah-mah-toehr / proh-feh-see-yoh-nehl*
Is there a game I could play in?	**Y a-t-il un événement sportif auquel je pourrais participer ?** *yah-teel uh~-nay-vay-nuh-maw~ spohr-teef oh-kehl zhuh pooh-ray pahr-tee-see-pay*
Which is the best team?	**Quelle est la meilleure équipe ?** *keh-lay lah may-yoehr ay-keep*
Will the game be on television?	**Le match va-t-il passer à la télévision ?** *luh mahtch vah-teel pah-say ah lah tay-lay-veez-yoh~*
Where can I buy tickets?	**Où puis-je acheter des places ?** *oo pwee-zhuh ahsh-tay day plahs*
The best seats, please.	**Les meilleures places, s'il vous plaît.** *lay may-yoehrs plahs seel voo play*

The cheapest seats, please.	**Les places les moins chères, s'il vous plaît.** *lay plahs lay mweh~ shayhr seel voo play*
How close are these seats?	**Ces places sont-elles près du terrain ?** *say plahs soh~-tehl pray due tuh-reh~*
Where are these seats?	**Où sont ces places ?** *oo soh~ say plahs*
May I have a private box?	**Puis-je avoir un box privé ?** *pwee-zhuh ah-vwahr uh~ bohks pree-vay*
Wow! What a game!	**Quel match !** *kehl mahtch*
Go! Go! Go!	**On va gagner !** *repeat several times* *oh~ vah gah-nyay*
Go for it!	**Vas-y !** *vah-zee*
Score!	**Marque un but !** *mahrk uh~ bue*
What's the score?	**Quel est le score ?** *keh-lay luh skohr*
Who's winning?	**Qui est en train de gagner ?** *kee eh-taw~ treh~ duh gah-nyay*

HIKING

Is there a trail map?	**Y a-t-il une carte des pistes ?** *yah-teel oon kart day peest*
Do we need to hire a guide?	**Est-il nécessaire de prendre un guide ?** *ey-teel nay-suh-sayhr duh praw~-druh uh~ gheed*
Where can I rent equipment?	**Où puis-je louer du matériel d'escalade ?** *oo pwee-zhuh loo-ay due mah-tayh-ree-yehl dehs-kah-lahd*

Do they have rock climbing there?

Y a-t-il des endroits où on peut faire de la varappe ?
yah-teel day-zaw~-dhwah oo oh~-poeh fayhr duh lah vah-rahp

We need to get more ropes and carabiners.

Nous avons besoin de cordes et de mousquetons supplémentaires.
noo-zah-voh~ buh-zweh~ duh kohrd ay duh moos-kuh-toh~ sue-play-maw~-tayhr

Where can we go mountain climbing?

Où est-il possible de faire de l'escalade ?
oo ey-teel poh-see-bluh duh fayhr duh lehs-kah-lahd

Are the routes well marked?

Les routes sont-elles bien signalisées ?
lay root soh~-tehl bee-yeh~ see-nyah-lee-zay

Are the routes in good condition?

Les chemins sont-ils en bon état ?
lay shuh-meh~ soh~-teel aw~-boh~-nay-tah

What is the altitude there?	**Quelle est l'altitude là-haut ?** *keh-lay lahl-tee-tued lah oh*
How long will it take?	**Combien de temps cela prendra-t-il ?** *koh~-bee-yeh~ duh taw~ suh-lah* *praw~-drah-teel*
Is it very difficult?	**Est-ce très difficile ?** *ehs tray dee-fee-seel*
I'd like a challenging climb, but I don't want to take oxygen.	**Je voudrais faire un parcours d'escalade difficile mais je ne veux pas porter d'oxygène.** *zhuh voo-dray fehr uh~ pahr koor* *dehs-kah-lahd may zhuh nuh voeh* *pah pohr-tay duh lohk-seezhehn*
I want to hire a porter.	**Je voudrais embaucher un porteur.** *zhuh voo-dray aw~-bo-shay uh~* *por-toehr*
We don't have time for a long route.	**Nous n'avons pas le temps de faire une longue sortie.** *noo nah-voh~ pah luh taw~ duh* *fayhr oon loh~g sohr-tee*
I don't think it's safe to proceed.	**Je ne pense pas qu'il soit prudent de continuer.** *zhuh nuh paw~s pah keel swah* *prue-daw~ duh koh~-tee-nue-ay*
Do we have a backup plan?	**Avons-nous un plan en cas de problème ?** *ah-voh~-noo-zuh~ plaw~ aw~ kah* *duh proh-blehm*
If we're not back by tomorrow, send a search party.	**Si nous ne sommes pas revenus demain, envoyez quelqu'un à notre recherche.** *see noo nuh sohm pah ruhv-noo* *duh-meh~ aw~-vwah-yay kehl-* *kuh~ ah noh-truh ruh-shersh*

Are the campsites marked?

Les emplacements de camping sont-ils balisés ?
layz aw~-plahs-maw~ duh kaw~-peeng soh~-teel bah-lee-zay

Can we camp off the trail?

Est-il possible de camper en pleine nature ?
ey-teel poh-see-bluh duh kaw~-pay aw~ plehn nah-tuehr

Is it okay to build fires here?

A-t-on le droit de faire des feux de camp ici ?
ah-toh~ luh dhwah duh fayhr day foeh duh kaw~ ee- see

Do we need permits?

A-t-on besoin d'une autorisation ?
ah-toh~ buh-zweh~ doon oh-toh-ree-zah-see-yoh~

For more camping terms, see p87.

BOATING OR FISHING

I'd like to go fishing.

J'aimerais aller pêcher.
zhay-meh-ray ah-lay pay-shay

When do we sail?

À quelle heure appareillons-nous ?
ah keh-loehr ah-pah-ray-oh~-noo

Where are the life preservers / vests?

Où sont les bouées / gilets de sauvetage ?
oo soh~ lay boo-ay / zhee-lay duh sohv-tazh

Can I purchase bait?

Puis-je acheter des appâts ?
pwee-zhuh ahsh-tay days ah-pah

Can I rent a rod / pole?

Puis-je louer une canne à pêche ?
pwee-zhuh loo-ay oon kahn

How long is the trip?

Combien de temps dure le voyage ?
koh~-bee-yeh~ duh taw~ duehr luh vwa-yahz

Are we going up river or down?	**Remontons-nous ou descendons-nous la rivière ?** *ruh-moh~-toh~-noo oo duh-saw~-doh~-noo lah ree-vee-yayhr*
How far out are we going?	**Jusqu'où allons-nous ?** *zhues-koo ah-loh~-noo*
How fast are we going?	**On va à quelle vitesse ?** *oh~ vah ah kehl vee-tehs*
How deep is the water here?	**Quelle est la profondeur de l'eau ici ?** *keh-lay lah proh-foh~-doehr duh loh ee-see*
I got one!	**J'ai attrapé un poisson !** *zhay ah-trah-pay uh~ pwah-soh~*
I can't swim.	**Je ne sais pas nager.** *zhuh nuh say pah nah-zhay*
Help! Lifeguard!.	**À l'aide ! Sauveteur !** *ahl-ayd soh-veh-toehr*
Can we go ashore?	**Pouvons-nous aller à terre ?** *poo-voh~-noo-zah-lay ah tayhr*

For more boating terms, see p70.

DIVING

I'd like to go snorkeling.	**Je voudrais faire de la plongée avec masque et tuba.** *zhuh voo-dray fayhr duh lah ploh~-zhay ah-vek mahsk ay tue-bah*
I'd like to go scuba diving.	**Je voudrais faire de la plongée sous-marine.** *zhuh voo-dray fayhr duh lah ploh~-zhay soo mah-reen*
I have a NAUI / PADI certification.	**J'ai le brevet de plongeur NAUI / PADI.** *zhay luh bruh-vay duh ploh~-zhoehr enn-ah-oo-ee / pay-ah-day-ee*

I need to rent gear.

Je voudrais louer du matériel de plongée.
zhuh voo-dray loo-ay due mah-tayh-ree-yehl duh ploh~-zhay

We'd like to see some shipwrecks if we can.

Nous aimerions si possible voir des épaves.
noo-zeh-meh-ree-yoh~ see poh-see-bluh vwahr day-zay-pahv

Are there any good cave / reef dives?

Y a-t-il de bonnes plongées dans des grottes / récifs ?
yah-teel duh buhn ploh~-zhay duh groht / ray-seef

I'd like to see a lot of diverse sea-life.

Je voudrais voir un milieu sous-marin diversifié.
zhuh voo-dray vwahr uh~ meel-yoeh soo-mah-reh~ dee-vayhr-see-fee-yay

Are the currents strong?

Le courant est-il fort ?
luh kooh-raw~ ey-teel fohr

How is the clarity?

Les eaux sont-elles claires ?
lay-zoh soh~-tehl klayhr

I want / don't want to go with a group.

Je voudrais / je ne veux pas me joindre à un groupe.
zhuh voo-dray / zhuh nuh voeh pah muh zhweh~-druh ah uh~ groohp

Do we have to go with a group, or can we charter our own boat?

Devons-nous nous joindre à un groupe, ou pouvons-nous louer notre propre bateau ?
duh-voh~-noo noo zhweh~-druh ah uh~ groop oo poo-voh~-noo loo-ay noh-truh proh-pruh bah-toh

SURFING

I'd like to go surfing.

Je voudrais aller faire du surf.
zhuh voo-dray ah-lay fayhr due suehrf

Are there any good beaches?

Y a-t-il de bonnes plages à surf ?
yah-teel duh buhn plahzh ah suehrf

Can I rent a board?

Puis-je louer une planche ?
pwee-zhuh loo-ay oon plaw~sh

How are the currents?

Y a-t-il beaucoup de courant ?
yah-teel boh-koo duh kooh-raw~

How high are the waves?

Les vagues sont de quelle hauteur ?
lay vahg soh~ duh kehl oh-toehr

Is it usually crowded?

Y a-t-il du monde d'habitude sur la plage ?
yah-teel due moh~d dah-bee-tued suehr lah plahzh

Are there facilities on that beach?

Y a-t-il des infrastructures sur la plage ?
yah-teel day-zeh~-frah-struek-tuehr suehr lah plahzh

Is there wind surfing there also?

Est-il possible de faire de la planche à voile ?
ey-teel poh-seeb-luh duh fayhr duh lah plaw~sh ah vwahl

GOLFING

I'd like to reserve a
tee-time, please.

**Je voudrais réserver un parcours
de golf, s'il vous plaît.**
*zhuh oo-dray ray-zehr-vay uh~
pahr-koor duh golf seel voo play*

Do we need to be members
to play your course?

**Ce terrain de golf est-il réservé
aux membres ?**
*suh tuh-reh~ duh gohlf ey-teel
ray-zehr-vay oh maw~-bruh*

How many holes is your
course?

C'est un golf à combien de trous ?
*seht uh~ gohlf ah koh~-bee-yeh~
duh troo*

What is par for the course?

Combien de pars sur ce terrain ?
*koh~-bee-yeh~ ay pahr suhr suh
teh-reh~*

What is the dress code
for players?

**Quel est le code vestimentaire
pour les joueurs ?**
*kehl ay luh kod vay-stee-maw~tayr
poor lay zhoehr*

I need to rent clubs.

**J'ai besoin de louer des clubs de
golf.**
*zhay buh-zweh~ duh loo-ay day
club~ duh gohlf*

I need to purchase
some balls.

**J'ai besoin d'acheter des balles de
golf.**
*zhay buh-zweh~ dahsh-tay day
bahl duh gohlf*

I need a glove.

J'ai besoin d'un gant.
zhay buh-zweh~ duh~ gaw~

Do you require soft spikes?	**Exigez-vous des crampons mous ?** *ek-zee-zhay-voo day kraw~-poh~-moo*
Do you have carts?	**Avez-vous des voiturettes ?** *ah-vay-voo day vwah-tueh-reht*
I'd like to hire a caddie.	**Je voudrais embaucher un caddie.** *zhuh voo-dray aw~-boh-shay uh~-kah-dee*
Do you have a driving range?	**Avez-vous un terrain d'exercice ?** *ah-vay-voo-zuh~ tuh-reh~ dayk-sayhr-sees*
How much are the greens fees?	**Combien coûte l'entrée ?** *koh~-bee-yeh~ koot law~-tray*
Can I book a lesson with the pro?	**Puis-je prendre rendez-vous pour une leçon avec un professionnel ?** *pwee-zhuh praw~-druh raw~-day-voo poohr oon leh-soh~ ah-vek uh~ proh-feh-see-yoh-nehl*
I need to have a club repaired.	**J'ai besoin de faire réparer l'un de mes clubs.** *zhay buh-zweh~ duh fayhr ray-pah-ray luh~ duh may club~*
Is the course dry?	**L'herbe du golf est-elle sèche ?** *layhrb due gohlf ey-tehl sehsh*
Are there any wildlife hazards?	**Est-ce qu'on risque de rencontrer des animaux sauvages ?** *ehs koh~ reesk duh raw~-koh~-tray day-zah-nee-moh soh-vahzh*
How many total meters is the course?	**Quelle est la longueur totale du golf ?** *keh-lay lah loh~-goehr toh-tahl due gohlf*
Is it very hilly?	**Y a-t-il beaucoup de bosses sur le terrain ?** *yah-teel bo-koo duh boss suhr luh tay-reh~*

CHAPTER TEN

NIGHTLIFE

For coverage of movies and cultural events, see Chapter 7, Culture.

NIGHTCLUBBING

Would you please tell me where to find ____	**Pourriez-vous m'indiquer ____, s'il vous plaît ?** *poo-vay-voo meh~-dee-kay ___ seel voo play*
a good nightclub?	**une bonne boîte de nuit** *oon buhn bwaht duh nwee*
a club with a live band?	**une boîte où un groupe joue de la musique** *oon bwaht oo uh groop zhoo duh lah mue-zeek*
a reggae club?	**une boîte où l'on joue du reggae** *oon bwaht oo loh~ zhoo due reh-gay*
a hip hop club?	**une boîte de hip-hop** *oon bwaht duh eep-ohp*
a techno club?	**une boîte avec de la musique techno** *oon bwaht ah-vek duh lah mue-zeek tehk-noh*
a jazz club?	**un club de jazz** *oon club duh zhahz*
a country / western club?	**une boîte avec de la musique country** *oon bwaht ah-vek duh lah mue-zeek kuhn-tree*
a gay / lesbian club?	**une boîte pour homosexuels / lesbiennes** *oon bwaht poohr oh-moh-sehk-sue-ehl / lehz-bee-yehn*

a club where I can dance?	**une boîte où l'on danse vraiment** *oon bwaht oo loh~ daw~s vray-maw~*
a club with French music?	**une boîte avec de la musique française** *oon bwaht ah-vek duh lah mue-zeek fraw~-sehz*
the most popular club in town?	**la boîte la plus chaude du quartier** *lah bwaht lah plue shohd-duh due kahr-tee-yay*
a singles bar?	**un bar pour célibataires ?** (unmarried) *uh~ bahr poor say-lee-bah-tayhr*
a piano bar?	**un piano-bar** *oon pee-yah-noh-bahr*
the most upscale bar?	**le bar le bar le plus luxueux / chic** *luh bahr luh bahr luh plue lueks-wue / cheek*
What's the hottest bar these days?	**Quel est le bar le plus chaud du moment ?** *keh-lay luh bahr luh plue shohd due mo-maw~*
What's the cover charge?	**Combien coûte l'entrée ?** *koh-byeh~ koot law~-tray*
Do they have a dress code?	**Y a-t-il une tenue correcte exigée ?** *yah-teel oon teh-nue correct ex-ee-zhay*
Is that an expensive club?	**Est-ce une boîte chère ?** *es oon bwaht shayhr*
What's the best time to get there?	**Quelle est la meilleure heure pour arriver ?** *keh-lay lah may-yoeh-roehr poor ah-ree-vay*

Do You Mind If I Smoke?

Est-ce qu'on a le droit de fumer ?
ehs-koh~ ah luh dhwah duh fue-may

May I smoke?

Avez-vous _____, s'il vous plaît ?
ah-vay-voo _____ seel voo play

Do you have _____

  une cigarette
  oon see-gah-reht

a cigarette?

  du feu
  due foeh

a light?

Puis-je vous offrir du feu ?
pwee-zhuh voo-zoh-freer due foeh

May I offer you a light?

What kind of music do they play there?

Quel type de musique y joue-t-on ?
kehl teep duh mue-zeek ee zhoo-toh~

Is there an outside area where I can smoke?

Puis-je fumer à l'extérieur ?
pwee-zhuh fue-may ahl-ex-tay-ryeur

I'm looking for _____

Je cherche _____
zhuh shayhrsh

  a good cigar shop.

  un bon magasin de cigares.
  uh~ boh mah-gah-zaw~ duh see-gahr

  a pack of cigarettes.

  un paquet de cigarettes.
  uh~ pah-kay duh see-gah-reht

I'd like _____

Je voudrais _____
zhuh voo-dray

a drink, please!

à boire, s'il vous plaît !
ah bwahr seel voo play

a bottle of beer, please!

une bouteille de bière, s'il vous plaît !
oon boo-tay duh bee-yayhr seel voo play

a beer on tap, please.

une bière pression, s'il vous plaît.
oon bee-yayhr pruh-syoh~ seel voo play

a shot of _____, please.

un verre de _____, s'il vous plaît.
uh~ vayhr duh _____ seel voo play

For a full list of beverages, see p96.

Make it a double, please!

Un double verre de _____, s'il vous plaît !
uh~ doo-bluh vayhr duh _____ seel voo play

May I have that with ice, please?

Avec des glaçons, s'il vous plaît ?
ah-vek day glah-soh~ seel voo play

I'd like to buy a drink for that girl / guy over there.

Je voudrais offrir un verre à la jeune fille / au jeune homme là-bas.
zhuh voo-dray oh-freer uh~ vayhr ah lah zhoehn fee / oh zhoeh-nuhm lah-bah

How much for a bottle / glass of beer?

Combien coûte une bouteille / un verre de bière ?
koh~-bee-yeh~ koot oon boo-tay / uh~ vayhr duh bee-yayhr

May I have a pack of cigarettes, please?

Puis-je avoir un paquet de cigarettes, s'il vous plaît ?
pwee-zhuh ah-vwahr uh~ pah-kay duh seeg-ah-reht, seel voo play

Do you have a lighter or matches?

Avez-vous un briquet ou des allumettes ?
ah-vay-voo uh~ bree-kay oo day-zah-lue-meht

Do you smoke?

Vous fumez ?
voo fue-may

Would you like a cigarette?

Voulez-vous une cigarette ?
voo-lay-voo-zoon see-gah-reht

May I run a tab?

Puis-je mettre cela sur une note ?
Pwee-zhuh meh-truh seh-lah suehr oon noht ?

ACROSS A CROWDED ROOM

You look like the most interesting person in the room.

Vous semblez être la personne la plus intéressante ici.
voo saw~-blay ay-tr~ lah payhr-suhn lah plue zeh~-tay-ray-saw~t ee-see

Can I buy you a drink?

Pardon, puis-je vous offrir un verre ?
pahr-doh~ pwee-zhuh voo-zoh-freer uh~ vayhr

I wanted to meet you. **Je voulais vous rencontrer.**
zhuh voo-lay voo raw~-coh~tray

Are you single? **Êtes-vous célibataire ?**
eht voo say-lee-bah-tayr

You look amazing! **Vous avez l'air fantastique !**
voo-zah-vay layhr faw~-tahs-teek

Would you like to dance? **Voulez-vous danser avec moi ?**
voo-lay-voo daw~-say ah-vek
mwah

Do you like to dance fast **Aimez-vous danser le rock ou le**
or slow? **slow ?**
ey-may-voo daw~-say luh rohk oo
luh sloh

Here, give me your hand. **Donnez-moi la main.**
duh-nay mwah lah meh~

What would you like to **Qu'est-ce que vous voulez boire ?**
drink? *kehs-kuh voo voo-lay bwahr*
You're a great dancer! **Vous dansez très bien !**
voo daw~-say tray bee-yeh~

Do you like this song? **Vous aimez cette chanson?**
voo-zey-may seht shaw~-soh~

You have nice eyes! **Vous avez de beaux yeux !**
voo-zah-vay duh bohz yoeh

For a full list of features, see p126.
May I have your phone **Puis-je avoir votre téléphone /**
number / email address ? **votre adresse mail ?**
pwee-zhuh ah-vwahr voh-truh
nue-may-roh duh tay-lay-fohn/
voh-truh ah-dress mail

Would you like to go out **Voulez-vous sortir (avec moi) ?**
(with me)? *voo-lay-vous sohr-tee-ruh (ah-vek*
mwah)

I'd love to. **J'aimerais bien.**
jay-meu-ray bee-yeh~

GETTING CLOSER

You're very attractive.

Tu es très séduisant *m* / **très jolie** *f.*
tueh ay tray say-dwee-zaw~ / tray zhoh-ee

I like being with you.

Je me sens bien avec toi.
zhuh muh saw~ bee-yeh~ ah-vek twah

I like you.

Tu me plais beaucoup.
tueh muh play boh-koo

I want to hold you.

Je veux te serrer dans mes bras.
zhuh voeh tuh suh-ray daw~ may brah-s

Kiss me.

Embrasse-moi.
aw~-brah-say mwah

May I give you a kiss?

Puis-je t'embrasser ?
pwee-zhuh taw~-brah-say

Would you like a massage / a back rub?

Veux-tu un massage / que je te masse le dos ?
voeh-tueh uh~ mah-sazh / kuh zhuh tuh mahs luh doh

GETTING INTIMATE

Would you like to come inside?	**Veux-tu entrer ?** *voeh-tueh aw~-tray*
May I come inside?	**Puis-je entrer ?** *pwee-zhuh aw~-tray*
Let me help you out of that.	**Laisse-moi l'enlever pour toi.** *leh-suy mwah law~-luh-vay poohr twah*
Would you help me out of this?	**Peux-tu m'aider à l'enlever ?** *poeh-tueh may-day ah law~-luh-vay*
You smell so good.	**Tu sens si bon.** *tueh saw~ see boh~*
You're handsome / beautiful.	**Tu es très beau** m / **très belle** f. *tueh ay tray boh / tray bell*
May I?	**Je peux ?** *zhuh puh*
OK?	**Tu es d'accord ?** *tueh ay dah-kohr*
Like this?	**Comme ça ?** *kohm sah*
How?	**Comment ?** *koh-maw~*

HOLD ON A SECOND

Please, don't do that.	**Ne fais pas ça s'il te plaît.** *nuh fay pah sah seel tuh play*
Stop, please.	**S'il te plaît, arrête.** *seel tuh play ah-reht*
Do you want me to stop?	**Tu veux que j'arrête ?** *tueh voeh kuh zhah-reht*
Let's just be friends.	**Si on restait amis ?** *see oh~ ray-stay ah-mee*

For a full list of features, see p126.
For a full list of body parts, see p196.

Do you have a condom?	**Est-ce que tu as un préservatif?** *ehs-kuh tueh ah uh~ prey-zehr-vah-teef*
Are you on birth control?	**Est-ce que tu prends la pilule ?** *ehs-kuh tueh praw~ lah peel-uel*
Hold on, I have a condom here.	**Attends, laisse-moi prendre un préservatif.** *ah-taw~ lehs-mwah praw~druh uh prey-zehhr-vah-teef*
You don't have anything you want to tell me first, do you?	**Y a-t-il quelque chose dont tu voudrais me parler ?** *yah-teel kehl-kuh shohz doh~ tueh voo-dray muh pahr-lay*

BACK TO IT

That's it!	**Oui, comme ça !** *wee kohm sah*
That's not it!	**Non, pas comme ça !** *noh~ pah kohm sah*
Here.	**Ici !** *ee-see*
There.	**Par là !** *pahr-lah*
More!	**Continue comme ça !** *koh~-tee-nue kohm sah*
Harder!	**Plus fort !** *plue fohr*
Faster!	**Plus vite !** *plue veet*
Deeper!	**Va plus loin !** *vah plue lweh~*
Slower!	**Moins vite !** *mweh~ veet*
Easier!	**Plus doucement !** *plue doos-maw~*

COOLDOWN

You're great!

Tu as été formidable !
tueh ah ay-tay fohr-mee-dah-bluh

That was great.

C'était magnifique.
seh-tay mah-nyee-feek

Would you like _____

Tu veux _____
tueh voeh

  a drink?

  quelque chose à boire ?
  kehl-kuh shohz ah bwahr

  a snack?

  manger quelque chose ?
  maw~-zhay kehl-kuh shohz

  a shower?

  prendre une douche ?
  praw~-druh oon doosh

May I stay here?

Puis-je passer la nuit ici ?
pwee-zhuh pah-say lah nwee ee-see

Would you like to stay here?

Veux-tu passer la nuit ici ?
voeh-tueh pah-say lah nwee ee-see

I'm sorry, I have to go now.

Je suis désolé(e), je dois m'en aller maintenant.
zhuh swee day-zoh-lay zhuh dwah maw~-nah-lay meh~t-naw~

Where are you going?

Où vas-tu ?
oo vah-tueh

I have to work early.

Je dois me lever tôt pour mon travail.
zhuh dwah muh leh-vay toh poohr moh~ trah-vie

I'm flying home in the morning.

Je prends l'avion demain matin.
zhuh praw~ lah-vee-yon duh-meh~ mah-teh~

I have an early flight.

Mon vol part très tôt.
moh~ vohl pahr tray toh

NIGHTLIFE

I think this was a mistake.	**Nous n'aurions pas dû.** *noo noh-ree-yoh~ pah due*
Will you make me breakfast?	**Peux-tu me préparer un petit déjeuner ?** *poeh-tueh muh pray-pah-ray uh~ puh-tee day-zhoeh-nay*
Stay, I'll make you breakfast.	**Reste, je te prépare le petit déjeuner.** *rehst zhuh tuh pray-pahr luh puh-tee day-zhoeh-nay*

IN THE CASINO

How much is this table?	**Combien sont les mises à cette table ?** *koh~-bee-yeh~ soh~ lay meez ah seht tah-bluh*
Deal me in.	**Donnez-moi des cartes, s'il vous plaît.** *doh-nay mwah day kahrt seel voo play*
Put it on red!	**Sur le rouge, s'il vous plaît !** *suehr luh roozh seel voo play*
Put it on black!	**Sur le noir, s'il vous plaît !** *suehr luh nwahr seel voo play*
Let it ride!	**Je conserve ma mise.** *zhuh koh~-sayr-uh mah meez*
21!	**Vingt-et-un !** *veh~-tay-uh~*
Snake-eyes!	**Paire d'as !** *payhr dahs*
Seven.	**Sept.** *seht*

For a full list of numbers, see p7.

Damn, eleven.	**Mince, ça fait onze.** *meh~s say fay oh~z*
I'll pass.	**Passe.** *pahs*
Hit me!	**Donne !** *duhn*
Split.	**Le split.** *luh spleet*
Are the drinks complimentary?	**Les boissons sont-elles comprises ?** *lay bwah-soh~ soh~-tehl* *koh~-preez*
May I bill it to my room?	**Puis-je mettre cela sur ma note ?** *pwee-zhuh meh-truh seh-lah suehr* *mah noht*
I'd like to cash out.	**Je voudrais récupérer mes gains.** *zhuh voo-dray ray-kue-pay-ray* *may gah~*
I'll hold.	**Je reste.** *zhuh rehst*
I'll see your bet.	**Je mets autant.** *zhuh may oh-tah~*
I call.	**J'abandonne.** *zhah-baw~-duhn*
Full house!	**Full !** *fuehl*
Royal flush!	**Quinte flush royale !** *keh~t fluesh rwah-yahl*
Straight!	**Suite !** *sweet*

CHAPTER ELEVEN

This chapter covers the terms you'll need to maintain your health and safety—including the most useful phrases for the pharmacy, doctor's office, and police station.

AT THE PHARMACY

Would you please fill this prescription?	**Pouvez-vous exécuter cette ordonnance, s'il vous plaît ?** *poo-vay-voo-zehk-say-kue-tay seht ohr-duh-naw~s seel voo play*
Do you have anything for a cold?	**Avez-vous quelque chose contre le rhume ?** *ah-vay-voo kehl-kuh shohz koh~-truh luh ruem*
I have a cough.	**Je tousse.** *zhuh toos*
I need something to help me sleep.	**J'ai besoin de quelque chose pour m'aider à dormir.** *zhay buh-zweh~ duh kehl-kuh shohz poohr may-day ah dohr-meer*
I need something to help me relax.	**J'ai besoin de quelque chose pour m'aider à me détendre.** *zhay buh-zweh~ duh kehl-kuh shohz poohr may-day ah muh day-taw~-druh*
I want to buy ____	**Je voudrais acheter ____** *zhuh voo-dray ahsh-tay*
condoms.	**des préservatifs.** *day prey-zayhr-vah-teef*
an antihistimine.	**de l'antihistaminique.** *duh law~-tee-ees-tah-mee-neek*
antibiotic cream.	**une pommade antibiotique.** *oon poh-mad aw~-tee-byoh-teek*

aspirin.	**de l'aspirine.**
	duh lah-spreen
nonaspirin pain reliever.	**un antidouleur sans aspirine.**
	uh~ naw~-tee doo-luhr saw~-zas-pee-reen
medicine with codeine.	**d'un médicament à la codéine.**
	daw~ may-deek-ah-maw~ ah lah koh-day-in
insect repellant.	**d'un insectifuge.**
	daw~ eh~-sehk-tee-fuezh
I need something for _____	**J'ai besoin de quelque chose contre _____**
	zhay buh-zweh~ duh kehl-kuh shohz koh~-tr
corns.	**les cors au pied.**
	lay kohr oh pee-yay
congestion.	**la congestion.**
	lah koh~-zhay-stee-yoh~
warts.	**les verrues.**
	lay vay-rue
constipation.	**la constipation.**
	lah koh~-stee-pah-see-yoh~
diarrhea.	**la diarrhée.**
	lah dee-yah-ray
indigestion.	**l'indigestion.**
	leh~-dee-zhay-stee-yoh~
nausea.	**la nausée.**
	lah noh-zay
motion sickness.	**le mal des transports.**
	luh mahl day traw~-spohr
seasickness.	**le mal de mer.**
	luh mahl duh mayhr
acne.	**l'acné.**
	lahk-nay
I need a band-aid.	**J'ai besoin d'un pansement.**
	zhay buh-zweh~ duh~ paw~-s-maw~

AT THE DOCTOR'S OFFICE

I would like to see ____	**Je voudrais consulter ____** *zhuh voo-dray koh~-suel-tay*
a doctor.	**un médecin.** *uh~ may-duh-seh~*
a chiropractor.	**un chiropraticien.** *uh~ kee-roh-prah-tees-yeh~*
a gynecologist.	**un gynécologue.** *uh~ zhee-nay-koh-lohg*
an eye specialist / an ear, nose, and throat (ENT) specialist.	**un ophtalmologue / un ORL** *uh~ noh-ftahl-moh-loh-g / uh~ noh-ayrh-ehl*
a dentist.	**un dentiste.** *uh~ daw~-teest*
an optometrist.	**un optométriste.** *uh~ ohp-toh-may-treest*
a dermatologist.	**un dermatologue.** *uh~ dayhr-mah-toh-lohg*
Do I need an appointment?	**Ai-je besoin d'un rendez-vous ?** *ay-zhuh buh-zweh~ duh~ raw~-day-voo*
Do I have to pay upfront?	**Dois-je payer d'avance ?** *dwah-zhuh pay-yeah dah-va~-s*
I have an emergency.	**C'est une urgence.** *seh-toon oohr-zhaw~s*
I need an emergency prescription refill.	**J'ai besoin de faire renouveler mon ordonnance en urgence.** *zhay buh-zweh~ duh fayhr ruh-noov-lay moh~-nohr-doh-naw~s duehr-zhaw~s*
Please call the doctor.	**Appelez un médecin, s'il vous plaît.** *ah-play uh~ may-duh-seh~ seel voo play*
I need an ambulance.	**Faites venir une ambulance.** *feht veh-neer oon aw~-bue-law~s*

SYMPTOMS

My _____ hurts.

J'ai mal au m / à la f / aux pl _____.
zhay mahl oh / ah lah / oh _____.

My _____ is stiff.

mon m / ma f _____ est raide.
moh / mah _____ ay rehd

I think I'm having a heart attack.

Je crois que je vais faire une crise cardiaque.
zhuh kwah kuh zhuh vay fayhr oon kreez kahr-dee-yahk

I can't move.

Je ne peux pas bouger.
zhuh nuh poeh pah boo-zhay

I fell.

Je suis tombé(e).
zhuh swee toh~-bay

I fainted.

J'ai perdu connaissance.
zhay payhr-due koh~-nay-saw~s

I have a cut on my _____.

Je me suis coupé(e) le m / la f / les pl._____.
zhuh muh swee koo-pay luh / lah / lay _____.

I have a headache.

J'ai mal à la tête.
zhay mahl ah lah teht

My vision is blurry.

Je vois trouble.
zhuh vwah troo-bluh

I feel dizzy.

J'ai des vertiges.
zhay day vayhr-teezh

I think I'm pregnant.

Je crois que je suis enceinte.
zhuh kwah kuh zhuh swee-zaw~-sehnt

I don't think I'm pregnant.

Je ne pense pas être enceinte.
zhuh nuh paw~s pah aytr aw~-suh~t

I'm having trouble walking.

J'ai du mal à marcher.
zhay due mahl ah mahr-shay

My back hurts.

J'ai mal au dos.
zhay mahl oh doh

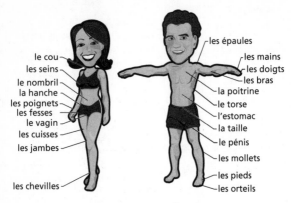

le cou
les seins
le nombril
la hanche
les poignets
les fesses
le vagin
les cuisses
les jambes

les chevilles

les épaules
les mains
les doigts
les bras
la poitrine
le torse
l'estomac
la taille
le pénis
les mollets
les pieds
les orteils

I can't get up.	**Je ne peux pas me lever.** *zhuh nuh poeh pah muh luh-vay*
I was mugged.	**J'ai été attaqué(e) par des voleurs.** *zhay ay-tay ah-tah-kay pahr day voh-loehr*
I was raped.	**J'ai été violé(e).** *zheh-tay vee-yoh-lay*
A dog attacked me.	**J'ai été attaqué(e) par un chien.** *zhay ay-tay ah-tahk-ay pahr uh shee-yeh~*
A snake bit me.	**J'ai été mordu(e) par un serpent.** *zhay ay-tay mohr-due pahr uh~ sayhr-paw~*
I can't move my _____ without pain.	**Cela fait mal lorsque je bouge le *m* / la *f* / les *pl*.____.** *suh-lah fay mahl lohr-skuh zhuh boozh luh / lah / lay ____.*
I think I sprained my ankle.	**Je crois que j'ai la cheville foulée.** *zhuh kwah kuh zhay lah shuh-vee foo-lay*

MEDICATIONS

I need morning-after pills. **J'ai besoin de la pilule du lendemain.**
zhay buh-sweh~ duh lah peel-uel
duh law~-d-meh

I need birth control pills. **J'ai besoin de pilules contraceptives.**
zhay buh-zweh~ duh peel-uel
koh~-trah-sehp-teev

I lost my eyeglasses and **J'ai perdu mes lunettes et ai**
need new ones. **besoin d'une nouvelle paire.**
zhay payhr-due may lue-net eh ay
buh-zweh~ duhn noo-vehl payhr

I lost a contact lens. **J'ai perdu une lentille de contact.**
zhay payhr-due oon law~-tee duh
koh~-tahkt

I need erectile **J'ai besoin de médicaments**
dysfunction pills. **favorisant l'érection.**
zhay buh-zweh~ duh may-deek-
ah-maw~ fa-vo-ree-zaw~ lay-rayk-
syoh~

I am allergic to _____ **Je suis allergique _____**
zhuh swee-zah-layhr-zheek

   penicillin. **à la pénicilline.**
   ah lah pay-nee-see-leen

   antibiotics. **aux antibiotiques.**
   oh-zaw~-tee-bee-yoh-teek

   sulfa drugs. **aux sulfamides.**
   oh suel-fah-meed

   steroids. **aux stéroïdes.**
   oh stay-roh-eed

I have asthma. **Je suis asthmatique.**
zhuh swee-zahst-mah-teek

DENTAL PROBLEMS

I have a sore tooth.

J'ai mal à une dent.
zhay mahl ah oon daw~

I chipped a tooth.

Je me suis cassé une dent.
zhuh muh swee ka-say oon daw~

My bridge came loose.

Mon bridge s'est défait.
moh~ breedzh say day-fay

I lost a crown.

J'ai perdu une couronne.
zhay payhr-due oon koo-rohn

I lost a denture plate.

J'ai perdu une prothèse dentaire.
zhay payhr-due oon pro-thay~z daw~ter

DEALING WITH POLICE

I'm sorry, did I do something wrong?

Pardon, j'ai fait quelque chose de mal ?
pahr-doh~ zhay fay kehl-kuh shohz duh mahl

I am _____

Je suis _____
zhuh swee

American.

américain *m* **/ américaine** *f.*
ah-may-ree-kah / ah-may-ree-kehn

Canadian.

canadien *m* **/ canadienne** *f.*
kah-nah-dee-eh~ / kah-nah-dee-ehn

Irish.

irlandais *m* **/ irlandaise** *f.*
eer-law~-day / eer-law~-dehz

English.

anglais *m* **/ anglaise** *f.*
aw~-glay / aw~-glehz

Australian.

australien *m* **/ australienne** *f.*
oh-strah-lee-eh~ / oh-strah-lee-ehn

New Zealander.

néo-zélandais *m* **/ néo-zélandaise** *f.*
nay-oh-zay-law~-dey / nay-oh-zay-law~-dehz

For more languages and nationalities, see the English / French dictionary.

Listen Up: Police Lingo

**Permis de conduire et
carte grise, s'il vous plaît.**
*payhr-mee duh koh~-dweer
ay kahrt greez seel voo play*

Your license, registration,
and insurance, please.

**L'amende est de ___ euros,
et vous pouvez me la régler
directement.**
*lah-maw~d ay duh ___ oehr-oh
ay voo poo-vay muh lah reh-glay
dee-rehkt-maw~*

The fine is ___, and you
can pay me directly.

Votre passeport, s'il vous plaît ?
voh-truh pahs-pohr seel voo play

Your passport please?

Où allez-vous ?
oo ah-lay-voo

Where are you going?

**Pourquoi êtes-vous si
pressé(e) ?**
*poohr-kwah eht-voo see
prehs-say*

Why are you in such a hurry?

The car is a rental.

C'est une voiture de location.
*seh-toon vwah-tuehr duh loh-kah-
see-yoh~*

Am I supposed to pay the
fine to you?

**Dois-je vous régler directement
l'amende ?**
*dwah-zhuh voo reh-glay dee-
rehkt-maw~ lah-maw~d*

Do I have to go to court?
When?

Dois-je passer en justice ? Quand ?
*dwah-zhuh pah-say aw~ zhue-
stees; kaw~*

I'm sorry, my French isn't
very good.

**Je suis désolé(e), je ne parle pas
bien le français.**
*zhuh swee day-zoh-lay zhuh nuh
pahrl pah bee-yeh~ luh fraw~-say*

I need an interpreter.

J'ai besoin d'un interprète.
*zhay buh-zweh~ duh~-neh~-tayhr-
preht*

I'm sorry, I don't understand the ticket.	**Désolé(e), je ne comprends pas pourquoi vous voulez me donner une amende.**
	day-zoh-lay zhuh nuh koh~- praw~pah poohr-kwah voo voo- lay muh duh-nay oon ah-maw~d
May we call the embassy?	**Pouvons-nous appeler l'ambassade de notre pays ?**
	poo-voh~-noo-zah-play law~-bah- sahd duh noh-truh pay-ee
I was robbed.	**J'ai été victime d'un vol.**
	zhay ay-tay veek-teem duh~ vohl
I was mugged.	**J'ai été attaqué(e).**
	zhay ay-tay ah-tah-kay
I was raped.	**J'ai été violé(e).**
	zhay ay-tay vee-yoh-lay
May I make a report?	**Puis-je faire une déclaration ?**
	pwee-zhuh fayhr oon day-klah- rah-see-yoh~
Somebody broke into my room.	**Quelqu'un s'est introduit dans ma chambre.**
	kehl-kuh~ say-teh~-tro-dwee daw~ mah shaw~-bruh
Someone stole my ____.	**On m'a volé mon ____.**
	mah voh-lay mon
purse.	**sac.**
	sack
wallet.	**porte-feuille.**
	pohrt-foehy
telephone.	**téléphone.**
	tay-lay-fohn
passport.	**passeport.**
	pahs-pohr
computer.	**ordinateur.**
	orh-dee-nah-toehr
backpack.	**sac à dos.**
	sack ah doh
camera.	**appareil photo.**
	ah-pah-ray foh-toh

DICTIONARY KEY

n	noun	*m*	masculine
v	verb	*f*	feminine
adj	adjective	*s*	singular
prep	preposition	*pl*	plural
adv	adverb	*interj*	interjection

All verbs are listed in infinitive (to + verb) form, cross-referenced to the appropriate conjugations page. Adjectives are listed first in masculine form, followed by the feminine ending.

For food terms, see the Menu Reader (p98) and the Grocery section (p105) in Chapter 4, Dining.

ENGLISH–FRENCH

A

able, to be able to (can) *v* pouvoir **p34**

above *adv* au-dessus de **p86**

accept, to accept *v* accepter **p24**

Do you accept credit cards? *Acceptez-vous les cartes de crédit ?*

accident *n* l'accident *m*

I've had an accident. *J'ai eu un accident.* **p64**

account *n* le compte *m* **p142**

I'd like to transfer to / from my checking / savings account. *Je désire transférer des fonds sur / de mon compte courant / épargne.*

acne *n* l'acné *f* **p193**

across *prep* en face de / de l'autre côté de **p5**

across the street *de l'autre côté de la rue* **p6**

actual *adj* réel / réelle

adapter plug *n* l'adaptateur *m* **p163**

address *n* l'adresse *f*

What's the address? *Quelle est l'adresse ?*

admission fee *n* le prix d'entrée

in advance *adv* à l'avance

African American *n adj* afro-américain(e)

afternoon *n* l'après-midi *m*

in the afternoon *durant l'après-midi*

age *n* l'âge *m* **p124**

What's your age? *Quel âge avez-vous ?*

agency *n* l'agence *f* **p58**

car rental agency *l'agence de location de voitures*

agnostic n adj agnostique
air conditioning n la climatisation f p76

Would you lower / raise the air conditioning? Pouvez-vous baisser / monter la climatisation ?

airport n l'aéroport m p44

I need a ride to the airport. Je désire aller à l'aéroport.

How much does the trip to the airport cost? Combien coûte le trajet jusqu'à l'aéroport ?

airsickness bag n sac pour le mal de l'air m p56

aisle (in store) n le rayon m

Which aisle is it in? Dans quel rayon cela se trouve-t-il ? p106

alcohol n l'alcool m p96

Do you serve alcohol? Vendez-vous de l'alcool ?

I'd like nonalcoholic beer. Je voudrais une bière sans alcool.

all n tout m

all of the time tout le temps

all adj tout(e) / tous (toutes) pl p11

allergic adj allergique p197

I'm allergic to _____. Je suis allergique à _____. See p197 for common allergens.

altitude n l'altitude f
aluminum n l'aluminium m
ambulance n l'ambulance f
American n adj américain(e)
amount n le montant m
angry adj fâché(e) p128
animal n l'animal m
another adj autre
answer n la réponse f
answer, to answer v répondre (à) p25

Answer me, please. Répondez-moi, s'il vous plaît.

antibiotic n l'antibiotique m

I need an antibiotic. J'ai besoin d'un antibiotique.

antihistamine n l'antihistaminique m p192

anxious adj impatient(e)
any adj n'importe lequel m / laquelle f
anything n n'importe quoi
anywhere adv n'importe où
April n avril m p14
appointment n le rendez-vous m p130

Do I need an appointment? Est-ce que j'ai besoin d'un rendez-vous ?

are v See être **(to be)** p27.
Argentinian n adj argentin(e)
arm n le bras m p196
arrive, to arrive v arriver p24

ENGLISH–FRENCH

arrival(s) *n l'arrivée f / les arrivées f pl* p44

art *n l'art m*
 exhibit of art *l'exposition d'art*
 art museum *le musée d'art*

artist *n l'artiste m f*

Asian *n adj asiatique*

ask, to ask *v poser une question* p24 *(request) / poser (ask)* p24
 to ask for a drink *demander une boisson*
 to ask a question *poser une question*

aspirin *n l'aspirine f* p193

assist, to assist *v aider* p24

assistance *n l'assistance f*

asthma *n l'asthme m* p197
 I have asthma. *Je suis asthmatique.*

atheist *adj athée*

ATM *n le distributeur automatique de billets (DAB) m f*
 I'm looking for an ATM. *Je cherche un distributeur automatique de billets.*

attend, to attend *v participer (à) / assister (à)* p24

audio *adj audio* p73

August *n août m* p15

aunt *n la tante f* p123

Australia *n l'Australie f*

Australian *n adj australien m / australienne f*

autumn *n l'automne m* p15

available *adj disponible*

B

baby *n le bébé m*

baby *adj pour bébés*
 Do you sell baby food? *Vendez-vous des aliments pour bébés ?*

babysitter *n le / la baby-sitter*
 Do you have babysitters who speak English? *Avez-vous des baby-sitters qui parlent anglais ?*

baby stroller *n la poussette f*

back *n le dos m* p195
 My back hurts. *J'ai mal au dos.*

back rub *n le massage dorsal m*

backed up (toilet) *adj bouchées f pl*
 The toilet is backed up. *Les toilettes sont bouchées.*

bag *n le sac m*
 airsickness bag *sac pour le mal de l'air* p56
 My bag was stolen. *On a volé mon sac.*
 I lost my bag. *J'ai perdu mon sac.*

bag, to bag v emballer **p24**

baggage n le bagage m

baggage adj des bagages m pl

baggage claim la récupération des bagages **p56**

bait n l'appât m **p174**

balance (bank account) n le solde m **p142**

balance, to balance n équilibre m, v équilibrer **p24, 38**

balcony n le balcon m **p77**

ball (sport) n le ballon m / la balle f

ballroom dancing n la danse de salon f

band (musical ensemble) n le groupe m

band-aid n le pansement (adhésif) m **p193**

bank n la banque f **p140**

Can you help me find a bank? Pouvez-vous m'indiquer une banque ?

bar n le bar m **p90**

barber n le coiffeur m **p164**

bass (instrument) n la basse f

bath n le bain m

bathe, to bathe v (se) baigner **p24, 38**

bathroom (restroom) n les toilettes f pl / les WC m pl

Where is the nearest public bathroom? Où sont les toilettes publiques les plus proches ?

bathtub n la baignoire f

battery n la pile **(for flashlight)** f / la batterie **(for car)** f

be, to be v être **p27**

beach n la plage f **p177**

beard n la barbe m **p166**

beautiful adj beau m / belle f

bed n le lit m **p75**

pull-out bed le canapé-lit

bed-and-breakfast (B & B) la chambre d'hôte / le bed-and-breakfast **p74**

bee n l'abeille f

I was stung by a bee. J'ai été piqué(e) par une abeille.

beer n la bière f **p96**

draft beer la bière pression

begin, to begin v commencer (à) **p24**

behave, to behave v se tenir **p38**

behind prep derrière **p5**

beige adj beige

Belgian n adj belge

Belgium n la Belgique f

below prep en dessous de

belt n la ceinture **(clothing)** f

bet, to bet v *miser / parier (sur)* p24

best adj *le / la meilleur(e)*

best adv *le mieux pl*

better adv *mieux*

big adj *grand(e)* p12

bilingual adj *bilingue*

bill n *le billet* **(currency)** m / *la note / la facture* **(tab)** f

bill, to bill v *facturer* p24

biography n *la biographie* f

biracial adj *biracial(e)*

bird n *l'oiseau* m

birth control (pill) n *la pilule* f

> **I need more birth control pills.** *J'ai besoin d'une ordonnance pour la pilule.* p197

bit (small amount) n *un peu* m

black adj *noir(e)*

blanket n *la couverture* f p55

bleach n *l'eau de Javel* f

blind (visually impaired) adj *aveugle / malvoyant(e)*

block, to block v *bloquer* p24

blond(e) adj *blond(e)*

blouse n *le chemisier* m

blue adj *bleu(e)*

blurred vision n *la vision trouble* f

board (transportation) n *le bord* m

> **on board** *à bord*

board, to board v *embarquer* p24

boarding pass n *la carte d'embarquement* f p54

boat n *le navire* m p70

bomb n *la bombe* f

book n *le livre* m p162

bookstore n *la libraire* f p162

boss n *le / la patron(ne)* m f

bottle n *la bouteille* f / *le biberon* **(baby)** m

> **May I heat this bottle someplace?** *Puis-je réchauffer ce biberon quelque part ?*

box (seat) n *la loge* m

box office n *le guichet* m

boy n *le garçon* m

boyfriend n *le petit ami* m

braid n *la natte* f p164

braille, American n *le braille américain* m

brake, to brake v *freiner* p24

brandy n *le brandy* m p97

bread n *le pain* m

break n *la rupture* **(in general)** f / *la fracture* **(broken bone)** f

break, to break v *(se) casser* p24, 38

breakfast n *le petit déjeuner* m

> **What time is breakfast?** *À quelle heure est le petit déjeuner ?* p81

bridge *n le pont* (across a river) *m / le bridge* (dental structure) *m*

briefcase *n la serviette f* p57

bright *adj lumineux m / lumineuse f*

broadband *n adj à haut débit f*

bronze (color) *adj mordoré*

brother *n le frère m* p120

brown *adj marron*

brunette *n le / la brun(e) m f*

Buddhist *n adj bouddhiste*

budget *n le budget m*

buffet *n le buffet m* p89

bug *n l'insecte m* p85

burn, to burn *v brûler* (fire) */ graver* (disk) p24

Can I burn a CD here?
Puis-je graver un CD ici ?

bus *n le car* (school bus, motorcoach) *m / l'autobus* (city bus) *m / la navette* (shuttle bus) *f*

Where is the bus stop?
Où se trouve l'arrêt d'autobus ?

Which bus goes to ____?
Quel autobus va à ____ ?

business *n l'entreprise* (a business) *f / les affaires* (in general) *f pl*

Here's my business card.
Voici ma carte de visite.

business center *le centre d'affaires*

busy *adj plein* (restaurant) *m / occupée* (phone line) *f*

but *conjunction mais*

butter *n le beurre m*

buy, to buy *v acheter* p24

C

café *n le café m*

Internet café *le cybercafé*

call, to call *v (s')appeler* p24, 39

camp, to camp, to go camping *v camper* p24

Do we need a camping permit? *Avons-nous besoin d'une autorisation pour camper ?*

camper (motor home) *n le camping-car m*

campsite *n le terrain de camping m*

can *n la boîte de conserve f*

can (to be able to) *v pouvoir* p34

Canada *n le Canada m*

Canadian *n adj canadien / canadienne*

cancel, to cancel *v annuler* p24

My flight was canceled.
Mon vol a été annulé.

canvas *n la toile f* p57

cappuccino *n le cappuccino m*

car *n la voiture f* p58

  car rental agency *l'agence de location de voitures*

  I need to rent a car. *Je voudrais louer une voiture.*

card *n la carte f* p141

  Do you accept credit cards? *Acceptez-vous les cartes de crédit ?*

  May I have your business card? *Puis-je avoir votre carte de visite ?*

car seat (child's safety seat) *n le siège auto m* p59

  Do you rent car seats for children? *Louez-vous des sièges auto pour enfants ?*

car sickness *n le mal des transports m*

cash *n les espèces f* p141

  cash only *espèces uniquement*

cash, to cash *v encaisser* p24

  to cash out (gambling) *v toucher les gains* p24

cashmere *n le cachemire m*

casino *n le casino m* p190

cat *n le / la chat(te) m f*

Catholic *adj catholique*

cavity (tooth) *n la carie f*

  I think I have a cavity. *Je pense que j'ai une carie.*

CD *n le CD m*

CD player *n le lecteur de CD m*

celebrate, to celebrate *v fêter* p24

cell phone *n le téléphone portable m*

centimeter *n le centimètre m*

chamber music *n la musique de chambre f*

change (money) *n la monnaie f* p141

  I'd like change, please. *Je voudrais de la monnaie, s'il vous plaît.*

  This isn't the correct change. *Ce n'est pas la monnaie exacte.* See p7 for numbers.

change, to change *v changer (de) / langer* **(a baby diaper)** p24

  changing room *n la cabine d'essayage f*

charge, to charge *v mettre* **(money)** p25 / *recharger* **(battery)** p24

charmed *adj enchanté(e)*

charred (meat) *adj très cuite (viande)* p93

charter, to charter (transportation) *v affréter* p24

cheap *adj pas cher / pas chère* p59

check *n le chèque* (money) *m / l'addition* (tab) *f*

 Check, please! *L'addition, s'il vous plaît!* p98

check, to check *v vérifier* p24

checked (pattern) *adj à carreaux m*

check-in *n l'enregistrement m* p44

 What time is check-in? *À quelle heure est l'enregistrement ?*

check-out *n la libération de la chambre f*

 What time is check-out? *À quelle heure doit-on libérer la chambre ?*

check out, to check out (of hotel) *v libérer la chambre* p24

cheese *n le fromage m* p107

chicken *n le poulet* (meat) *m*

child *n l'enfant m f*

children *n les enfants m f*

 Are children allowed? *Les enfants sont-ils acceptés ?*

 Do you have children's programs? *Avez-vous des spectacles pour enfants ?*

 Do you have a children's menu? *Avez-vous un menu pour enfants ?* p93

China *n la Chine f*

Chinese *n adj chinois(e)*

chiropractor *n le chiropracticien m / la chiropracticienne f* p194

Christian *adj chrétien m / chrétienne f*

church *n le messe f* p134

cigar *n le cigare m*

cigarette *n la cigarette f*

 pack of cigarettes *le paquet de cigarettes*

city *n la ville f*

claim *n la réclamation f*

 I'd like to file a claim. *Je voudrais faire une réclamation.*

clarinet *n la clarinette f*

class *n la classe f* p49

 business class *la classe affaires*

 economy class *la classe économique*

 first class *la première classe*

classical (music) *adj de musique classique f*

clean *adj propre*

clean, to clean *v nettoyer* p24

 Please clean the room today. *Veuillez nettoyer la chambre aujourd'hui.*

clear, to clear *v enlever* p24

clear *adj clair(e)*

climbing n l'escalade f / la varappe **(rock climbing)** f

climb, to climb v escalader **(mountain)** p24 / monter **(stairs)** p24

close, to close v fermer p24

close (near) adj près de, proche de

closed adj fermé(e)

cloudy adj nuageux p131

clover n le trèfle m

go clubbing, to go clubbing v sortir en boîte **p36**

coat n le manteau m

coffee n le café **(espresso)** m
iced coffee le café glacé

cognac n le cognac m p97

coin n la pièce f p139

cold n le rhume m p192
I have a cold. J'ai un rhume.

cold adj froid(e)
I'm cold. J'ai froid.

collect adj en PCV
I'd like to place a collect call. Je voudrais passer un appel en PCV.

collect, to collect v ramasser / collectionner p24

college n l'université f

color n la couleur f

color, to color v colorer p24

come, to come v venir p36

computer n l'ordinateur m

concert n le concert m p137

condition n l'état m
in good / bad condition en bon / mauvais état

condom n le préservatif m
Do you have a condom? As-tu un préservatif sur toi ?
not without a condom pas sans préservatif

confirm, to confirm v confirmer p24
I'd like to confirm my reservation. Je voudrais confirmer ma réservation. p50

confused adj confus(e) p128

congestion n la congestion **(respiratory)** f / l'embouteillage **(traffic)** m

connection speed n la vitesse de connexion f p147

constipated adj constipé(e)
I'm constipated. Je suis constipé(e).

contact lens n la lentille de contact f p197

continue, to continue v continuer p24

convertible (car) n la voiture décapotable f / le cabriolet m

cook, to cook v cuisiner p24
  I'd like a room where I can cook. Je voudrais une chambre où il est possible de cuisiner.
cookie n le petit gâteau m
copper adj cuivre (color)
cork n le bouchon m
corkscrew n le tire-bouchon m
corner n le coin m
  on the corner au coin p6
correct, to correct v corriger p24
correct adj bon m / bonne f
  Am I on the correct train? Suis-je dans le bon train ?
cost, to cost v coûter p24
  How much does it cost? Combien est-ce que cela coûte ?
costume n le déguisement m
cotton n le coton m
cough n la toux f p192
cough, to cough v tousser p24
counter (in bar) n le comptoir m
country-and-western n la country f
country-and-western adj country
court n la justice (legal) f / le court (sports) m
courteous adj courtois(e)
cousin n le / la cousin(e) m f

cover charge (in bar) n l'entrée f p181
cow n la vache f
crack (in glass object) n la fissure f
craftsperson n l'artisan(e) m f
cream n la crème f
credit card n la carte de crédit f p139
  Do you accept credit cards? Acceptez-vous les cartes de crédit ?
crib n le lit d'enfant m p77
crown (dental) n la couronne f
curb n le bord du trottoir m
curl n la boucle f
curly adj bouclé(e)
currency exchange n le change m p140
  Where is the nearest currency exchange? Où se trouve le bureau de change le plus proche ?
current (water) n l'eau courante f
customs n la douane f p52
cut (wound) n la coupure f / l'entaille f
  I have a bad cut. Je me suis fait une vilaine entaille.
cut, to cut v couper p24
cybercafé n le cybercafé m
  Where can I find a cybercafé? Où puis-je trouver un cybercafé ?

D

damaged adj abîmé(e)

Damn! expletive Mince!

dance, to dance v danser **p24**

danger n le danger m

dark n le noir m

dark adj sombre

daughter n la fille f p122

dawn n l'aube f p13

at dawn à l'aube

day n le jour m

the day before yesterday
avant-hier

these last few days ces
derniers jours

deaf adj sourd(e) / malentendant(e)
(hearing-impaired)

deal (issue) n l'affaire f

deal, to deal (cards) v donner
p24

Deal me in. Tu peux
compter sur moi! p190

December n décembre m

declined adj rejeté(e)

Was my credit card
declined? Ma carte de
crédit a-t-elle été rejetée ?

declare, to declare v déclarer
p24

I have nothing to declare.
Je n'ai rien à déclarer. p52

deep adj profond(e)

delay n le retard m p51

How long is the delay? De
combien est le retard ?

delighted adj ravi(e) p120

democracy n la démocratie f

dent, to dent v cabosser **p24**

He / She dented the car. Il /
Elle a cabossé la voiture.

dentist n le / la dentiste m f

denture n la prothèse
dentaire f p198

denture plate la plaque de
prothèse dentaire

departure(s) n les départs m pl

designer n le / la styliste m f

dessert n le dessert m p102

dessert menu la carte des
desserts

destination n la destination f

diabetic adj diabétique

dial, to dial (phone number)
v composer **p24**

to dial direct composer
directement le numéro

diaper n la couche f

Where can I change a
diaper? Où puis-je langer
mon enfant ?

diarrhea n la diarrhée f p193

dictionary n le dictionnaire m

different (other) adj
différent(e)

difficult adj difficile

dinner n le dîner m

directory assistance (phone) *n les renseignements m pl*

disability *n le handicap m*

disappear, to disappear *v disparaître* p25

disco *n la disco f*

disconnected *adj coupé(e)*

Operator, I was disconnected. *Monsieur / Madame, j'ai été coupé(e).*

discount *n la réduction (store) f / le tarif réduit (ticket) m*

Do I qualify for a _____ discount? *Ai-je droit à une réduction pour _____ ?*
children's *enfants*
senior *personnes âgées*
student *étudiants*

dish (meal) *n le plat m*

dive, to dive *v plonger* p24
scuba diving *la plongée sous-marine* p175

divorced *adj divorcé(e)* p123

dizzy (to be) *adj avoir des vertiges* p195

do, to do *v faire* p33

doctor *n le médecin m f* p194
doctor's office *n le cabinet du médecin m*

dog *n le chien m / la chienne f*
guide dog *le chien guide*

door *n la porte f*

double *adj à deux / double*

double bed *lit pour deux*
to have double vision *voir double*

down *adj déprimé(e)* (mood) / *bas/basse* (position)

download, to download *v télécharger* p24

downtown *n le centre-ville m*

dozen *n la douzaine f* p11

drain *n le tuyau d'évacuation m*

drama *n le drame m*

drawing *n le dessin m*

dress (garment) *n la robe f*

dress code *n la tenue de rigueur f / le code vestimentaire m*

What's the dress code? *Quel est le code vestimentaire ?*

dress, to dress *v s'habiller* p24, 39

dressing (salad) *n la sauce f*

dried *adj séché(e)*

drink *n la boisson f* p96

I'd like a drink. *Je voudrais quelque chose à boire.*

drink, to drink *v boire* p31

drip, to drip *v fuir*

drive, to drive *v conduire*

driver *n le conducteur m / la conductrice f*

driving range *n le terrain d'exercice m*

drum *n la batterie f / le tambour m*

ENGLISH–FRENCH

dry *adj sec m / sèche f*
This towel isn't dry. *Cette serviette n'est pas sèche.*
dry, to dry *v sécher* p24
I need to dry my clothes. *J'ai besoin de sécher mes vêtements.*
dry cleaner *n le pressing m*
dry cleaning *n le nettoyage à sec m* p82
duck *n le canard m*
duty-free *adj hors-taxe*
duty-free shop *n la boutique hors-taxe f* p46
DVD *n le DVD m* p59
Do the rooms have DVD players? *Les chambres ont-elles des lecteurs de DVD ?*
Where can I rent DVDs ? *Où puis-je louer des DVD ?*

E

early *adv tôt* p13
It's early. *Il est tôt.*
eat, to eat *v manger / déjeuner* (lunch) */ dîner* p24
to eat out *sortir dîner*
economy *n l'économie f* p58
editor *n le rédacteur m / la rédactrice f* p129
educator *n l'éducateur m / l'éducatrice f* p129

eight *adj huit* p7
eighteen *adj dix-huit* p7
eighth *adj huitième m* p7
eighty *adj quatre-vingts* p7
election *n l'élection f*
electrical hookup *n le raccordement m* p87
elevator *n l'ascenseur m* p73
eleven *adj onze* p7
e-mail *n le mail m*
May I have your e-mail address? *Puis-je avoir votre adresse mail ?*
e-mail message *le mail*
e-mail, to send e-mail *v envoyer mail* p24
embarrassed *adj embarrassé(e)*
embassy *n l'ambassade f*
emergency *n l'urgence f*
emergency brake *n le frein à main m*
emergency exit *n l'issue de secours f* p49
employee *n l'employé(e) m f*
employer *n l'employeur m / l'employeuse f*
engine *n le moteur m* p62
engineer *n l'ingénieur m f*
England *n l'Angleterre f*
English *n adj anglais(e)*
Do you speak English? *Parlez-vous anglais ?*
enjoy, to enjoy *v aimer* p24

enter, to enter v entrer p24
enthusiastic adj enthousiaste
entrance, entry n l'entrée f
  Do not enter. Entrée
  interdite.
environment n
  l'environnement m
escalator n l'escalier roulant m
espresso n le café m
exchange rate n le taux de
  change m p140
  **What is the exchange rate
  for U.S. / Canadian
  dollars?** Quel est le taux
  de change du dollar
  américain / canadien ?
excuse, to excuse (pardon) v
  excuser / pardonner p24
  Excuse me. Excusez-moi.
exhausted adj épuisé(e)
exhibit n l'exposition f
exit n la sortie f
exit, to exit v sortir p36
  not an exit ne pas sortir par
  cette issue
expensive adj cher m / chère f
explain, to explain v
  expliquer p24
express adj express
  express check-in
  l'enregistrement express p48
extra (additional) adj
  supplémentaire

extra-large adj très grand(e)
eye n l'œil m / les yeux m pl
eyebrow n le sourcil m p126
eyeglasses n les lunettes f pl
eyelash n le cil m p127

F

fabric n le tissu m / la matière f
face n le visage f p128
faint, to faint v perdre
  connaissance p25
fall (season) n l'automne m
fall, to fall v tomber p24, 38
family n la famille p120
fan n le ventilateur m p85
far adv loin p5
  How far is it to _____?
  Combien y a-t-il jusqu'à
  _____ ?
fare n le prix m
fast adj adv rapide / vite
fat adj gros m / grosse f p12
father n le père m p122
faucet n le lavabo m
  (bathroom) / l'évier m
  (kitchen)
fault n / **at fault** adj la faute f
  / fautif m / fautive f
  I'm at fault. c'est moi qui
  suis responsable. p64
  It was his / her fault. C'est
  sa faute.
fax n la télécopie m p130

February n février m p14

fee n le prix m

female adj féminin(e)

fiancé(e) n le / la fiancé(e) m f

fifteen adj quinze p7

fifth adj cinquième p9

fifty adj cinquante p7

find, to find v trouver p24

fine (for traffic violation) n l'amende f p64

fine adv bien

I'm fine. Bien merci. p1

Fire! Au feu!

first adj premier m / première f

fishing pole n la canne à pêche f p175

fitness center n le club de remise en forme f

fit, to fit (clothes) v aller p30

This doesn't fit. Cela ne va pas.

Does this look like it fits? Est-ce que ça a l'air d'aller ?

fitting room n la cabine d'essayage f

five adj cinq p7

flight n le vol m p46

Where do domestic flights arrive / depart? Où se trouve la zone d'arrivée / de départ des lignes intérieures ?

Where do international flights arrive / depart? Où se trouve la zone d'arrivée / de départ des vols internationaux ?

What time does this flight leave? À quelle heure part ce vol ?

flight attendant le steward m / l'hôtesse de l'air f

floor (level) n l'étage m

ground floor le rez-de-chaussée

first floor le premier étage

flower n la fleur f

flush (gambling) n le flush m

flush, to flush v tirer la chasse d'eau p24

This toilet won't flush. La chasse d'eau de ces toilettes ne marche pas.

flute n la flûte f

food n la nourriture f / les aliments m pl

foot n le pied m p196

forehead n le front m p126

format n le format m

formula n la préparation lactée **(baby)** f / la formule **(math)** f

Do you sell infants' formula? Est-ce que vous vendez des préparations lactées pour nourrisson ?

forty adj quarante p7

forward adv en avant

four adj quatre p7

fourteen adj quatorze p7

fourth adj le quart m / la quatrième f p9

one-fourth un quart

fragile adj fragile

freckle n la tache de rousseur f

free adj gratuit(e) (complimentary) / libre (having freedom) / disponible (available, open)

French n adj français(e)

fresh adj frais m / fraîche f

Friday n le vendredi m p14

friend n l'ami(e) m f p122

front adv de devant

front desk n la réception f

front door n la porte d'entrée f

fruit n le fruit m p113

fruit juice n le jus de fruit m

full adj / **to be full (after a meal)** v ne plus avoir faim

Full house! Full! p191

fuse n la bougie (car) f / le fusible (home) m

G

gallon n le gallon m

garlic n l'ail m p115

gasoline n l'essence f p160

gas gauge la jauge d'essence p62

I'm out of gas. Je suis en panne d'essence.

gate (at airport) n la porte f

German n adj allemand(e)

gift n le cadeau m

gin n le gin m p97

girl n la fille f

girlfriend n la petite amie f

give, to give v donner p24

glass n le verre m

Do you have it by the glass? Est-ce qu'il est possible de le commander au verre ?

I'd like a glass, please. Je voudrais un verre, s'il vous plaît.

glasses (spectacles) n les lunettes f pl p159

I need new glasses. J'ai besoin de nouvelles lunettes.

glove n le gant m

go, to go v aller p30

goal (sport) n le but m

goalie n le gardien de but m

goat n la chèvre f

gold n l'or (metal)

golden adj doré (color)

golf n le golf m p178

golf, to golf v jouer au golf p24

good *adj* bon *m* / bonne *f*
goodbye *n* au revoir
goose *n* l'oie *m*
grade school *n* l'école primaire *f*
gram *n* le gramme *m*
grandfather *n* le grand-père *m*
grandmother *n* la grand-mère *f*
grandparents *n* les grands-parents *m pl* p123
grape *n* le raisin *m*
gray *adj* gris(e)
Great! *adj* Super!
Greek *n adj* grec *m* / grecque *f*
green (golf) *n* le vert *m*
green (color) *adj* vert(e)
groceries *n* les provisions *f pl*
group *n* le groupe *m*
grow, to grow (get larger) *v* grandir p24

Where did you grow up?
Où avez-vous grandi ?

guard *n* le garde *m* / l'agent *m*

security guard *l'agent de sécurité* p45

guest *n* l'hôte *m* / l'hôtesse *f*
guide (tour) *n* le / la guide *m f*
guide (publication) *n* le guide *m*
guide, to guide *v* guider p24
guided tour *n* la visite guidée *f* p155

guitar *n* la guitare *f*
gym *n* la gymnastique *f*
gynecologist *n* le / la gynécologue *m f* p194

H

hair *n* le cheveu *m* / les cheveux *m pl*
haircut *n* la coupe *f*

I need a haircut. *J'ai besoin d'une coupe.*
How much is a haircut?
Combien coûte une coupe ?

hairdresser *n* le coiffeur *m* / la coiffeuse *f*
hair dryer *n* le sèche-cheveux *m* p84
half *n* la moitié *n*
half *adj* demi(e)

one half *une moitié*

hallway *n* le couloir (building) *m* / l'entrée (house) *f* / le hall d'entrée *m*
hand *n* la main *f*
handicapped-accessible *adj* accessible aux personnes à mobilité réduite p73
handle, to handle *v* manipuler p24
handsome *adj* beau *m* / belle *f*
hangout (hot spot) *n* lieu de rencontre *m*

hang out, to hang out (to relax) v traîner / passer du temps p24

hang up (end a phone call) v raccrocher p24

happy adj heureux m / heureuse f p128

hard adj dur(e)

hat n le chapeau m p159

have, to have v avoir p25

hazel adj noisette

headache n le mal de tête m

headlight n le feu (avant) m

headphones n le casque m s

hear, to hear v entendre p25

hearing-impaired adj malentendant(e) p73

heart n le cœur m

heart attack n la crise cardiaque f

hectare n l'hectare m p10

hello n bonjour / salut (informal) / allô (telephone)

Help! Au secours!

help, to help v aider p24

hen n la poule f

her adj sa f / son m / ses m f pl

herb n l'herbe f

here adv ici p5

high adj haut(e)

highlights (hair) n les mèches f pl p165

highway n l'autoroute f

hike, to hike v faire de la marche p33

him pron lui

Hindu n adj hindou(e) adj

hip-hop n le hip-hop m

his adj son m / sa f / ses m f pl

historical adj historique

history n l'histoire f

hobby n le passe-temps m

hold, to hold v tenir **(something)** / attendre **(pause)** p25 / rester en ligne **(on telephone)** p24 / conserver **(gambling)** p24

to hold hands se tenir par la main

Would you hold this for me? Pouvez-vous tenir cela pour moi ?

Hold on a minute! Attendez une minute!

I'll hold. Je reste en ligne.

holiday n les vacances f pl

home n le domicile m

homemaker n l'homme m / la femme f au foyer p129

horn (automobile) n le klaxon m

horse n le cheval m

hostel n l'auberge f p74

hot adj chaud(e)

hot chocolate n le chocolat chaud m p97

hotel n l'hôtel m p74

Do you have a list of local hotels? Avez-vous une liste des hôtels de la région ?

hour n l'heure f p12

hours (at museum) n les heures d'ouverture f pl

how adv comment (manner) / combien (amount) p3

humid adj humide p132

hundred n adj cent p8

hurry, to hurry v être pressé(e) p27 / se dépêcher p24, 38

I'm in a hurry. Je me suis pressé(e). p65

Hurry, please! Dépêchez-vous, s'il vous plaît!

hurt, to hurt v avoir mal p25 / faire mal p33

Ouch! That hurts! Aïe ! Ca fait mal !

My head hurts. J'ai mal à la tête.

husband n le mari m p122

I

I pron je p22

ice n la glace f / le glaçon m (ice cube)

with ice cubes avec des glaçons

identification n la pièce d'identité f

inch n le pouce m

include, to include v comprendre p25

Is breakfast included? Le petit-déjeuner est-il compris ?

India n l'Inde f

Indian n adj indien m / indienne f

indigestion n l'indigestion f

inexpensive adj pas cher m / pas chère f

infant n l'enfant en bas âge m

Are infants allowed? Les enfants en bas âge sont-ils acceptés ?

information n l'information f / les renseignements m pl

information booth n le stand d'information

injury n la blessure f

insect repellent n l'insectifuge m

inside prep dans / à l'intérieur de

insult, to insult v insulter p24

insurance n l'assurance f

intercourse (sexual) n les rapports sexuels m pl

interest rate n le taux d'intérêt m p140

intermission n l'entracte m
Internet n l'Internet m p145
  high-speed Internet
    l'Internet à haut débit
  **Do you have Internet
  access?** Offrez-vous un
    accès à Internet ?
  **Where can I find an Internet
  café?** Où puis-je trouver
    un cybercafé ?
interpreter n l'interprète m f
  I need an interpreter. J'ai
    besoin d'un interprète.
introduce, to introduce v
    présenter p24
  **I'd like to introduce you to
  _____.** Laissez-moi vous
    présenter _____.
Ireland n l'Irlande f
Irish n adj irlandais(e)
is v est See être (to be) p27.
Italian n adj italien m /
    italienne f

J
jacket n le blouson m / la
    veste f
January n janvier m p14
Japanese n adj japonais(e)
jasmine n le jasmin m
jazz n le jazz m
Jewish adj juif m / juive f

jogging n le jogging m
jog, to go jogging v faire du
    jogging p33
juice n le jus m
June n juin m p15
July n juillet m p15

K
keep, to keep v / **to mind
  (children)** v garder p24
kilo n le kilo m p10
kilometer n le kilomètre m
kind (type) n la sorte f
kind (nice) adj gentil m /
    gentille f
  What kind of car is it?
    Quelle sorte de voiture
    est-ce ?
  You're very kind! C'est très
    gentil de votre part!
kiss n le baiser m
kiss, to kiss v embrasser p24
kitchen n la cuisine f
know, to know v savoir **(a
  fact) p35** / connaître **(a
  person or place) p31**
kosher adj kasher

L
lactose-intolerant adj
    allergique aux produits
    laitiers p94
land, to land v atterrir p24
language n la langue f

laptop n l'ordinateur portable m

large adj grand(e)

last, to last v durer p24

last adj dernier m / dernière f

late adj en retard p13

Please don't be late. Ne soyez pas en retard, s'il vous plaît.

later adv plus tard p4

See you later. À bientôt.

laundry n la lessive f

lavender adj bleu lavande

law n la loi f

lawyer n l'avocat(e) m f

least adv le moins

leather n le cuir m p57

leave, to leave (depart) v partir p34

left n la gauche f p5

on the left à gauche

leg n la jambe f p196

less adj moins

license n le permis m

driver's license le permis de conduire

life preserver n le gilet m / la bouée de sauvetage f

light n la lumière (lamp) f / le voyant (car) m / le feu (for cigarette) m

May I offer you a light? Puis-je vous offrir du feu ?

lighter (cigarette) n le briquet m

like, to like v vouloir (want) p37 / aimer (take pleasure in) p24

I would like ____. Je voudrais ____.

limousine n la limousine f

liqueur n la liqueur f p97

liquor n les boissons alcoolisées f

liter n le litre m p10

little adj petit(e)

live, to live v vivre p25 / habiter (place) p24

Where do you live? Où habitez-vous ?

living n la vie f

What do you do for a living? Que faites-vous dans la vie ?

local adj local(e)

lock n le verrou (on door) m / le cadenas (on locker) m

lock, to lock v verrouiller p24

I'm locked out. Je me suis enfermé(e) dehors.

locker (storage) n le local de stockage m

locker room n le vestiaire m

long adj longtemps p10

For how long? Pendant combien de temps ?

long adj long m / longue f

look, to look *v regarder*
(observe) p24 / *aller*
(clothing) p30
 I'm just looking. *Je ne fais*
 que regarder.
 Look here! *Regarde ça!*
 How does this look?
 Comment ça me va ?
look for, to look for (search)
v chercher **p24**
 I'm looking for a porter. *Je*
 cherche un porteur.
loose *adj flottant(e)*
lose, to lose *v perdre* **p25**
 I lost my passport / wallet.
 J'ai perdu mon passeport /
 porte-monnaie.
 I'm lost. *Je suis perdu(e).*
lost *adj perdu(e)*
loud *adj fort(e)*
loudly *adv fort*
 Please speak more loudly.
 Parlez plus fort, s'il vous
 plaît.
lounge *n le salon m / le bar m*
lounge, to lounge *v se*
prélasser **p24, 38**
love *n l'amour m*
love, to love *v aimer* **p24**
 to love (family) *aimer*
 to love (a friend) *bien aimer*
 to love (a lover) *aimer*
 to make love *faire l'amour*

low *adj bas m / basse f*
lunch *n le déjeuner m*
luggage *n le bagage m*
 Where do I report lost
 luggage? *Où puis-je*
 déclarer la perte d'un
 bagage ?
 Where is the lost luggage
 claim? *Où se trouve la*
 zone de récupération des
 bagages ?

M

machine *n la machine f*
made of *adj en / fait à partir*
de
magazine *n le magazine m*
maid (hotel) *n la femme de*
chambre f
maiden *adj de jeune fille*
 That's my maiden name.
 C'est mon nom de jeune
 fille.
mail *n le courrier m*
 registered mail *courrier*
 recommandé
make, to make *v faire* **p33**
makeup *n le maquillage m*
make up, to make up *v se*
réconcilier (apologize)
p24, 38 / *se maquiller*
(apply cosmetics) **p24, 38**
male (man) *n l'homme m*
male *adj masculin*

mall *n le centre commercial m*

manager *n le directeur m / la directrice f* p80

manual (instruction booklet) *n le guide d'utilisation m*

many *adj beaucoup de* p11

map *n la carte f / le plan* **(subway)** *m* p71

March (month) *n mars m*

market *n le marché m* p160

flea market *le marché aux puces*

open-air market *le marché en plein air*

married *adj marié(e)* p123

marry, to marry *v (s')épouser* **p24, 39**

massage, to massage *v masser* **p24**

match *n le match (sport) m / l'allumette (fire) f*

book of matches *la boîte d'allumettes*

match, to match *v aller avec* **p30**

May (month) *n mai m* p15

may (permission) *v pouvoir* **p34**

May I ____? *Puis-je ____ ?*

meal *n le repas m*

meat *n la viande f*

medication *n le médicament m*

medium (size) *adj moyen(ne)*

medium rare (meat) *adj à pointe* p92

medium well (meat) *adj cuit* p92

member *n le / la membre mf*

menu *n le menu m* p93

May I see a menu? *Puis-je avoir un menu ?*

metal detector *n le détecteur de métaux m*

meter *n le mètre m*

Mexican *n adj mexicain(e)*

middle *prep au milieu de*

midnight *n minuit* p13

mile *n le mile m* p10

military *n l'armée f / le militaire m*

milk *n le lait m* p97

milk shake *le milk-shake*

milliliter *n le millilitre m* p10

millimeter *n le millimètre m*

minute *n la minute f* p12

in a minute *dans une minute*

miss, to miss *v manquer* **(a flight)** p24

missing *adj absent(e)*

mistake *n l'erreur f*

moderately priced *adj pas trop cher m / chère f*

mole (facial feature) *n le grain de beauté m*

Monday *n le lundi m* p13

money *n l'argent m / les fonds m* p139

money transfer *le virement* p139

month *n le mois m*

morning *n le matin m* p13

in the morning *le matin*

mosque *n la mosquée f* p133

mother *n la mère f* p120

motorcycle *n la moto f* p58

mountain *n la montagne f*

mountain climbing *l'escalade f*

mouse *n la souris f*

moustache *n la moustache*

mouth *n la bouche f* p126

move, to move (change homes) *v déménager* p24

movie *n le film m* p151

movie theater *n le cinéma m* p151

moving walkway *n le tapis roulant m*

much *adv beaucoup*

mugged *adj attaqué(e)* p196

museum *n le musée m* p155

music *n la musique*

live music *la musique live*

musician *n le musicien m / la musicienne f* p129

muslim *adj musulman(e)*

mystery (novel) *n le roman policier m*

N

name *n le nom m*

My name is ___. *Je m'appelle ___.* p1

What's your name? *Comment vous appelez-vous ?*

first name *le prénom*

last name *le nom de famille*

napkin *n la serviette f*

narrow *adj étroit(e)* p12

nationality *n la nationalité f*

nausea *n la nausée f* p193

near *adj proche* p5

nearby *adv près d'ici*

neat (tidy) *adj bien rangé(e)*

need, to need *v avoir besoin de* p25

neighbor *n le / la voisin(e) m f* p123

nephew *n le neveu m* p123

network *n le réseau m*

new *adj nouveau m / nouvelle f*

news (current events) *n les actualités f pl*

newspaper *n le journal m*

newsstand *n le kiosque à journaux m* p162

New Zealand *n la Nouvelle-Zélande f*

New Zealander *adj néo-zélandais(e)*

next *adj prochain(e)*

next *prep à côté de* p5

 the next station *la prochaine station*

next *adv puis* **(then)** */ après* **(later)**

nice *adj gentil m / gentille f*

niece *n la nièce f* p123

night *n la nuit f* p13

 at night *pendant la nuit*
 per night *par nuit* p78

nine *adj neuf* p7

nineteen *adj dix-neuf*

ninety *adj quatre-vingt-dix*

ninety-one *adj quatre-vingt-onze* p8

ninth *adj neuvième* p9

no *non* p1

no (not any) *adv pas de*

noisy *adj bruyant(e)*

none *pron aucun(e)* p11

nonsmoking *adj non-fumeur*

noon *n le midi m* p13

nose *n le nez m* p126

novel *n le roman m*

November *n novembre m*

now *adv maintenant* p4

number *n le numéro m / le chiffre* **(digit, figure)** p7

 Which room number? *Quel numéro de chambre ?*
 May I have your phone number? *Puis-je avoir votre numéro de téléphone ?*

nurse *n l'infirmier m / l'infirmière f* p129

nurse, to nurse (breastfeed) *v allaiter* p24

 Do you have a place where I can nurse? *Y a-t-il un endroit où je puisse allaiter ?*

nursery *n la crèche f*

 Do you have a nursery or playground? *Avez-vous une crèche ou une aire de jeu ?*

nut *la noix f* p95

O

o'clock *adv heures* p13

October *n octobre m* p15

offer, to offer *n offre f, v offrir* p33

officer *n l'officier m / l'agent m*

oil *n l'huile f*

Ok *D'accord* p1

 Are you okay? *Ça va ?*

old *adj vieux m / vieille f / âgé(e)* **(person)**

 I'm six years old. *J'ai six ans.* See p7 for numbers.

olive *n l'olive f*

one *adj un(e)*

one way (traffic sign) *adj sens unique m*

open (business) *adj ouvert(e)*

 Are you open? *Êtes-vous ouvert ?*

open *v ouvrir* **p33**

opera *n l'opéra m* **p153**

opera house *n l'opéra m*

operator (phone) *n l'opérateur m / l'opératrice f*

optometrist *n l'optométriste*

orange *adj orange* **(color)**

orange juice *n le jus d'orange m*

order, to order *v ordonner / demander / commander* **(a meal)** **p24**

organic *adj biologique*

Ouch! *Aïe!*

outside *adv dehors*

overcooked *adj trop cuit(e)*

overheat, to overheat *v* **(car)** *chauffer* **p24**

The car is overheating. *La voiture chauffe.*

overflow, to overflow *v déborder* **p24**

oxygen tank *n la bouteille d'oxygène f*

P

package *n le colis m* **p147**

pacifier *n la tétine f*

page, to page (someone) *v faire appeler* **p33**

paint, to paint *n peinture, v peindre* **p25**

painting *n la peinture f*

pale *adj pâle*

paper *n le papier m*

parade *n le défilé m*

parent *n le parent m* **p123**

park *n le parc m*

parking *n le parking m / le stationnement m*

no parking *stationnement interdit* **p61**

park, to park *v se garer* **p24, 38**

parking fee *le prix du stationnement* **p61**

parking garage *le parking couvert* **p61**

partner *n le / la partenaire m f*

party *n la soirée* **(event)** *f / le parti* **(political)** *m*

pass, to pass (gambling) *v passer* **p24**

I'll pass / double. *Je passe.*

passenger *n le passager m / la passagère f*

passport *n le passeport m*

I've lost my passport. *J'ai perdu mon passeport.* **p54**

password *n le mot de passe m*

pay, to pay *v payer* **p24**

peanut *n la cacahuète f* **p95**

pedestrian *n le piéton m / la piétonne f*

pediatrician *n le / la pédiatre m f*

Can you recommend a pediatrician? *Pouvez-vous me recommander un(e) pédiatre ?*

permit n le permis f
Do we need a permit?
Avons-nous besoin d'un
permis ?
permit, to permit v
permettre p25
phone n le téléphone m
**Do you have a phone
directory?** Avez-vous un
annuaire (téléphonique) ?
**May I have your phone
number?** Puis-je avoir
votre numéro de
téléphone ?
**Where can I find a public
phone?** Où puis-je trouver
un téléphone public ?
phone operator l'opérateur
l l'opératrice téléphonique
**Do you sell prepaid
phones?** Vendez-vous des
téléphones portables
prépayés ?
phone call n l'appel m p143
**I need to make a collect
phone call.** Je dois faire un
téléphoner en PCV.
an international phone call
un appel à l'étranger
photocopy, to photocopy v
photocopier p24
piano n le piano m
pillow n l'oreiller m p82
down pillow l'oreiller en
duvet d'oie

pink adj rose
pint n la pinte f / la bière
(pint of beer) f p10
pizza n la pizza f
place, to place v mettre p25
plastic n le plastique m
play n la pièce de théâtre f
play, to play v jouer (à) (de)
(game, instrument) p24
playground n l'aire de jeu f
**Do you have a playground
or nursery?** Avez-vous une
aire de jeu ou une crèche ?
please (polite entreaty) adv
s'il vous plaît p1
please, to be pleasing to v
plaire p25 / faire plaisir (à)
p33
pleasure n le plaisir m
It's a pleasure. C'est un
plaisir.
plug n la prise (electrical
outlet) f
plug in, to plug in v brancher
p24
point, to point v montrer p24
**Would you point me in the
direction of ___?** Pouvez-
vous me montrer dans
quelle direction se trouve
___ ?
police n la police f
police station n le poste de
police m / la gendarmerie
f p45

pool n la piscine **(swimming)** f / le billard **(game)** m
pop music n la musique pop f
popular adj populaire
port n le porto **(beverage)** m / le port **(ship)** m
porter n le porteur m p44
portrait n le portrait m
postcard n la carte postale f
post office n le bureau de poste m p140

Where is the nearest post office? Où se trouve le bureau de poste le plus proche ?

poultry n la volaille f p101
pound n la livre f
prefer, to prefer v préférer p24
pregnant adj enceinte p195
prescription n l'ordonnance f
price n le prix m
print, to print n impression f v imprimer p24
private berth / cabin n la couchette individuelle f / le compartiment privé m
problem n le problème m
process, to process (transaction) v traiter p24
product n le produit m
professional adj professionnel m / professionnelle f
program n le programme m / le spectacle m

May I have a program? Puis-je avoir un programme ?
Protestant n adj le / la protestant(e)
publisher n l'éditeur m / l'éditrice **(person)** f / la maison d'édition **(publishing house)** f
pull, to pull v tirer p24
pump n la pompe f
purple adj violet
purse n le sac à main m p54
push, to push v pousser p24
put, to put v mettre

Q

quarter adj le quart m
one-quarter un quart
Quebec n le Québec m
Quebecois n adj québécois(e)
quiet adj calme

R

rabbit n le lapin m p101
radio n la radio f
satellite radio la radio par satellite
rain, to rain v pleuvoir
Is it supposed to rain? Est-ce qu'il va pleuvoir ?
It's rainy. Le temps est pluvieux. p131
ramp, wheelchair n la rampe d'accès f p65

rape n le viol m p196
I was raped. J'ai été violé(e).

rare (meat) adj bleue p92

rate (car rental, hotel) n le tarif m p60
What's the rate per day? Quel est le tarif par jour ?
What's the rate per week? Quel est le tarif hebdomadaire ?

rate plan (cell phone) n le forfait m
Do you have a rate plan? Offrez-vous des forfaits ?

rather adv mieux

read, to read v lire p32

really adv vraiment

receipt n le reçu m p140

receive, to receive v recevoir p37 (like VOIR)

recommend, to recommend v recommander p24

red adj rouge

redhead n le roux m / la rousse f

refill n la même boisson (beverage) f / le renouvellement d'une ordonnance (prescription) m

reggae n le reggae m

relative n le membre de la famille m

remove, to remove v ôter p24

rent, to rent v louer p24

I'd like to rent a car. Je voudrais louer une voiture.

repeat, to repeat v répéter p24
Would you please repeat that? Pourriez-vous répéter ce que vous venez de dire, s'il vous plaît ?

reservation n la réservation f
I'd like to make a reservation for ___ people. Je voudrais faire une réservation pour ___ personnes. See p7 for numbers.

restaurant n le restaurant m
Where can I find a good restaurant? Où puis-je trouver un bon restaurant ? p88

restroom n les toilettes f pl / les WC m pl p44
Do you have a public restroom? Avez-vous des toilettes publiques ?

return, to return v retourner p24

ride, to ride v conduire p25

right adj droit(e) p5
It is on the right. C'est à droite.
Turn right at the corner. Tournez à droite au coin de la rue.

rights n les droits m pl
  civil rights les droits civiques
river n la fleuve f / la rivière f
road n la route f / la rue
  (street) f
road closed (sign) n route
  fermée f p61
rob, to rob v voler p24
  I've been robbed. J'ai été
  victime d'un vol. p200
rock and roll n le rock m
rock climbing n la varappe f
rocks (iced beverage) adj
  avec des glaçons p96
  **I'd like it on the rocks,
  please.** Avec des glaçons,
  s'il vous plaît.
romantic adj romantique
room (hotel) n la chambre f
  room service le service en
  chambre p81
rooster n le coq m
rope n la corde f
rose n la rose f
royal flush n la quinte royale f
rum n le rhum m p97
run, to run v courir p34

S

sad adj triste p128
safe (for valuables) n le
  coffre-fort m p83
  Do the rooms have safes?
  Les chambres sont-elles
  équipées de coffres-forts ?

safe (secure) adj sûr(e) / sans
  danger
  Is this area safe? Ce
  quartier est-il sûr ?
sail n la voile f / la navigation f
sail, to sail v appareiller p24
  When do we sail? À quelle
  heure le navire appareille-
  t-il ?
salad n la salade f
salesperson n le vendeur m /
  la vendeuse f
salt n le sel m p93
  Is that low-salt? Est-ce à
  faible teneur en sel ? p93
satellite n le satellite m p76
  satellite radio la radio par
  satellite
Saturday n le samedi m p14
sauce n la sauce f p103
say, to say v dire p32
scan, to scan (document) v
  scanner p24
schedule (of events) n le
  programme m
school n l'école f
  high school le lycée
  law school l'université de
  droit
scooter n le scooter m p58
score n le score m
Scottish n adj écossais(e)
scratched adj rayé(e)

scuba dive, to scuba dive *v faire de la plongée sous-marine* **p33**

sculpture *n la sculpture f*

seafood *n les poissons et fruits de mer* **p99**

search *n la fouille f* **p53**

search, to search *v chercher* **p24**

seasick (to be) *adj avoir le mal de mer* **p25**

I am seasick. *J'ai le mal de mer.* **p70**

seasickness pill *n le cachet contre le mal de mer* **p25**

seat *n la place f / le siège m*

child seat *le siège pour enfant* **p59**

second *adj second(e)*

security *n la sécurité f*

security guard *l'agent de sécurité* **p45**

sedan *n la berline f*

see, to see *v voir* **p37**

May I see it? *Puis-je le / la voir de plus près ?*

self-serve *adj en libre-service m*

sell, to sell *v vendre* **p25**

seltzer *n l'eau de Seltz f*

send, to send *v envoyer* **p24**

separated (marital status) *adj séparé(e)* **p123**

September *n septembre m*

serve, to serve *v servir* **p24**

service *n le service m / l'office (religious) m*

out of service *hors service*

service charge *n frais de traitement m*

seven *adj sept*

seventy *adj soixante-dix*

seventeen *adj dix-sept*

seventh *adj septième*

sew, to sew *v coudre* **p25**

sex (gender) *n le sexe m*

sex, to have intercourse *v avoir des rapports sexuels* **p25**

sheet *n le drap (bed) m / la feuille (paper) f*

shellfish *n les fruits de mer m*

ship *n le navire m* **p70**

ship, to ship *v expédier* **p24**

How much to ship this to ____? *Combien cela coûte-t-il pour expédier cela en ____ ?*

shipwreck *n le naufrage m*

shirt *n la chemise f*

shoe *n la chaussure f*

shop *n la boutique f*

shop, to shop *v faire des achats / chercher (to look for) / faire des courses* **p33**

I'm shopping for ____ clothes. *Je cherche des vêtements pour ____*

men's *hommes.*

women's *femmes.*

children's *enfants.*

short *adj court(e)* p10

shorts *n le short m*

shot (liquor) *n le verre m*

shout, to shout *v crier* p24

show (performance) *n le spectacle m* p155

What time is the show? *À quelle heure est le spectacle ?*

show, to show *v montrer* p24

Would you show me? *Pouvez-vous me montrer ?*

shower *n la douche f* p76

Does it have a shower? *Est-ce qu'il y a une douche ?*

shower, to shower *v se doucher* p24, 38

shrimp *n la crevette f*

shuttle bus *n la navette f*

sick *adj malade*

I feel sick. *Je ne me sens pas bien.*

side *adv à part*

sidewalk *n le trottoir m*

sightseeing *n l'excursion m*

sightseeing bus *n le car d'excursion m*

sign, to sign *v signer* p24

Where do I sign? *Où dois-je signer ?*

silver *adj argent*

sing, to sing *v chanter* p24

single *n adj le / la célibataire (unmarried) / seul(e) (alone, only)* p123

Are you single? *Êtes-vous célibataire ?*

single bed *le lit à une place*

sink *n le lavabo (bathroom) m / l'évier (kitchen) m /*

sister *n la sœur f* p120

sit, to sit *v s'asseoir* p39

six *adj six* p7

sixteen *adj seize* p7

sixty *adj soixante* p7

size (clothing, shoes) *n taille (clothing) f / pointure (shoes) f* p158

skin *n la peau f*

sleeping berth *n la couchette f*

sleeping car *n le wagon-lit m*

slow *adj lent(e)*

slow, to slow *v ralentir* p24

Slow down! *Ralentissez! / Veuillez ralentir!* p65

slowly *adv lentement*

Please speak more slowly. *Parlez plus lentement, s'il vous plaît.*

slum *n les bas quartiers m pl*

small *adj petit(e)* p11

smell, to smell *v sentir* p24

smoke, to smoke *v fumer* p24

smoking *adj (pour) fumeurs*

smoking area *la zone fumeurs*

no smoking *interdit de fumer*

ENGLISH—FRENCH

snack *n le snack m*

Snake eyes! *Paire d'as!* p190

snorkel, to snorkel *v faire de la plongée avec un tuba* **p175**

soap *n le savon m*

sock *n la chaussette f* p159

soda *n le soda m* p96

  diet soda *le soda allégé*

soft *adj doux m / douce f*

software *n le logiciel m*

sold out *adj complet m / complète f*

some *adj du m / de la f / des m f pl* p21

someone *n quelqu'un* **(definite)** / *on* **(indefinite)**

something *n quelque chose f*

son *n le fils m* p120

song *n la chanson f*

sorry *adj désolé(e)*

  I'm sorry. *Je suis désolé(e).*

soup *n la soupe f* p98

spa *n le spa m* p75

Spain *n l'Espagne f*

Spanish *n adj espagnol(e)*

spare tire *n la roue de secours f*

sparrow *n le moineau m*

speak, to speak *v parler* **p24**

  Do you speak English? *Parlez-vous anglais ?* p120

  Please speak louder. *Parlez plus fort s'il vous plaît____.*

Please speak more slowly. *Parlez plus lentement s'il vous plaît.* p120

special (featured meal) *n le plat du jour m*

specify, to specify *v spécifier* **p24**

speed limit *n la limitation de vitesse f* p64

  What's the speed limit in town? *Quelle est la limitation de vitesse en ville ?*

speedometer *n l'indicateur de vitesse m*

spell, to spell *v épeler* **p24**

  Would you spell that, please? *Pourriez-vous épeler ce mot, s'il vous plaît ?*

spices *n les épices f pl* p104

spill, to spill *v renverser* **p24**

split (gambling) *v partager* **p24**

sports *n les sports m pl*

spring (season) *n le printemps m* p15

stadium *n le stade m* p169

staff (employees) *n le personnel m / les employés m pl*

stamp (postage) *n le timbre m*

stair *n l'escalier m*

  Where are the stairs? *Où sont les escaliers ?*

stand, to stand v *se tenir debout* **p24, 38**

start, to start v *commencer* **(begin)** / *démarrer* **(a car)** **p24**

state n *l'état* m

station n *la station* f

Where is the nearest gas station? *Où se trouve la station essence la plus proche ?*

Where is ____ *Où se trouve* ____

the bus station? *la station de bus ?*

the subway station? *la station de métro ?*

the train station? *la gare ?*

stay, to stay v *rester* **p24**

We'll be staying for ____ **nights.** *Nous resterons* ____ *nuits.* See **p7** for numbers.

steakhouse n *le grill* m **p88**

steal, to steal v *voler* **p24**

stolen adj *volé(e)*

stop n *l'arrêt* m **p71**

Is this my stop? *Est-ce mon arrêt ?*

I missed my stop. *J'ai manqué mon arrêt.*

stop, to stop v *(s')arrêter* **p24, 39**

Please stop. *Arrêtez-vous, s'il vous plaît.*

STOP (traffic sign) *STOP*

Stop, thief! *Au voleur! Arrêtez-le!*

store n *le magasin* m **p156**

straight (gambling) n *la suite* f **p191**

straight adj *droit(e)* / *raide* **(hair)** / *sec* **(drink)**

straight ahead adv *tout droit*

street n *la rue* f

across the street *de l'autre côté de la rue*

down the street *en bas de la rue*

Which street? *Quelle rue ?*

How many more streets? *Dans combien de rues ?*

stressed adj *stressé(e)*

striped adj *à rayures* f pl

stroller n *la poussette* f

Do you rent baby strollers? *Est-ce que vous louez des poussettes ?*

suburb n *la banlieue* f

subway n *le métro* m **p71**

subway line *la ligne de métro*

subway station *la station de métro* **p71**

Which subway do I take for ____? *Quelle ligne de métro dois-je prendre pour aller à* ____ *?*

subtitle n le sous-titre m

suitcase n la valise f p57

suite n la suite f p74

summer n l'été m p15

sun n le soleil m

sunburn n le coup de soleil m

I have a bad sunburn. J'ai un mauvais coup de soleil.

Sunday n le dimanche m p14

sunglasses n les lunettes de soleil f

sunny adj ensoleillé(e) p131

It's sunny out. Il fait du soleil.

sunroof n le toit ouvrant m

sunscreen n la crème solaire f

Do you have sunscreen SPF ___? Avez-vous une crème solaire indice ___ ? See p7 for numbers.

supermarket n le supermarché m p105

surf, to surf v surfer p24

surfboard n la planche de surf f

suspiciously adv bizarrement p56

swallow, to swallow v avaler p24

sweater n le pull m p159

swim, to swim v nager p24

Can one swim here? Peut-on nager ici ?

swimsuit n le maillot de bain m

swim trunks n le caleçon de bain m

Swiss n adj suisse

Switzerland n la Suisse f

symphony n l'orchestre symphonique m

T

table n la table f p90

table for two la table pour deux p90

tailor n faire des retouches m p82

Can you recommend a good tailor? Pourriez-vous me recommander un bon couturier ?

take, to take v prendre p35 / emmener p24

Take me to the station. Emmenez-moi à la gare, s'il vous plaît.

How much to take me to ___? Quel est le prix de la course d'ici à ___ ?

takeout menu n le menu des plats à emporter m

talk, to talk v parler p24

tall adj grand(e)

taste n le goût m

taste, to taste v goûter / déguster p24

tax n la taxe f p161

value-added tax (VAT) la taxe sur la valeur ajoutée (TVA)

taxi n le taxi m p65

Taxi! *Taxi!*

Would you call me a taxi?
Pouvez-vous m'appeler un taxi ?

tea n le thé m p97

herbal tea *la tisane*

team n l'équipe f p169

techno n la musique techno f

television n la télévision f p76

temple n le synagogue m p133

ten adj dix p7

tennis n le tennis m p168

tennis court *le court de tennis*

tent n la tente f p87

tenth adj dixième p10

terminal n le terminal m

Thank you. Merci. p1

that (nearby) pron celui-ci m / celle-ci f p21

that (far away) pron celui-là m / celle-là f p21

theater n le théâtre m p151

them pron pl eux m / elles f

then adv alors **(so, in that case)** / puis **(next)**

there adv là

Is / Are there ___? *Est-ce qu'il y a ___ ?*

over there *là-bas*

these adj ces p21

thick adj épais m / épaisse f

thin adj fin(e)

third adj troisième p9

thirteen adj treize p7

thirteenth adj treizième p9

thirty adj trente p7

this adj ce m / cette f p21

those adj ces p21

thousand adj mille p8

three adj trois p7

Thursday n le jeudi m p14

ticket n le billet m p67

ticket counter *le guichet*

one-way ticket *un aller simple* p67, 72

round-trip ticket *un aller-retour* p67, 72

tight adj serré(e)

time n l'heure f p12

Is it on time? *Est-il / Est-elle à l'heure ?*

At what time? *À quelle heure ?*

What time is it? *Quelle heure est-il ?* p12

timetable n l'horaire m

tip (gratuity) le pourboire m

tip included *service compris*

tire n le pneu m p61

I have a flat tire. *J'ai un pneu crevé.*

tired adj fatigué(e)

today n adv aujourd'hui p14

toilet n les toilettes f pl / la cuvette des toilettes f

The toilet is overflowing.
Les toilettes débordent.
p84

The toilet is backed up. *Les toilettes sont bouchées.*

toilet paper n *le papier de toilette m*

You're out of toilet paper. *Il n'y a plus de papier toilette.*

toiletries n *le nécessaire de toilette m*

toll n *le péage m*

tomorrow n adv *demain* p14

ton n *la tonne f*

too adv *trop* **(excessively)** / *aussi* **(also)** p12

tooth n *la dent f*

I lost my tooth. *J'ai perdu une dent.*

toothache n *la rage de dents f*

I have a toothache. *J'ai mal à une dent.*

total adv *en tout*

What is the total? *Ca fait combien en tout ?*

tour n *l'excursion f* p155

Are guided / audio tours available? *Y a-t-il des visites guidées / avec audioguide ?*

towel n *la serviette f* p82

May we have more towels? *Pouvons-nous avoir plus de serviettes ?*

toy n *le jouet m*

toy store *le magasin de jouets*

Do you have any toys for the children? *Avez-vous des jouets pour enfants ?*

traffic n *la circulation f*

How's traffic? *Comment est la circulation ?*

traffic rules *le code de la route*

trail n *le sentier m*

Are there trails? *Y a-t-il des sentiers ?*

train n *le train m* p66

express train *le train express*

local train *la ligne régionale*

Does the train go to ____? *Le train va-t-il à ____ ?*

Where is the train station? *Où se trouve la gare ?*

train, to train v *(s)entraîner* p24,38

transfer, to transfer v *transférer* p24

I need to transfer funds. *J'ai besoin de transférer des fonds.*

wire transfer *le virement*

transmission n *la transmission f*

automatic transmission *la transmission automatique*

standard transmission *la transmission standard*

travel, to travel v *voyager* **p24**

trim, to trim v *couper* (hair) **p24**

trip n *le voyage* m

triple adj *triple* **p8**

trumpet n *la trompette* f

trunk n *le coffre* m **p62**

try, to try v *essayer* **p24**

Tuesday n *le mardi* m **p13**

turkey n *la dinde* f

turn, to turn v *tourner* **p24**

to turn left / right *tourner à gauche / à droite*

to turn off / turn on *éteindre / allumer*

turn signal n *le clignotant* m

twelve adj *douze* **p7**

twelfth adj *douzième*

twenty adj *vingt* **p7**

twentieth adj *vingtième*

two adj *deux* **p7**

U

umbrella n *le parapluie* m

uncle n *l'oncle* m **p123**

undercooked adj *pas assez cuit(e)*

understand, to understand v *comprendre* **p25**

I don't understand. *Je ne comprends pas.* **p2**

Do you understand? *Vous comprenez ?*

underwear n *le sous-vêtement* m

United States n *les États-Unis* m

university n *l'université* f

up adv *en haut* **p5**

update, to update v *mettre à jour* **p25**

upgrade n *la mise à niveau* f

upload, to upload v *télécharger* **p24**

upscale adj *huppé(e)*

us pron *nous*

USB port n *le port USB* m

use, to use v *utiliser* **p24**

V

vacation n *les vacances* f

on vacation *en vacances*

to go on vacation *partir en vacances*

vacancy n *les chambres libres* f pl

no vacancy *complet*

van n *le fourgon* m **p58**

VCR n *le magnétoscope* m

vegetable n *le légume* m

vegetarian n *végétarien* m / *végétarienne* f

vending machine n *le distributeur* m

version n *la version* f

very adj *très*

video n *la vidéo / la cassette vidéo* f

view n *la vue* f p76

   beach view *la vue sur la mer*

   city view *la vue sur la rue*

vineyard n *le vignoble* m

vinyl adj en *vinyle* m p57

violin n *le violon* m

visa n *le visa* m

   Do I need a visa? *Ai-je*
   besoin d'un visa ?

vision n *la vision* f

visit, to visit v *visiter* (a place)
   p24 / *rendre visite à*
   (person) p25

visually-impaired adj
   malvoyant(e) p73

vodka n *la vodka* f p97

volume n *le volume* m

   Please turn up / turn down
   the volume. *Veuillez*
   augmenter / baisser le
   volume.

vote, to vote v *voter* p24

voucher n *le bon* m / *le*
   coupon m p52

   meal voucher *le chèque-*
   repas

   room voucher *le bon pour*
   une chambre

W

wait, to wait v *attendre* p25

   Please wait. *Attendez, s'il*
   vous plaît!

waiter n *le serveur* m / *la*
   serveuse f

waiting area n *la salle*
   d'attente f p44

wake-up call n *le réveil*
   téléphonique m p83

wallet n *le portefeuille* m

   I lost my wallet. *J'ai perdu*
   mon portefeuille. p54

   Someone stole my wallet.
   On a volé mon
   portefeuille.

walk, to walk v *marcher* p24
   / *aller à pied* p28, 30

walker (ambulatory device)
   n *le déambulateur* m

walkway n *le trottoir* m

want, to want v *vouloir* p37

war n *la guerre* f

warm adj *chaud(e)* p132

watch, to watch v *regarder*
   p24

water n *l'eau* f

   Is the water drinkable?
   L'eau est-elle potable ?
   p87

   Do you have sparkling
   water? *Avez-vous de l'eau*
   pétillante ?

wave n *la vague* (water)

waxing n *l'épilation à la cire* f

weapon n *l'arme* f

wear, to wear *v* porter **p24**
weather forecast *n* les
prévisions
météorologiques *f pl*
Wednesday *n* le mercredi *m*
week *n* la semaine *f* **p4**
  this week cette semaine
  last week la semaine dernière
  next week la semaine
  prochaine
weigh *v* peser **p24**
  I weigh ____. Je pèse ___.
  It weighs ____. Cela pèse
  ___. See **p7** for numbers.
weights *n* les haltères *f pl*
welcome *adv* bienvenue
  You're welcome. Vous êtes
  le bienvenu / la bienvenue.
well *adv* bien
  well done (meat) bien cuite
  well done (task) bon travail
  I don't feel well. Je ne me
  sens pas bien.
western *adj* western (movie)
whale *n* la baleine *f*
what *adv* quel *m* / quelle *f* **p3**
  What sort of ____? Quelle
  sorte de ____ ?
  What time is it? Quelle
  heure est-il ?
wheelchair *n* le fauteuil
roulant *m* **p73**

wheelchair access l'accès
pour fauteuils roulants
p73
  wheelchair ramp la rampe
  d'accès pour fauteuils
  roulants
  power wheelchair le
  fauteuil roulant motorisé
wheeled (luggage) *adj* à
roulettes
when *adv* quand **p1**
where *adv* où **p1**
  Where is it? Où est-ce ?
which *adj* lequel *m* / laquelle *f* /
lesquels *m pl* / lesquelles *f pl*
  Which one? Lequel /
  Laquelle ?
  Which is it? Lequel /
  Laquelle est-ce ?
white *adj* blanc *m* / blanche *f*
who *pron* qui **p3**
whose *pron* à qui
wide *adj* large **p12**
widow / widower *n* la veuve
f / le veuf *m* **p123**
wife *n* la femme *f* **p122**
Wi-Fi *n* le Wi-Fi *m*
window *n* la fenêtre *f*
  drop-off window le guichet
  de dépôt **p149**
  pickup window le guichet
  de récupération **p149**
windshield *n* le pare-brise *m*

windshield wiper *n l'essuie-glace m* p62

windsurf, to windsurf *v faire de la planche à voile* p33

windy *adj du vent* p132

wine *n le vin m* p96

winery *n le vignoble m*

winter *n l'hiver m* p15

wiper *n l'essuie-glace m*

with *prep avec*

withdraw *v retirer* p24

I need to withdraw money. *J'ai besoin de retirer de l'argent.*

withdrawal *n le retrait m*

without *prep sans*

woman *n la femme f*

work, to work *v travailler* (job) p24 / *marcher* (function) p24

This doesn't work. *Cela ne marche pas.*

workout *n l'entraînement m*

worse *adj pire*

worst *adj le pire*

write, to write *v écrire* p32

Would you write that down for me? *Pourriez-vous m'écrire cela ?*

writer *n l'écrivain* p129

X

x-ray machine *n l'appareil de radiographie m*

Y

yellow *adj jaune*

yes *adv oui* p1

yesterday *n hier m* p4

the day before yesterday *avant-hier*

yield sign *n panneau de priorité m*

you *pron tu s / vous pl* p22

you (s. informal) *tu*
you (s. formal) *vous*
you (pl. informal) *vous*
you (pl. formal) *vous*

your, yours *adj ton m / ta f / tes pl*

young *adj jeune*

Z

zoo *n le zoo m* p137

ENGLISH—FRENCH

A

l'abeille *f* bee *n*

abîmé(e) *damaged adj* p57

accepter *to accept v* **p24**

accessible aux personnes à mobilité réduite *handicapped-accessible adj* p73

l'accident *m* accident *n*

D'accord. *Okay. adv* p2

acheter *to buy v* **p24**

l'acné *f* acne *n*

l'acompte *f* advance (money) *n*

à côté de *next to adj* p5

actuel *actual adj*

l'adaptateur *m* adapter plug *n*

l'addition *f* check (tab) *n*

l'adresse *f* address *n*

à droite *f* right *n* p5

les droits civiques *civil rights*

droit(e) / raide *straight adj* / *right adj*

tout droit *straight ahead*

C'est à droite. *It is on the right.*

Tournez à droite au coin de la rue. *Turn right at the corner.*

l'aéroport *m* airport *n* p44

l'affaire *f s* deal *n*

les affaires *f pl* business *n*

Voici ma carte de visite. *Here's my business card.*

affréter *to charter v* **p24**

afro *afro n adj*

afro-américain(e) *m f* African-American *n adj*

l'âge *m* age *n* p124

Quel âge avez-vous ? *What's your age?*

l'agence *f* agency *n* p58

l'agence de location de voitures *car rental agency*

l'agent *m* guard *n*

agnostique *agnostic adj*

l'aide *f* help *n*

aider *to help v* **p24**

Aïe! *Ouch! exclamation*

l'ail *m* garlic *n* p115

aimer *to like, to enjoy / to love v* **p24**

faire l'amour *to make love*

l'aire de jeu *f* playground *n*

l'alcool *m* alcohol *adj* p96

allaiter *to nurse v* **p24**

allemand(e) *German n adj*

aller *to go / to look (appear) / to fit (clothes) / to go with (match) v* **p30**

l'aller simple *m* one-way ticket *n* p67, 72

l'aller-retour *m* round-trip ticket *n* p67, 72

l'allergie *f allergy n*

allergique *allergic adj* See p197 for common allergens.

allumer *to turn on v* **p24**

l'allumette *f match n*

  la boîte d'allumettes *book of matches*

alors *then adv / yet adv / so*

l'altitude *f altitude n*

l'ambassade *f embassy n*

l'ambulance *f ambulance n*

l'amende *f fine (for traffic violation) n* **p64**

américain(e) *American n adj*

l'ami(e) *m f friend n* **p122**

l'amour *m love n*

l'amphithéâtre *m colisseum n*

anglais(e) *English n adj*

l'Angleterre *f England n*

l'animal *m animal n*

annuler *to cancel v* **p24**

  Le vol _____ a été annulé. *Flight _____ has been canceled.*

l'antibiotique *m antibiotic n*

l'antihistaminique *m antihistamine n adj* **p192**

anxieux *m /* anxieuse *f anxious adj*

août *August n* **p15**

à point *medium rare (meat) / bloody adj* **p92**

l'appareil de radiographie *m x-ray machine n*

appareiller *to sail away v* **p24**

l'appel *m phone call n* **p143**

  un appel en PCV *collect phone call*

  l'appel à l'étranger *international phone call*

appeler *to call (on the phone) / to call (shout) v* **p24**

l'après-midi *m afternoon n*

l'argent *m money n / silver n*

l'arme *f weapon n*

l'armée *f military, army n*

l'arrêt *m stop n* **p71**

  l'arrêt de bus *bus stop*

arrêter *to stop v* **p24, 39**

  Arrêtez-vous, s'il vous plaît. *Please stop.*

  Je veux que vous vous arrêtiez. *I need you to stop.*

  STOP *STOP (traffic sign)*

l'arrivée *f /* les arrivées *f pl arrival(s) n* **p44**

arriver *to arrive v* **p24**

l'art *m art n*

  exposition d'art *exhibit of art*

d'art *art adj*

  le musée d'art *art museum*

l'artisan(e) *m f craftsperson n*

l'artiste *m f artist n* **p129**

l'ascenseur *m elevator n* p73
asiatique *Asian n adj*
l'aspirine *f aspirin n* p193
s'asseoir *to sit v* p39
l'assistance *assistance, help n*
assister *to assist, to help v*
 p24
l'assurance *f insurance n*
 assurance de tierce collision
 collision insurance
 l'assurance responsabilité
 civile *liability insurance*
asthmatique *asthmatic adj*
 p197
athée *atheist adj*
attaqué(e) *mugged adj* p196
attendre *to wait / to hold*
 (telephone) v p25
 Attendez, s'il vous plaît!
 Please wait.
 Attendez une minute! *Hold*
 on a minute!
l'attente *f wait n*
atterrir *to land v* p24
l'aube *f dawn n* p13
l'auberge *f hostel n* p74
aucun(e) *none n* p11
au-dessus de *above prep* p86
audio *audio adj* p73
 l'assistance audio *audio*
 assistance
aujourd'hui *today n*
aussi *too (also) adv*
l'Australie *f Australia n*

australien *m* / **australienne** *f*
 Australian n adj
l'autobiographie *f*
 autobiography n
l'autobus *m bus n*
l'automne *m autumn (fall) n*
l'autoroute *f highway n*
autre *another adj*
de l'autre côté de *across adv*
 de l'autre côté de la rue /
 en face *across the street*
avaler *to swallow v* p24
à l'avance *in advance adv*
en avant *forward adj*
avec *with prep*
 avec des glaçons *on the*
 rocks (beverage) p96
 Avec des glaçons ou sec ?
 On the rocks or straight?
aveugle *blind adj*
l'avocat(e) *m f lawyer n*
avoir *to have v* p25
avoir besoin de *to need v*
 p25
avoir des rapports sexuels *to*
 have intercourse v p25
avoir mal *to hurt v* p25
 Aïe ! Ca fait mal ! *Ouch!*
 That hurts!
avril *m April n* p14

B
le / la baby-sitter *m f*
 babysitter n

**Les baby-sitters parlent
anglais.** *The babysitters
speak English.*

le(s) bagage(s) *m pl*
baggage, luggage n

bagages perdus *lost
baggage*

récupération des bagages
baggage claim p56

se baigner *to bathe v* **p24, 38**

la baignoire *f bathtub n*

le bain *m bath n*

le baiser *m kiss n*

baiser *vulgar to fuck v* **p24**

la branche d'essuie-glace *m
wiper blade n*

le balcon *m balcony n* **p77**

le ballon *m* / **la balle** *f ball
(sport) n*

la banlieue *f suburb n*

la banque *f bank n* **p140**

bancaire *bank, banking adj*

le compte bancaire *bank
account*

la carte bancaire *bank card*

le bar *m bar, lounge n* **p90**

la barbe *f beard n*

bas *m* / **basse** *f low adj*

les bas quartiers *m slum(s) n*

la batterie *f battery (car) n*

le tambour *m drum n*

beau *m* / **belle** *f handsome,
beautiful adj*

beaucoup *much n*

beaucoup de *many adj*

le bébé *m baby n*

beige *beige adj*

belge *Belgian n adj*

la Belgique *f Belgium n*

le berceau *m crib n*

la berline *f sedan n*

le beurre *m butter n*

le biberon *m baby bottle n*

bien *fine / well adv*

Bien, merci. *I'm fine.* p1

Je ne me sens pas bien. /
don't feel well.

bien cuite *well done adj*

bienvenue *welcome adv*

De rien. *You're welcome.*
(response to « Thank you »)

la bière *f beer n* **p96**

la bière pression *draft beer*

bilingue *bilingual adj*

le billard *m pool (game) n*

le billet *m ticket n* / *bill
(currency) n*

la biographie *f biography n*

biologique *organic adj*

blanc *m* / **blanche** *f white adj*

la blessure *f injury n*

bleu(e) *blue adj*

bleue *rare (meat) adv* **p92**

bleu lavande *lavender adj*

blond(e) *blond(e) adj*

bloquer *to block v* **p24**

le blouson *m jacket n*

le **bœuf** m *beef (meat)* n
boire *to drink* v **p31**
la **boisson** f *drink* n

la **boisson comprise**
complimentary drink
**Voulez-vous quelque chose
à boire ?** *Would you like
something to drink?*

les **boissons alcoolisées** f
liquor n

la **boisson gazeuse allégée**
diet soda

la **boîte de nuit** f *nightclub* n
la **bombe** f *bomb* n
le **bon** m *voucher* n **p52**
bon m / **bonne** f *good /
correct* adj

Bonjour. *Good morning.*
Bon après-midi. *Good
afternoon.*
Bonsoir. *Good evening.*
Bonne nuit. *Good night.*
Bonjour. *Hello. (morning
and daytime)*

le **bord** m *board* n
à bord *on board*
la **bosse** f *dent* n
la **bouche** f *mouth* n **p126**
la **boucle** f *curl* n
bouclé(e) *curly* adj
bouddhiste m f *Buddhist* adj
bouger *to move* v **p24**
la **bougie** f *fuse (car) / candle* n
la **bouteille** f *bottle* n

la **bouteille de vin** *wine
bottle*
la **bouteille d'oxygène**
oxygen tank
la **boutique** f *shop* n
la **boutique hors-taxe**
duty-free shop **p46**
le **braille américain** m *braille,
American* n
brancher *to plug* v **p24**
le **brandy** m *brandy* n
le **bras** m *arm* n
le **bridge** m *bridge (dental)* n
le **briquet** m *lighter
(cigarette)* n
bronzé(e) *tanned* adj
brûler *to burn* v **p24**
brun *brown (hair)* adj
la **brune** f *brunette* n
bruyant(e) *noisy* adj
le **budget** m *budget* n
budgéter *to budget* v **p24**
le **buffet** m *buffet* n **p89**
le **bureau de poste** m *post
office* n **p147**
le **but (sport)** m *goal (sport)* n

C

la **cabine d'essayage** f
*changing room, fitting
room* n
le **cabinet du médecin** m
doctor's office n

cabosser *to dent* v **p24**
  Il / Elle a cabossé la voiture.
  He / She dented the car.
la cacahuète *f peanut* n **p95**
en cachemire *cashmere* adj
le cachet contre le mal de mer *m seasickness pill* n
le cadeau *m* / **les cadeaux** *m pl gift* n **p52**
le café *m coffee / café* n
  le café glacé *iced coffee*
  le café au lait *latte*
le caleçon de bain *m swim trunks* n
calme *quiet* adj
une camionnette *m van* n **p58**
camper *to camp* v **p24**
de camper *camping* adj
le camping-car *m camper* n
le Canada *m Canada* n
canadien *m* / **canadienne** *f Canadian* n adj
le canard *m duck* n
la canne à pêche *f fishing pole* n
le cappucino *m cappuccino* n
le car *m bus (coach)* n **p68**
  le car d'excursion *m sightseeing bus* n
la carie *f cavity (tooth)* n
la carte *f card* n
  Voici ma carte de visite.
  Here's my business card.

la carte *f map* n
  la carte de crédit *credit card* **p139**
  la carte d'embarquement *boarding pass* **p54**
  la carte postale *postcard*
le casier *m locker* n
le casino *m casino* n **p190**
(se) casser *to break* v **p24, 38**
le casque *m headphones* n
catholique *Catholic* adj
le CD *m CD* n
ce *m* / **cette** *f this* adj
la ceinture *f belt (clothing)* n
célébrer *to celebrate* v **p24**
célibataire *single (unmarried)*
  Êtes-vous célibataire ? *Are you single?*
celui-ci *m* / **celle-ci** *f that (nearby)* adj **p21**
celui-là *m* / **celle-là** *f that (far away)* adj **p21**
cent *hundred* adj **p8**
centaine *f hundred* n
le centimètre *m centimeter* n
le centre commercial *m mall* n
le centre-ville *m downtown* n
ces *these / those* adj **p21**
la chambre *f room* n
  le service en chambre *room service* **p81**
  la chambre d'hôte *bed-and-breakfast (B & B)*
  chambres libres *vacancy*
  complet *no vacancy*

le change *m currency exchange n*

changer *to change v* **p24**

la chanson *f song n*

chanter *to sing v* **p24**

le chapeau *m hat n* **p159**

charter *charter adj*

le chat *m /* **la chatte** *f cat n*

chaud(e) *hot / warm adj* **p132**

chauffer *to overheat, warm up v* **p24**

la chaussette *f sock n* **p159**

la chaussure *f shoe n* **p159**

la chemise *f shirt n* **p158**

le chemisier *m blouse n* **p158**

le chèque *m check n*

cher *m /* **chère** *f expensive adj*

pas cher *m /* **pas chère** *f cheap*

chercher *to look for, to search v* **p24**

le cheval *m horse n*

le cheveu *m /* **les cheveux** *m pl hair n*

la chèvre *f goat n*

le chien *m /* **la chienne** *f dog n*

la Chine *f China n*

chinois(e) *Chinese n adj*

le chiropraticien, m /
chiropraticienne *f chiropractor n* **p194**

le chocolat chaud *m hot chocolate n* **p97**

chrétien *m /* **chrétienne** *f Christian adj*

le cigare *m cigar n*

la cigarette *f cigarette n*

le cil *m eyelash n* **p127**

le cinéma *m movie theater n* **p151**

cinq *five adj* **p7**

cinquante *fifty adj* **p7**

le / la cinquième *fifth adj* **p9**

la circulation *f traffic n*

la citronnade *f lemonade n*

clair(e) *clear adj*

la clarinette *f clarinet n*

la classe *f class n* **p49**

la classe affaires *business class*

la classe économique *economy class*

la première classe *first class*

la climatisation *f air conditioning n* **p76**

le clos *vineyard / orchard n*

le club de remise en forme *f fitness center n* **p167**

le cochon *m pig n*

le code vestimentaire *m dress (general attire) n*

le cœur *m heart n*

le coffre (à bagages) *m trunk (luggage, car) n* **p57**

coffre-fort *m safe (for storing valuables)* n p83

le cognac *m cognac* n p97

le coiffeur *m* / **la coiffeuse** *f hairdresser* n

le coin *m corner* n

le colis *m package* n p147

collectionner *to collect* v p24

colorer *to color* v p24

commander *to order (a meal)* v p24

commencer *to start, to commence* v p24

comment / combien *how* adv

Comment allez-vous ? *How are you?*

Combien de temps cela va-t-il prendre ? *How long will it take?*

Combien est-ce que cela coûte ? *How much does this cost?*

commencer *to begin* v p24

compenser *to make up (compensate)* v p24

complet *full house* n

complet *m* / **complète** *f sold out* adj

composer *to dial (a phone number)* v p24

composer directement le numéro *to dial direct*

comprendre *to understand* v p25

Vous comprenez ? *Do you understand?* p1

compris(e) *included*

compte *m account* n p142

le comptoir *m counter (in bar)* n

le concert *m concert* n p137

le conducteur *m* / **la conductrice** *f driver* n

conduire *to drive / to ride* v p25

confirmer *to confirm* v p24

Vous n'avez pas confirmé votre réservation. *You didn't confirm your reservation.*

la confirmation *f confirmation* n

confus(e) *confused* adj p128

la congestion *f congestion (sinus)* n

connaître *to know (someone)* v p31

constipé(e) *constipated* adj

continuer *to continue* v p24

le coquillage *m shellfish* n

la corde *f rope, twine* n

corriger *to correct* v p24

à côté (de) *next (to)* prep

le coton *m cotton* n

la couche *f diaper* n

la couche jetable *disposable diaper*

la couchette individuelle *f*
private berth / cabin n

coudre *to sew v*

la couleur *f color n*

le coup de soleil *m sunburn n*

la coupe (de cheveux) *f*
haircut n

coupé(e) *disconnected adj*

couper *to cut / to trim (hair)*
v **p24**

le coupon *m voucher n* **p52**

le coupon-repas *meal*
voucher

le coupon d'hébergement
room voucher

courir *to run v*

la couronne *f crown (dental) n*

Puis-je avoir votre adresse
courriel ? *May I have your*
e-mail address?

le courrier *m mail n*

courrier par avion *air mail*

courrier en recommandé
avec accusé de réception
certified mail

courrier exprès *express mail*

courrier première classe
first class mail

courrier recommandé
registered mail

le court *m court (sport) n*

court(e) *short adj* **p10**

courtois(e) *courteous adj*

le / la cousin(e) *m f cousin n*

coûter *to cost v* **p24**

la couverture *f blanket n*
p55

la crèche *f nursery n*

la crème *f cream n*

la crème solaire *f sunscreen n*

la crème solaire indice ____
sunscreen SPF ____

la crevette *f shrimp n*

crier *to shout v* **p24**

la crise cardiaque *f heart*
attack n

le cuir *m leather n* **p57**

la cuisine *f kitchen n*

cuisiner *to cook v* **p24**

très cuite *charred (meat) adj*

trop cuit(e) *overcooked adj*

cuivre *copper (color) adj*

le culte *m service (religious) n*

le cybercafé *Internet café,*
cybercafé n

D

le danger *m danger n*

la danse *f dance n*

danser *to dance v* **p24**

dans *in, inside prep*

dans l'enseignement *f*
educator n **p129**

le déambulateur *m walker*
(ambulatory device) n

déborder *to overflow v* **p24**

décapotable *convertible (car)*
adj

décembre m *December* n
déclarer *to declare* v **p24**

Vous n'avez rien à déclarer ? *You don't have anything to declare?*

le déguisement m *costume* n
la dégustation f *tasting, sampling* n
déguster *to taste* v **p24**
dehors *outside* n
le déjeuner m *lunch* n
déjeuner *to eat (lunch)* v **p24**
demain *tomorrow* adv p14
demander / poser *to ask* v **p24**
démarrer *to start (car)* v **p24**
déménager *to move (household)* v **p24**
demi(e) *half* adj
la démocratie f *democracy* n
la dent f *tooth* n
le / la dentiste m f *dentist* n
les départs m *departure(s)* n
se dépêcher *to hurry* v **p24, 38**
déprimé(e) *down, depressed* adj
dernier m **/ dernière** f *last* adv
derrière *behind* prep p5
désolé(e) *sorry* adj

Je suis désolé(e), je ne comprends pas. *I'm sorry, I don't understand.*

le dessert m *dessert* n p102

la carte des desserts *dessert menu*

le dessin m *drawing* n
en dessous de *below* prep
la destination f *destination* n
le détecteur de métaux m *metal detector* n
deux *two* adj
à deux / double *double* adj

à deux lits *double room*

devant *front* prep
diabétique *diabetic* adj
la diarrhée f *diarrhea* n p193
le dictionnaire m *dictionary* n
différent(e) *different (other)* adj
difficile *difficult* adj
le dimanche m *Sunday* n p14
la dinde f *turkey* n
le dîner m *dinner* n
dîner *to eat* v **p24**

sortir dîner *to eat out*

dire *to say* v **p32**
le directeur m **/ la directrice** f *manager* n **p84**
la discothèque / la boîte de nuit f *disco / nightclub* n
disparaître *disappear* v
disponible *available* adj
le distributeur m *vending machine* n

le distributeur automatique f
ATM / cash machine n

**DAB (distributeur
automatique de billets)**
ATM p142

divorcé(e) *divorced adj* p193

dix *ten adj* p7

dix-huit *eighteen adj* p7

dix-neuf *nineteen adj* p7

dix-sept *seventeen adj* p7

dixième *tenth adj* p8

le docteur m / **la docteresse** f
doctor n

le dollar m *dollar* n

le domicile m *home* n

donner *to give / to deal
(cards)* v **p24**

doré(e) *golden adj*

le dos m *back (body)* n

la douane f *customs* n

la douche f *shower* n p76

se doucher *to shower* v **p24,
38**

doux m / **douce** f *soft adj*

la douzaine f *dozen* n p11

douze *twelve adj* p7

douzième *twelfth adj*

le drame m *drama* n

le drap m *sheet (bed linen)* n

dur(e) *hard adj*

durer *to last* v **p24**

le DVD m *DVD* n p59

E

l'eau f *water* n

l'eau chaude *hot water*

l'eau froide *cold water*

l'eau courante f *current
(water)* n

l'eau de Javel f *bleach* n

l'eau de Seltz f *seltzer* n

échouer *to beach, to fail* v **p24**

l'école f *school* n

l'économie f *economy* n p58

l'Écosse f *Scotland* n

écossais(e) *Scottish* n adj

écrire *to write* v **p32**

**Pourriez-vous m'écrire
cela ?** *Would you write
that down for me?*

l'écrivain m f *writer* n p129

l'église f *church* n p133

l'égratignure f *scratch* n

l'élection f *election* n

emballer *to bag* v **p24**

embarquer *to board* v **p24**

embarrassé(e) *embarrassed
adj*

l'embouteillage m
congestion (traffic) n

l'employé(e) m f *employee* n

l'employeur m /
l'employeuse f *employer* n

encaisser *to cash* v **p24**

en-cas m *snack* n

enceinte *pregnant adj* p195

enchanté(e) *charmed adj*

l'enfant *m* *infant / child* n

enlever *to clear, delete, remove* v **p24**

l'enregistrement *m* *check-in* n

l'enregistrement électronique *electronic check-in*

ensoleillé(e) *sunny* adj

l'entaille *f* *cut (wound)* n

entendre *to hear* v **p25**

enthousiaste *enthusiastic* adj

l'entracte *m* *intermission* n

l'entraînement *m* *workout* n

(s')entraîner *to train* v **p24**

l'entrée *f* *entrance / cover charge (in bar)* n **p184**

entrée interdite *do not enter*

l'entreprise *f* *business* n

entrer *to enter* v **p24**

l'enveloppe *f* *envelope* n

l'environnement *m* *environment* n

envoyer *to send* v **p24**

épais *m* / épaisse *f* *thick* adj

épeler *to spell* v **p24**

Pourriez-vous épeler ce mot, s'il vous plaît ? *Can you spell this word, please?*

les épices *f* *spice* n **p104**

l'épilation à la cire *f* *waxing* n

l'épilation _____ à la cire _____ *waxing*

du maillot *bikini*

des sourcils *eyebrow*

des jambes *leg*

(s')épouser *to marry, to get married* v **p24, 39**

épuisé(e) *exhausted* adj

l'équipe *f* *team* n **p169**

l'erreur *f* *mistake* n

l'escalade *f* *climbing* n

escalader *to climb* v **p24**

l'escalier *m* *stair* n

l'escalier roulant *m* *escalator* n

l'Espagne *f* *Spain* n

espagnol(e) *Spanish* n adj

les espèces *f* *cash* n **p141**

espèces uniquement *cash only*

essayer *to try* v **p24**

l'essence *f* *gas* n **p60**

l'essuie-glace *m* *windshield wiper* n **p67**

est *is* v See être (to be) **p27**.

l'étage *m* *floor* n

le premier étage *first floor*

l'état *m* *condition / state* n

l'été *m* *summer* n **p15**

éteindre *to turn off* v **p25**

êtes *are* v See être (to be) **p27**.

être *to be* v **p27**

étroit(e) *narrow* adj **p12**

eux *m* pl / elles *f* pl *them* pron

s'évanouir *to faint* v **p24, 39**
l'évier *m sink (kitchen)* n
la visite *f sightseeing / tour* n **p155**

les excursions guidées *guided tours*

les excursions audio guidées *audio tours*

(s') excuser *to excuse (pardon)* v **p24**

Excusez-moi. *Excuse me.*

expédier *to ship* v **p24**
expliquer *to explain* v **p24**
l'exposition *f exhibit* n

F

fâché(e) *angry* adj **p128**
facturer *to bill* v **p24**
faire *to do, to make* v **p33**
fait à partir de *made of* adj
la famille *f family* n **p120**
fatigué(e) *tired* adj
la faute *f fault* n
le fauteuil roulant *f wheelchair* n

l'accès aux fauteuils roulants *wheelchair access* **p73**

la rampe d'accès pour handicapés *wheelchair ramp*

le fauteuil roulant motorisé *power wheelchair*

le fautif *m /* **la fautive** *f at fault* adj

C'est moi le fautif / la fautive. *I'm at fault.*

C'est sa faute. *It is his / her fault.*

féminin(e) *female* adj
la femme *f woman / wife* n
la femme au foyer *f homemaker* n **p129**
la femme de chambre *f maid (hotel)* n
la fenêtre *f window* n
fermé(e) *closed* adj
fermer *to close* v **p24**
le festival *m festival* n

le festival de rue *street festival*

Au feu! *Fire!* n
le feu *m light* n

Puis-je vous offrir du feu ? *May I offer you a light?*

février *m February* n **p14**
le fiancé *m /* **la fiancée** *f fiancé(e)* n **p123**
la fille *f girl, daughter* n **p122**

le film *m movie* n **p151**

le fils *m son* n **p122**
fin(e) *thin* adj
finir *to finish* v **p24**
la fissure *f crack (in glass object)* n
la fleur *f flower* n
flottant(e) *loose* adj
le flush *m flush (gambling)* n

la flûte f flute / small baguette n

les fonds m pl money (in an account) / stocks, securities n

le forfait m rate plan n

le format m format n

fort(e) loud adj

fort loudly adv

Parlez plus fort, s'il vous plaît. *Please speak more loudly.*

la fouille f search n

fragile fragile adj

frais m / **fraîche** f fresh adj

frais de traitement m service charge n

la France f France n

français(e) French n adj

le frein m brake n

le frein à main emergency brake

freiner to brake v p24

le frère m brother n p122

froid(e) cold adj

le fromage m cheese n p107

le front m forehead n p126

le fruit m fruit n p113

les fruits de mer seafood n

fuir to drip v p25

fumer to smoke v p24

les fumeurs m pl smokers n

la zone fumeurs smoking area

interdit de fumer no smoking

le fusible m fuse (home) n

G

le gallon m gallon n

le gant m glove n

le garçon m boy n

le garde m guard n

garder to keep v p24

se garer to park v p24, 38

la gauche f left n p5

à gauche on the left

gentil m / **gentille** f kind (nice) adj

le gilet m / **la bouée** f de sauvetage life preserver n

le gin m gin n p97

la glace f ice / ice cream n

avec des glaçons with ice cubes / on the rocks

la machine à glaçons ice machine

le golf m golf n p178

le terrain de golf golf course

le club de golf golf club

le goût m taste n

goûter to taste v p24

le grain de beauté m mole (facial feature) n

le gramme m gram n

grand(e) big / tall adj p12

très grand(e) extra-large adj

la grand-mère f *grandmother* n

le grand-père m *grandfather* n

les grands-parents m f pl *grandparents* n p123

grandir to *grow (get larger)* v p24

Où avez-vous grandi ? *Where did you grow up?*

gratter to *scratch* v p24

gratuit(e) *complimentary, free* adj

graver to *burn (CD)* v p24

grec m / **grecque** f *Greek* adj

le grill m *steakhouse* n

gris(e) *gray* adj

gros m / **grosse** f *fat* adj p12

le groupe m *band (musical ensemble) / group* n

la guerre f *war* n

le guichet m *ticket counter, box office* n

le / la guide m f *guide (of tours)* n

le guide m *guide (publication)* n

le guide d'utilisation m *manual (instruction booklet)* n

guider to *guide* v p24

la guitare f *guitar* n

la gymnastique f *gym* n

le / la gynécologue m f *gynecologist* n p194

H

s'habiller to *dress* v p24, 39

Vous devriez vous habiller pour cet événement. *You should dress up for that affair.*

habiter to *live* v p24

le hall d'entrée m *hallway* n

le handicap m *handicap, disability* n

haut(e) *high* adj

à haut débit m *broadband* n

l'hectare m *hectare* n

l'herbe f *herb* n

l'heure f *hour / time* n p12

les heures d'ouverture f pl *hours (of operation)* n

heureux m / **heureuse** f *happy* adj p128

hier *yesterday* adv p4

avant-hier *the day before yesterday*

hindou(e) *Hindu* adj

hip-hop *hip-hop* n

l'histoire f *history* n

historique *historical* adj

l'hiver m *winter* n p15

l'homme au foyer m *homemaker* n

l'homme m / **la personne de sexe masculin** f *man / male* n

l'horaire m *timetable* n

hors-taxe *duty-free* adj

l'hôte *m* / l'hôtesse *f guest n*

l'hôtel *m hotel n* p74

l'huile *f oil n*

huit *eight adj*

huitième *eighth adj*

humide *humid adj* p132

huppé(e) *upscale adj*

I

ici *here n* p5

il est tard *it is late adj* p13

n'importe lequel *m* / laquelle *f any adj*

n'importe quoi *m f anything n*

n'importe où *anywhere adv*

imprimer *to print v* p24

l'Inde *f India*

indien *m* / indienne *f Indian n adj*

l'indicateur de vitesse *m speedometer n*

l'indigestion *f indigestion n*

l'infirmier *m* / l'infirmière *f nurse n* p129

l'information *f information n*

l'ingénieur *mf engineer n*

l'inscription *f membership n*

l'insecte *m bug n* p85

l'insectifuge *m insect repellent n*

l'institution de crédit *f credit bureau n*

insulter *to insult v* p24

à l'intérieur de *inside prep*

Internet *m Internet n*

Internet à haut débit *high-speed Internet*

l'interprète *m f interpreter n*

l'Irlande *f Ireland n*

irlandais(e) *Irish n adj*

l'issue de secours *f emergency exit n* p49

l'Italie *f Italy n*

italien *m* / italienne *f Italian n adj*

J

la jambe *f leg n*

janvier *m January n* 14

le Japon *m Japan n*

japonais(e) *Japanese n adj*

jaune *yellow adj*

le jazz *m jazz n*

je *I pron* p22

le jeudi *m Thursday n* p14

jeune *young adj*

de jeune fille *maiden adj*

J'ai gardé mon nom de jeune fille. *I kept my maiden name.*

le jogging *m jogging n*

jouer *to play v* p24

le jouet *m toy n*

le magasin de jouets *toy store*

le jour *m day n*

le journal *m* / **les journaux** *m pl* newspaper *n*

juif *m* / **juive** *f* Jewish *adj*

juillet *m* July *n* p15

juin *m* June *n* p15

le jus *m* juice *n*

 le jus de fruit *fruit juice*

la justice *f* / **le tribunal** *m* court (legal) *n*

K

kasher *kosher adj*

le kilo *m* kilo *n* p10

le kilomètre *m* kilometer *n*

le kiosque à journaux *m* newsstand *n* p162

la kitchenette *f* kitchenette *n*

le klaxon *m* horn *n*

L

là *there adv* p5

 là-bas *over there*

le lait *m* milk *n* p97

 le milkshake *milkshake*

la langue *f* language *n*

le lapin *m* rabbit *n* p101

large *wide adj* p12

le lavabo *m* sink (bathroom) *n*

la leçon *f* lesson *n*

le lecteur de CD *m* CD player *n*

le légume *m* vegetable *n*

lent(e) *slow adj*

lentement *slow(ly) adv*

 Parlez plus lentement, s'il vous plaît. *Please speak more slowly.* p120

les lentilles de contact *f* contact lens *n* p197

lequel *m* / **laquelle** *f* / **lesquels** *m pl* / **lesquelles** *f pl* which adj

 Lequel ? *m* / **Laquelle ?** *f* Which one?

 Lequel *m* / **Laquelle** *f* **est-ce ?** *Which is it?*

la lessive *f* laundry *n*

la libération de la chambre *f* check-out *n* p24

 l'heure de libération de la chambre *check-out time*

la librairie *f* bookstore *n*

en libre-service *self-serve adj*

le lieu de rencontre *m* hangout (hot spot) *n*

la limitation de vitesse *f* speed limit *n* p64

la limousine *f* limo *n*

la liqueur *f* liqueur *n* 97

lire *to read v*

le lit *m* bed *n* 75

 le très grand lit *king-sized bed*

 le canapé-lit *pull-out bed*

 le grand lit *queen-sized bed*

 le lit à une place *single bed*

le litre *m liter n* p10
le livre *m book n* p162
la livre *f pound n*
local(e) / locaux *pl local adj*
la loge *m box (seat) n*
le logiciel *m software n*
la loi *f law n*
loin *far adj* p5
long *m /* **longue** *f long adj*
longtemps *for a long time adv* p10
louer *to rent v* p24
lui *him pron*
la lumière *f light (lamp) n*
lumineux *m /* **lumineuse** *f bright adj*
le lundi *m Monday n* p13
les lunettes *f pl glasses (spectacles) n*

les lunettes de protection *safety glasses*
les lunettes de soleil *sunglasses*

M

la machine *f machine n*
le magasin *m store n* p156
le magazine *m magazine n*
le magnétoscope *m VCR n*
mai *m May (month) n* p14
le mail *m e-mail n*
le maillot de bain *m swimsuit n*
la main *f hand n*

mais *but conjunction*
maintenant *now adv* p4
malade *sick adj*
le mal de tête *m headache n*
le mal des transports *m car sickness n*
malentendant(e) *hearing-impaired adj* 73
malvoyant(e) *visually-impaired adj* p73
manger *to eat v* p24
d'une manière étrange *suspiciously adv*
manipuler *to handle v* p24
manquant(e) *missing adj*
manquer *to miss / to lack v* p24
le manteau *m coat n*
le maquillage *m makeup n*
se maquiller *to make up (apply cosmetics) v* p24, 38
le / la marchand(e) ambulant(e) *m f street vendor n*
la marche *f walk n*
le marché *m market n*
le marché aux puces *flea market*
le marché en plein air *open-air market*
marcher *to walk v* p24
le mardi *m Tuesday n* p13
le mari *m husband n* p122

marié(e) *married adj* p123
marron *brown adj*
mars *m March (month) n*
masculin *male adj*
le massage dorsal *m back rub n*
masser *to massage v* **p24**
le match (sport) *m match (sport) n*
la matière *f subject matter, content / fabric n*
le matin *m morning n* p13
les mèches *f highlights (hair) n*
le médecin *m f doctor n*
le médicament *m medication n*
meilleur(e) *best adj*
le / la membre *m f member n*
même *same adj*
le menu *m menu n* p90

le menu des plats à emporter *m takeout menu*

Merci. *Thank you.* p1
le mercredi *m Wednesday n*
la mère *f mother n* p122
Métis/métisse *biracial ad*
le mètre *m meter n*
le métro *m subway n* p71

la ligne de métro *subway line*

mettre *to place / to charge (money) v* p25
mettre à jour *to update v* p25
le Mexique *m Mexico n*

mexicain(e) *Mexican n adj*
midi *m noon n adv* p13
mieux *best / better / rather adj*
le mile *m mile n* p10
au milieu de *in the middle prep*
le / la militaire *m f military n*
mille *thousand adj* p8
le millilitre *m milliliter n* p10
le millimètre *m millimeter n*
mince *damn expletive / slender adj*
minuit *m midnight n* p13
minute *f minute n*
la mise *f / le pari m bet n*

Je veux connaître votre mise. *I'll see your bet.*

la mise à niveau *f upgrade n*
miser *to put / to bet v* p24
moins *less adv / least adv*
le mois *m month n*
la moitié *f half n*

une moitié *one half*

la monnaie *f change (money) n*

Vous voulez de la monnaie ? *Would you like change back?*

la montagne *f mountain n*
le montant *m amount n*
monter *to climb / to get in (a vehicle) v* **p24**

montrer *to show / to point v*
p24

mordoré(e) *bronze adj*

la mosquée *f mosque n* p133

le mot de passe *m password n*

le moteur *m engine n*

la moto *f motorcycle n* p58

le mousqueton *m carabiner n*

la moustache *f moustache n*

moyen(ne) *medium (size) adj*

le musée *m museum n* p155

le musicien *m /* **la musicienne**
f musician n p129

la musique *music n*

musulman(e) *Muslim adj*

N

nager *to swim v* p24

défense de nager *no
swimming*

la nationalité *f nationality n*

le naufrage *m shipwreck n*

la nausée *f nausea n* p193

la navette *f shuttle bus n* p68

le navire *m ship, boat n* p70

le nécessaire de toilette *m
toiletries n*

néo-zélandais(e) *New
Zealander n adj*

le nettoyage à sec *m dry
cleaning n* p82

nettoyer *to clean v* p24

neuf *nine adj* p7

neuvième *ninth adj* p9

le neveu *m /* **les neveux** *m pl
nephew n* p123

le nez *m nose n* p126

la nièce *f niece n* p123

le noir *m dark n*

noir(e) *black adj*

noisette *hazel adj*

la noix *f nut n* p95

le nom *m name n*

Quel est ton nom ? *What's
your (sur)name?*

le nom de famille *last name*

non-fumeur *nonsmoking adj*

zone non-fumeur
nonsmoking area

voiture non-fumeur
nonsmoking car

chambre non-fumeur
nonsmoking room

la nourriture *f food n*

nous *us pron*

nouveau *m /* **nouvelle** *f new
adj*

la Nouvelle-Zélande *f New
Zealand n*

novembre *m November n*

nuageux *cloudy adj*

la nuit *f night n* p13

par nuit *per night* p78

le numéro *m number n* p7

**Puis-je avoir votre numéro
de téléphone ?** *May I have
your phone number?*

O

occupé(e) *busy, occupied adj*

octobre *m October* p15

l'œil *m* / **les yeux** *m pl eye(s) n*

l'officier *m officer n*

offrir *to offer v* **p24**

l'oie *m goose n*

l'oiseau *m bird n*

l'olive *f olive n*

l'once *m ounce n*

l'oncle *m uncle n* p123

onze *eleven adj* p7

l'opéra *m opera / opera house n*

l'opérateur *m* / **l'opératrice** *f operator (phone) n*

l'optométriste *m f optometrist n*

l'or *m gold n adj*

l'orange *f orange n adj*

l'orchestre symphonique *m symphony n*

l'ordinateur *m computer n*

l'ordinateur portable *m laptop n*

l'ordonnance *f prescription n*

l'oreiller *m pillow n* p82

l'orgue *m organ n*

orthodoxe *orthodox adj*

ôter *to remove v* **p24**

où *where adv*

oui *yes adv*

ouvert(e) *open adj*

Nous ne sommes plus ouvert. *We're not open anymore.*

P

le pain *m bread n*

pâle *pale adj*

panneau de priorité *m yield sign n* p61

le pansement (adhésif) *m band-aid n* p193

le papier *m paper n*

le papier toilette *m toilet paper n*

le parapluie *m umbrella n*

le parc *m park n*

le pare-brise *m windshield n*

le parent *m parent n* p123

parier (sur) *to bet (on), to gamble (on) v* **p24**

le parking *m parking n*

parler *to speak, talk v* **p24**

Parlez-vous français ? *Do you speak French?* p120

Pouvez-vous parler plus fort, s'il vous plaît ? *Would you speak louder, please?*

partager *to divide / to split (gambling) v* **p24**

le / la partenaire *m f partner n*

le parti *m party n*

participer (à) *to attend v* **p24**

partir *to leave, depart v* p25
pas de *no adv*
le passager *m* / **la passagère** *f passenger n*
le passe-temps *m hobby n*
le passeport *m passport n*
le pâté de maisons *m block (residential) n*
le patron *m* / **la patronne** *f boss n*
payer *to pay v* p24
en PCV *collect adv*

Veuillez faire votre appel en PCV. *Please make your call collect.*

le péage *m toll n*
la peau *f skin n*
le / la pédiatre *m f pediatrician n*
peindre *to paint v*
la peinture *f painting n*
perdre *to lose v* p25
perdu(e) *lost adj*
le père *m father n* p120
permettre *to permit v* p25
le permis *m license, permit n*
le permis de conduire *driver's license*
le personnel *m staff, employees n*
peser *to weigh* p24

Combien de kilos peser-vous ? *How much do you weigh (in kilos)?*

petit(e) *little, small adj* p11
le petit ami *m* / **la petite amie** *f boyfriend / girlfriend n*
le petit déjeuner *m breakfast n*

On ne sert plus le petit déjeuner. *Breakfast is no longer being served.*

le petit gâteau *m cookie n*
un peu *m bit (small amount) n*
un peu de *some adj*
le phare *m headlight n*
le piano *m piano n*
la pièce *f coin / room (of house) / play (theater) n*
la pièce d'identité *f identification n* p54
le pied *m foot n*
à pied *walking, on foot adj*
le piéton *m* / **la piétonne** *f pedestrian n*
la pile *f battery (for flashlight) n*
la pillule contraceptive *f birth control pill n*
la pinte *f pint n* p11
pire *worse / worst adj adv*
la piscine *f swimming pool n*
la piste de décollage *f runway n*
la pizza *f pizza n*
la place *f seat n / plaza, square n*
la plage *f beach n*

le plaisir *m* pleasure *n*

le plastique *m* plastic *n*

le plat *m* dish *n*

le plat du jour *special (featured meal)*

plein *adj* busy (restaurant) *adj*

pleuvoir *to rain v*

plonger *to dive v* **p24**

pluvieux *m* / **pluvieuse** *f* rainy *adj* **p131**

le pneu *tire n*

la poignée *f* handle *n*

la police *f* police *n*

le pont *m* bridge (across a river) *n*

populaire *popular adj*

le port *m* port (for ship mooring) *n*

le port USB *m* USB port *n*

la porte *f* door *n* / gate (airport) *n*

le portefeuille *m* wallet *n*

porter *to wear v* **p24**

le porteur *m* porter *n* **p44**

le porto *m* port (beverage) *n*

poser une question *to ask a question v* **p24**

le poste de police *m* police station *n*

le potage *f* soup *n* **p98**

le pouce *m* inch *n*

le poulet *m* chicken *n*

le pourboire *m* tip (gratuity) *n*

pousser *to push v* **p24**

la poussette *f* stroller *n*

pouvoir *can (able to) v* / may *v* **p34**

Puis-je ____ ? *May I ____?*

préférer *to prefer v* **p24**

se prélasser *to lounge v* **p24, 38**

premier *m* / **première** *f* first *adj*

prendre *to take v* **p35**

Cette place est-elle prise ? *Is this seat taken?*

la préparation lactée *f* formula *n*

préparé(e) *adj* prepared *adj*

près de *close (near) prep*

présenter *to introduce v* **p24**

Laissez-moi vous présenter à ____. *I'd like to introduce you to ____.*

le préservatif *m* condom *n*

pas sans préservatif *not without a condom*

les prévisions météorologiques *f pl* weather forecast *n*

le printemps *m* spring (season) *n* **p15**

la prise *f* plug *n*

privé(e) *private adj*

le prix *m* fee *n* / price *n*

le prix d'entrée *m* admission
 fee *n*

le prix du trajet *m* fare *n*

le problème *m* problem *n*

le produit *m* product *n*

professionnel *m* /
 professionnelle *f*
 professional *adj*

profond(e) deep *adj*

le programme *m* schedule *n* /
 program *n*

propre clean *adj*

protestant(e) Protestant *adj*

la prothèse dentaire *f*
 denture *n* p198

les provisions *f pl* groceries *n*

puis next, then *adv*

le pull *m* sweater *n* p159

Q

Quand when *adv*

quarante forty *n* adj p7

le quart *m* quart *n* / fourth *n*
 / quarter *n* adj

quatorze fourteen *adj* p7

quatre four *adj* p7

quatre-vingts eighty *adj* p7

quatre-vingt-dix ninety *adj*

quatre-vingt-onze ninety-
 one *adj* p8

quatrième fourth *adj* p9

le Québec *m* Quebec *n*

québécois(e) Quebecois *n* adj

quel *m* / **quelle** *f* what *adv*

quelque chose *f* something

quelqu'un *m* someone *pron*

qui who *adv* p3

à qui whose *adj*

la quinte *f* straight
 (gambling) *n*

la quinte royale *f* royal flush *n*

quinze fifteen *adj*7

Quoi de neuf ? What's up?

R

le raccordement *m* electrical
 hookup *n* p87

raccrocher hang up (end a
 phone call) *v* **p24**

la radio *f* radio *n* p59

le raisin *m* grape *n*

ralentir to slow *v* **p24**

 Ralentissez! Slow down!

ramasser to collect *v* **p24**

la rampe d'accès *f* ramp
 (wheelchair) *n* p65

rapide fast *adj*

les rapports sexuels *m pl*
 intercourse (sexual) *n*

ravi(e) delighted *adj* p122

rayé(e) scratched *adj*

le rayon *m* aisle (in store) *n*

à rayures striped *adj*

recevoir to receive *v*

recharger to charge (a battery) v **p24**

le récif m reef (coral) n

la réclamation f claim n

Voulez-vous faire une réclamation ? Do you want to file a claim?

recommander to recommend v **p24**

se réconcilier to make up (apologize) v **p24, 38**

le reçu m receipt n p140

le rédacteur m / **la rédactrice** f editor n p129

la réduction f discount n

la réduction pour enfants children's discount

la réduction pour personnes âgées senior discount

la réduction étudiante student discount

regarder to look (observe) / to watch v **p24**

le reggae m reggae n

régler la note to check out (of hotel) v **p24**

rejeté(e) declined adj

Votre carte de crédit a été rejetée. Your credit card was declined.

le rendez-vous m appointment n p130

rendre visite à to pay a visit to v **p25**

renoncer à to wave v **p24**

le renouvellement m refill (prescription) n

les renseignements m pl information / directory assistance (phone) n

rentrer to return (to a place, usually home) v **p24**

renverser to spill v **p24**

le repas m meal n

répéter to repeat v **p24**

Pourriez-vous répéter ce que vous venez de dire, s'il vous plaît ? Would you please repeat that?

répondre to answer v **p25**

la réponse f answer n

le réseau m / **les réseaux** m pl network n

la réservation f reservation n

le restaurant m restaurant n

rester to stay v **p24**

Combien de nuits resterez-vous ? For how many nights will you be staying?

rester en ligne to hold (telephone) v **p24**

le retard m delay n p51

retirer withdraw v **p24**

retourner to return v **p24**

le retrait m withdrawal n

le réveil *m* alarm clock *n*

le réveil téléphonique *m*
  wake-up call *n* p83

Au revoir! *Goodbye!*

le rhum *m* rum *n* p97

le rhume *m* cold (illness) *n*

la rivière *f* river *n*

le robinet *m* faucet *n*

le rock *m* rock and roll *n*

la roue de secours *f* spare
  tire *n*

le roman *m* novel *n*

romantique romantic *adj*

la rose *f* rose *n*

rose pink *adj*

rouge red / medium well
  (meat) *adv* p92

à roulettes wheeled *adj*

la route *f* road *n*

route fermée *f* road closed
  (sign) *n* p61

le roux *m* / la rousse *f*
  redhead *n*

la rue *f* street *n*

  de l'autre côté de la rue
  across the street

la rupture *f* break *n*

  en bas de la rue *down the
  street*

la rupture *f* break *n*

S

sa *f* his, her *adj*

le sac bag *n*

le sac à main *m* purse *n* p54

le sac de vol *m* carry-on bag *n*

sac pour le mal de l'air *m*
  airsickness bag *n* p56

la salade *f* salad *n*

la salle d'attente *f* waiting
  area *n* p44

la salle de dégustation *f*
  tasting room *n*

le salon *m* lounge, bar *n*

le samedi *m* Saturday *n* p14

sans without *prep*

la sauce *f* dressing (salad) *n* /
  sauce *n* p103

savoir to know (something)
  v p35

le savon *m* soap *n*

scanner to scan (document) *v*
  p24

le scooter *m* scooter *n* p58

le score *m* score *n*

la sculpture *f* sculpture *n*

se oneself, himself, herself
  pron

sec *m* / **sèche** *f* dry *adj*

séché(e) dried *adj*

sécher to dry *v* p24

le sèche-cheveux *m* hair
  dryer *n* p83

second(e) *second n adj*

Au secours! *Help!*

la sécurité *f security n*

le contrôle de sécurité *security checkpoint*

l'agent de sécurité *security guard* p45

seize *sixteen adj* p7

le sel *m salt n* p93

Ce plat est à faible teneur en sel. *This is a low-salt dish.*

la semaine *f week n* p4

cette semaine *this week*

la semaine dernière *last week*

la semaine prochaine *next week*

sens unique *m one way adj*

le sentier *m trail n* p171

sentir *to smell v*

séparé(e) *separated (marital status) adj* p123

sept *seven adj* p7

septembre *m September n*

septième *seventh adj* p9

serré(e) *tight adj*

le serveur *m* / **la serveuse** *f waiter n* p94

le service *m service n*

hors service *out of service*

la serviette *f napkin / towel / briefcase n* p57, 82

servir *to serve v* p24

ses *mf pl his, her adj*

seul(e) *single (one) adj*

le sexe *m sex (gender) n*

le short *m shorts n*

siège pour enfant *m car seat (child's safety seat) n* p59

signer *to sign v* p24

Signez ici, s'il vous plaît. *Sign here, please.*

s'il te plaît *s please (informal)*

s'il vous plaît *please (formal)*

six *six adj* p7

le soda *m soda n*

la sœur *f sister n* p120

la soie *f silk n*

soixante *sixty adj* p7

soixante-dix *seventy adj* p7

le solde *m balance (bank account)* / *sale (discount) n*

le soleil *m sun n*

sombre *dark adj*

sommes *are v See* **être** *(to be)* p27

son *m* / **sa** *f* / **ses** *mf his, her adj*

sont *are v See* **être** *(to be)* p27

la sorte *f kind (type) n*

la sortie *f exit n*

sortir *to exit / to go out v* p36

ne pas sortir par cette issue *not an exit*

sortir en boîte *to go clubbing* v p36

le sourcil *m eyebrow n* p126

sourd(e) *deaf adj*

le sous-titre *m subtitle n*

le sous-vêtement *m underwear n*

le spa *m spa n* p75

spécifier *to specify v* p24

le spectacle *m show (performance) n*

les sports *m sports n*

le stade *m stadium n* p169

le stand d'information *m information booth n* p45

la station *f station n*

  la station essence *gas station*

  la station de bus *bus station*

  la station de métro *subway station* p71

stationner *to park (a vehicle) v* p24

  stationnement interdit *no parking* p61

stressé(e) *stressed adj*

le / la styliste *m f designer n*

la substitution *f substitution n*

la Suisse *f Switzerland n*

suisse *Swiss n adj*

la suite *f suite n* p74

la suite avec terrasse *f penthouse n*

super *great adj*

superficiel *shallow adj*

le supermarché *m supermarket n* 105

supplémentaire *extra (additional) adj*

sur *on, over prep*

sûr(e) *safe (secure) adj*

  Ce quartier n'est pas sûr. *This area isn't safe.*

surfer *to surf v* p24

T

ta *f* / **ton** *m* / **tes** *m f pl your, yours pron*

la table *f table n* p90

la taille *f size (clothing, shoes) n*

le tailleur *m tailor n* p158

la tante *f aunt n* p123

plus tard *adv later adv* p7

le tarif *m rate (car rental, hotel) n*

  le tarif par jour *daily rate*

  le tarif hebdomadaire *weekly rate*

le taux de change *m exchange rate n* p140

le taux d'intérêt *m interest rate n* p141

la taxe f tax n p161

la taxe sur la valeur ajoutée (TVA) value-added tax (VAT)

le taxi m taxi n p65

télécharger to download / to upload v **p24**

la télécopie m fax n p130

le téléphone m phone n

Nous n'avons pas de téléphone public. We don't have a public phone.

le téléphone portable m cell phone n

téléphonique phone adj

la carte téléphonique phone card

l'annuaire téléphonique phone directory

la télévision f television n

la télévision par câble cable television

la télévision par satellite satellite television

le temple m temple n p139

tenir to hold v **p24**

se tenir to behave v **p38**

se tenir debout to stand v **p24, 38**

le tennis m tennis n p168

la tente f tent n p87

la tenue de rigueur f / **le code vestimentaire** m dress (general attire) n

le terminal m terminal (airport) n

le terrain de camping m campsite n

le terrain d'exercice m driving range n

la terrasse f terrace / sidewalk seating n

Voulez-vous dîner en terrasse ? Would you like to be seated outdoors?

tes m f pl / **ton** m / **ta** f your, yours pron

la tétine f pacifier n

le thé m tea n p97

le théâtre m theater n p151

le timbre m stamp (postage) n

le tire-bouchon m corkscrew, bottle opener n

tirer to pull v **p24**

tirer la chasse d'eau to flush v **p24**

le tissu m fabric n

la toile f canvas n57

la toilette f s toilet (fixture) n

les toilettes f pl bathroom n

les toilettes pour hommes men's restroom

les toilettes pour femmes women's restroom

les toilettes publiques public restroom

le toit ouvrant m sunroof n

tomber *to fall v* **p24**

ton *m* / **ta** *f* / **tes** *mf pl your, yours adj*

la tonne *f ton n*

tôt *early adj* **p13**

tourner *to turn v* **p24**

tourner à gauche / à droite *to turn left / right*

tousser *to cough v* **p24**

tout *all n* **p11**

en tout *total adv*

Ca fait ___ euros en tout. *It comes to ___ euros.*

tout *m* / **toute** *f* / **tous** *m pl* / **toutes** *f pl all adj*

la toux *f cough n*

le train *m train n*

les horaires des trains *train schedule*

traîner *(passer du temps) to hang out (to relax) v* **p24**

traiter *to process (a transaction) v* **p24**

la transaction *f transaction n*

transférer *to transfer v* **p24**

le transfert *m transfer n*

la transmission *f transmission n*

la transmission automatique *automatic transmission*

la transmission standard *standard transmission*

travailler *to work v* **p24**

en travers de *across prep*

treize *thirteen adj* **p7**

treizième *thirteenth adj*

trente *thirty adj* **p7**

très *very adj*

la tresse *f braid n*

le tribunal *m court (legal) n*

le tribunal des infractions à la circulation *traffic court*

triple *triple adj* **p8**

triste *sad adj* **p128**

trois *three adj* **p7**

troisième *third adj* **p9**

la trompette *f trumpet n*

trop *too (excessively) adv* **p12**

le trottoir *m sidewalk n / walkway n*

trouble *blurry adj*

trouver *to find v* **p24**

tu *you (singular, informal) pron*

le tuyau d'évacuation *m drain n*

U

un(e) *one adj* **p1**

l'université *f university / college n*

l'urgence *f emergency n*

utiliser *to use v* **p24**

V

les vacances *f pl holidays n / vacation n*

la vache *f cow n*

la valise *f suitcase n* p57

la varappe *f rock climbing n*

végétarien *m /* **végétarienne** *f vegetarian adj*

vendre *to sell v* **p25**

le vendeur / la vendeuse *m f salesperson n*

vendredi *m Friday n* p14

le ventilateur *m fan n* p85

du vent *windy adj* p132

vérifier *to check v* **p24**

le verre *m glass n / shot (liquor) n*

Ce vin est servi au verre ou au pichet. *This wine is served by the glass or by the carafe.*

le verrou *m lock (on door) n*

verrouiller *to lock v* **p24**

vers le haut *up adv*

la version *f version n*

le vert *m green (golf) n*

vert(e) *green adj*

des vertiges (avoir) *dizzy (to be) adj* p194

la veste *f jacket n*

la veuve *f /* **le veuf** *m widow, widower n* p123

viande *f meat n* p108

la vidéocassette *f video n*

la vie *f living n / life n*

Que faites-vous dans la vie ? *What do you do for a living?*

vieux *m /* **vieille** *f old adj*

la vigne *f vine n*

le vignoble *m vinyard, winery n*

la ville *f city n*

le vin *m wine n* p96

la carte des vins *wine list*

le vin sec *dry wine*

le vin doux *sweet wine*

le vin rosé *blush wine*

le vin mousseux *sparkling wine*

vingt *twenty adj* p7

vingtième *twentieth adj* p9

le vinyle *m vinyl n* p57

violer *to rape v* **p24**

violet *purple adj*

le violon *m violin n*

le visa *m visa n*

le visage *f face n* p126

la vision *f vision n*

visiter *to visit v* **p24**

vite *fast adv*

vivre *to live v* **p25**

la vodka *f vodka n* 97

la voile *f sail n*

voir *to see v* **p37**

voir navire *ship n* **p70**

le voisin *m* / **la voisine** *f*
neighbor n **p121**

la voiture *f car n* **p58**

agence de location de
voitures *car rental agency*

le vol *m flight n* **p46**

Vous allez changer de vol.
*You have a connecting
flight.*

la zone d'arrivée des vols
internationaux
international arrivals

la zone de départ des vols
internationaux
international departures

la volaille *f poultry n* **p101**

volé(e) *stolen adj*

voler *to rob, to steal v* **p24**

le volume *m volume n*

voter *to vote v* **p24**

vouloir *to want, to desire v*
p37

le voyage *m trip n*

voyager *to travel v* **p24**

le voyant *m light (car) n*

le voyant de contrôle *check
engine light*

le voyant du niveau d'huile
oil light

vraiment *really adj*

la vue *f view n* **p76**

W

le wagon-lit *f sleeping car n*

les WC *f pl restrooms n*

le Wi-Fi *m Wi-Fi n*

Z

le zoo *m zoo n* **p137**

NOTES

NOTES

NOTES